The Passion of Music and Dance

The Passion of Music and Dance

Body, Gender and Sexuality

**Edited by
William Washabaugh**

Oxford • New York

First published in 1998 by
Berg
Editorial offices:
150 Cowley Road, Oxford, OX4 1JJ, UK
70 Washington Square South, New York, NY 10012, USA

Berg is the imprint of Oxford International Publishers Ltd.

Library of Congress Cataloging-in-Publication Data

A catalogue record for this book is available from the Library of Congress

British Library Cataloguing-in-Publication Date

A catalogue record for this book is available from the British Library

ISBN 1 85973 904 0 (Cloth)
      1 85973 909 1 (Paper)

Typeset by JS Typesetting, Wellingborough, Northants.
Printed in the United Kingdom by WBC Book Manufacturers, Mid-Glamorgan.

Contents

Contents

Acknowledgements

This collection of essays in comparative social history grew out of the papers that were presented at the 1996 meeting of the American Anthropological Association in a session entitled 'The Politics of Passion.' The idea for this exploration of the politics and ideology in flamenco, tango and other popular styles had occurred to me a number of years earlier, but my discussions with Gerhard Steingress in 1994 and 1995 helped to advance it by leaps and bounds – Gerhard's *Sociología del Cante Flamenco* (1993) ends with a discussion of *flamenco, tango, rebetika*, and *csárdás*. This present collection of essays, written by some of the world's most knowledgeable students of flamenco, tango, rebetika, and North American popular music, makes giant strides forward in our quest to understand the complex interweaving of gender, politics, music, and dance in modern life while simultaneously opening the way for future explorations of these phenomena.

The essays by Donald Castro, Gail Holst-Warhaft, Timothy deWaal Malefyt, Marta Savigliano, Jeffrey Tobin, and Susan Cook are revisions of the presentations they made at the San Francisco meeting. Gerhard Steingress, Angela Shand and I were involved in the organization of the session from its inception. Angela and I assisted at the presentations, participated in subsequent discussions, and contributed our editorial efforts to the present volume. Discussions with David Monroe enhanced my own essays. My wife Catherine talked me through a great number of intellectual and organizational knots. I thank all these people, but especially Catherine, for their participation in this project.

W. Washabaugh

Notes on Contributors

Donald Castro is Dean of Arts and Humanities at California State University at Fullerton. He has written numerous essays on the social history of tango and is author of *Tango as Social History 1880–1955* (1991).

Susan C. Cook is Associate Professor of Musicology at the University of Wisconsin-Madison. She co-edited *Cecilia Reclaimed* (1991).

Gail Holst-Warhaft is a lecturer in classics at Cornell University and has written extensively on rebetika, notably, *The Road to Rebetika* (1977), and *Theodorakis: Myth and Politics in Modern Greek Music* (1979). Her most recent book is *Dangerous Voices: Women's Lament and Greek Literature* (1992).

Timothy deWaal Malefyt completed his doctoral dissertation, "Gendered Authenticity: The Invention of Flamenco Tradition in Seville, Spain," at Brown University. He is currently a Senior Account Planner in Advertising.

Marta E. Savigliano is Associate Professor at UCLA in the Department of World Arts and Cultures, and is married to Jeffrey Tobin. She is the author of *Tango and the Political Economy of Passion* (1995).

Angela Shand is studying the history and practice of Greek dance as a graduate student of anthropology at the University of Wisconsin-Milwaukee.

Gerhard Steingress is professor of Sociology at the University of Seville and associate of the Fundación Machado. He authored the books *Sociología del Cante Flamenco* (1993) and *Cante flamenco: Zur Kulturkritik der andalusischen Moderne (1997)* as well as numerous essays on flamenco art and collective identity.

Jeffrey Tobin is a cultural anthropologist teaching in the Department of World Arts and Cultures at UCLA. His contribution to this volume is taken from his doctoral dissertation, "Ethnographic Interventions in the Manly Culture of Buenos Aires," completed at Rice University.

William Washabaugh is Professor of Anthropology at the University of Wisconsin-Milwaukee. He co-edited *The Social Context of Creolization* (1983), and authored *Five Fingers for Survival* (1986), *Speak into the Mirror: A Story of Linguistic Anthropology* (1988), and *Flamenco: Passion, Politics, and Popular Culture* (1996).

–1–

Introduction: Music, Dance, and the Politics of Passion

William Washabaugh

Popular music and dance are about changing the world. Such has been the case since the 1790s when modern life was formed out of the cultural crucible of the French Revolution. Then, as now, the energy of music and dance was shifted away from praising God and entertaining kings, and toward the reputedly more important tasks of contacting reality, locating wholeness, and rebuilding the tracks along which any good society should move. During this same post-Revolutionary period, the term 'popular' began operating as a kind of neon sign for marking the place where stars are made, tickets are sold, endorsements are secured, identities are created, and where cities, states, and nations are emboldened by the sounds of their own musical souls. And if these latter aspects of 'the popular' seem strange bedfellows for the former, then we have succeeded in outlining the problem at hand: popular music and dance are puzzlements, full of self-contradictions. They are treated with church-going respectfulness (Gay 1995: 18; Johnson 1995), yet they overflow with licentiousness and banality. They are firmly stitched into the eco-nomic and political fabric of a this-worldly existence, but they persistently stretch and strain towards ecstasy and transcendence.

More confusingly still, popular music and dance became knotted with gender and nation in the nineteenth century, a knot that tightened as patriarchal regimes of the old order came unraveled. In the new modern order of things, womanhood and nation became tightly wedded, the former being the master trope for the latter (Parker et al. 1992: 6; Kittler 1991). 'Nation' was then understood in feminine terms, as the nurturing fundament of social life, source of all warmth and security. 'In 1800 the system of equivalents Woman=Nature=Mother allowed acculturation to begin from an absolute origin' (Kittler 1991: 28). Womanhood became the rock on which nations were built. Not for nothing are nations referred to with feminine pronouns and their languages are called 'Mother tongues.' Accordingly, womanly sounds and womanly movements came to symptomatize the vital soul of 'a people.' More than just 'Mother', it was 'Mother-at-song' that knotted the knot of modern political life, creating the modern triad of nation-gender-music that changed the world while simultaneously mystifying it. Hence, our scholarly attentions are directed to the matters of politics, gender, and popular song and dance.

What linkage can we discern between politics and the gendering of song and dance in popular performances? In the very earliest popular performances – in the *cafés concerts* of Paris, in the *cafés cantantes* of Seville, and in the music halls of London (see Attali 1985; Middleton 1989) – what political repercussions were set into motion by the trilling voices and the delicate steps of women? Contrastively, where did men stand vis-à-vis those brazen but lovely singers and dancers of the mid-nineteenth century? And why were males so fascinated with the emotion-charged movements of women, most notably by the chorea that came to be known as hysteria (Hacking 1995: 212; McCarren 1995; Phelan 1996)? These questions draw us into the swirling energies of the gender and politics in the nineteenth century. Further, they prompt us to raise questions about who or what stands behind the scenes, pushing the buttons and pulling the strings that drive these performances forward. Is it the impresarios who produce the events? Or maybe the journalists and intellectuals who comment on them? Or perhaps, the audiences who attend them? Or is no one in charge? Perhaps popular music and dance phenomena piggy-back on, and spin-off from, the general force of bourgeois culture?

Twentieth-century developments have only complicated these questions, making them muddier rather than clearer, and distancing us from the possibility of generating satisfying answers. More than ever, we stand perplexed before musical events that have been inflated into extravaganzas, then amplified, recorded, and re-engineered before being selectively broadcast, competitively marketed, surreptitiously pirated, and conspicuously collected, classified, and displayed, all in keeping with the still developing profile of the global music industry. Through all these transformations, the critical features of popular music have been obscured and hidden from view. In short, popular music has become increasingly resistant to critical inquiry, discouraging the efforts of those who explore this domain in hopes of responding to it with just, equitable, and productive tactics.

As a guide to the musically perplexed, the insights that we offer here aim to penetrate some of these scumbling complexities of popular music and dance by going back in time to some of the earliest and most widely celebrated forms and styles that qualify as 'popular.' This is the reason for our focus on flamenco, tango, and rebetika. Each of these styles, more than merely emotional, is exaggeratedly so, as if each style had captured, distilled and crystallized the diffused discourses of womanhood that swirled about popular performances in the nineteenth century. Each remains highly gendered to this day. Each is distinctively national. All are vintage, with roots that stretch back deep into the nineteenth century. Moreover, their musical styles are riddled with traditionalisms that have been overlaid with discourses of authenticity and purity. With all these characteristics, flamenco-tango-rebetika cannot but offer us a coign of vantage onto the nineteenth-century triad of nation-gender-music.

In one sense, our method is age-old: we aim to attain an understanding of modern popular music and dance by tracing its development through time. In order to understand the majestic oak tree, one considers the lowly acorn. In order to understand Renaissance Europe, one studies ancient Greece. In our case, in order to understand contemporary popular music and dance, we consider early and elemental forms, flamenco, tango, and rebetika.

Such a strategy of gazing into the past in order to understand the present is common to the point of being conventional, but it is not without its dangers and traps. For one thing, such a strategy can often be manipulative. More than just attending to the past, we may well find ourselves co-opting it, enlisting our representation of the past into the service of a future that is never made explicit. Just so, Armbrust (1996), commenting on modernist aesthetics in Egyptian popular culture, found that the tradition-oriented song styles of al-Wahhab and Umm Kulthum drew from the humble and folkloric past, delighting audiences in the process. Paradoxically, however, their styles left the past all but eclipsed in the future. Modernism, Armbrust concludes, is a movement that pits tradition against itself. Such a co-optation is a trap that we aim to avoid here.

For another thing, rearward glances at music and dance may well result in essentialist visions, establishing a canon, and generating 'coherent, linear historico-aesthetic narratives' of the sort that raises red flags for Simon Frith (1996: 38). Under the influence of essentialist thinking, one might well be tempted to try to return to firm and fixed musical realities by peeling away stylistic accretions built up through time. But here, we aim to avoid such essentialist blunders. Like Steumpfle's concrete and detailed description of the development of steelband music in Trinidad and Tobago (1995), our studies must be historically well grounded. Like Finnegan's study of the musical practices of the people of Milton Keynes, we will discuss the behaviors of singing and dancing rather than the objectifications of such processes, the 'finalized results' of those behaviors (1989: 8). And following the lead of Middleton (1989), our discussions have been constructed with an eye to the aesthetic and political forces that have circulated as social energy, shifting and transforming as one era gives way to another.

We will elucidate elemental interconnections and negotiations rather than elemental forms, emphasizing moments of music and dance as occasions for people to relate to one another rather than as objects for them to trade. Moreover, while we will be attending to the local circumstances of performance, we will not neglect the large institutional forces that are continually introduced into the concrete events of music and dance. In line with Manuel, we will assume that 'popular music remains embedded in powerful commercial enterprises linked to dominant classes with their own ideological agendas' (1993: 6). As much as flamenco, tango, and rebetika might seem to be derived from and keyed to the national circumstances of Spain, Argentina and Greece, we will show that these styles spill beyond those borders, and in the current commercial scene, end up hybridizing the nationalist identities they themselves helped to create (Garcia Canclini 1995), deliberately disguising their own nationalist inventions in order to highlight aspects of their identity that cannot otherwise be expressed (Lipsitz 1994: 62). Like icebergs, the bulks of which are submerged and hidden from view, these musical styles, though seeming to be confined to properly national and musical spaces, are – and have been – on the move.

In general, then, our rearward glances will show that popular music and dance exercise influence in domains well beyond aesthetics, being deeply implicated in the struggles of genders and nations. In the end, by charting the connectivity of popular music, from past to present, we hope to draw a clearer picture of how popular music has contributed to changing the modern world.

For a number of reasons, the time seems right for a consideration of these elemental styles, not only in their earliest forms, but in their later stages of development, right down to the present. These reasons have everything to do with the current state of thought about social history and popular music. First, the staid discipline of musicology has been shaken since the late 1980s by scholars such as Richard Leppert, Lawrence Kramer, and Susan McClary[1] who have turned a critical eye on the gender relations that pervaded elite music in the nineteenth century. Their efforts guide this current investigation of root styles, paving the way for our reconsideration of the role of gender relations in flamenco, tango, rebetika, and other popular phenomena. Second, recent accounts of the history of bourgeois culture by Gay, Seigel, Hacking, and Huyssen have redirected scholarly attention to the ambivalence of gender identity in modern social life.[2] This ambivalence, we will show, is obvious and evident in the musical styles that we are considering here, thereby rendering these styles all the more promising as sites for critical study. Third, recent studies of flamenco, tango, and rebetika by Castro, Deval, Holst, García Gómez, Savigliano, and Steingress[3] have directed attention to musical experiences as cultural texts to which social energies gravitate and in which they circulate. In other words, musical performances are cultural lightning rods that have the power to reveal in condensed form the forces that are elsewhere diffuse. Accordingly and in contrast to earlier scholarship that confined itself to chronicling names, places, and events for purposes of applauding or lambasting artists and audiences, our discussions will treat these elemental musical styles as sites for understanding the general operations of modernity.

Popular Music, Gender, and Exoticism

Popular music has been turned into something of a commodity. It differs from singing-in-the-shower and from singing-in-the-choir insofar as it is bought and sold. Produced and consumed in the market place, it acquires exchange value, and, as such, a certain *concrete abstractness*. If we are speaking of a song sung in a coffee house or music hall, its *concreteness* is evident. The singers and the audiences are visible, audible, tangible, and palpable and, in all these respects, concrete. But in addition, the popular event is one that embeds this concreteness in a new context, one that silently redefines the music as a marketable object, a commodity. Ticket-sales, show-times, stage-lights, curtain-calls and, subtler yet, the practice, practice, practice that artists submit themselves to in order to market their musical virtuosity, all these serve to distinguish commodified music, invisibly hedging it off from street music on the one hand, and haute music on the other. This new and *abstractly* defined popular music never existed in the choir, or in the shower, or in the street or in the court. It is a distinctly modern phenomenon, produced, packaged, distributed, and consumed in the modern marketplace.

The commodification of music was a response in part to the dislocations associated with the French Revolution. Both Richard Terdiman and Paul Connerton have examined this period and have concluded that, while the king may have lost his head during this social upheaval, the far more distinguished victim of the Revolution and its aftershocks was social memory.[4] In the wake of the quake, citizens of the new order could no longer remember what was important and fundamental for their social lives. Their time-wrought ceremonies and traditional practices were swept away, and in the bombed out landscape of Europe during the first decades of the nineteenth century, modern people were forced to reinvent the social ground that they were then and there already walking on.

Musical commodities came to the rescue, plugging the dikes, filling the gaps, and rescuing all of Europe, momentarily at least, from the aimlessness that threatened everyone. Little wonder that musical experiences quickly emerged as *post-religious experiences* (Gay 1995: 24; Berlin 1996: 178). Music was the only and proper form of religion once religion itself had been discredited. It was considered by many to be, in Carlyle's words, 'the speech of angels,' and that was especially so for the growing urban middle classes. According to Peter Gay, urbanization, the rise of the world market, the modernization of banking and commerce, favored an already growing middle class that had 'more time, money and energy for luxuries, however modest, and the devout enjoyment of music ranked high among them.'

Early on, this nineteenth-century cultivation of music went hand in hand with the task of creating nations. This was as true of Spain as it was of Germany. In Germany, the linkage between music, poetry, language, and politics had been hammered out in the last quarter of the eighteenth century, then to become emphatically clear a hundred years later in Wagner's Romantic music. Spain and Greece followed Germany's footsteps. Stoetzer argues that 'Spain had suffered for too long the excessive French influence, and German Romanticism had actually dug up the glories of the Spanish past that the Spaniards themselves had forgotten during the period of the Enlightenment. Since the Germans fought this French cultural domination, it seemed logical for the Spaniards to look for solutions in Germany' (Stoetzer 1996: 90; see also Isaiah Berlin 1990: 207–37). In consequence, the music and dance academies that flourished in Spain in the first half of the nineteenth century used musical commodities to effectively underwrite state-level politics. In Greece, as Michael Herzfeld has shown, folkloristic nationalists encouraged the search for national identity in cultural legacies of the past. Simultaneously, they recommended that extraneous traditions be rooted out and purged so as to cleanse the culture.[5]

By mid-century, however, populist Romanticism had lost its edge and was replaced by a politically languorous but psychologically vitalizing gospel that was associated with the French avant garde. Spain, like England, followed France's lead towards this new aesthetics of, what

Peter Gay mimicking Baudelaire calls, 'the naked heart.' This new wave of Romanticism emphasized narcissistic introspection made possible by a self-indulgent inward turn. In contrast to the German Romantics who had predicted a *political* payoff for those who celebrated downtrodden people languishing on the borders of circles where power is played, this French version found *psychological* benefit in delivering oneself over to transgressive actions, to the lust for travel, and to passions and ecstasies of every sort. Sincerity, authenticity and intensity of feeling became sacred values. The heroes of this post-religion were the mavericks and misfits who spurned wealth, power, and fame so as to become emotionally rich.

Gypsies and the self-styled Gypsies known as bohemians were all the rage in Paris after 1840, as Seigel's history demonstrates. Defined by 'Carmen' on the front end (1845) and 'La Boheme' at the rear (1890), this era of bohemian Romanticism, with its tantalizing samplings of exotically edgy lifestyles, offers us a critical vantage point from which to appreciate modern popular music. Among the primary features of this era, we include its fascination with introspection, emotionality, and music all played out with fawning, though distant, regard for marginalized and downtrodden communities.

Inevitably, gender was woven into this mix. When popular music took off in the late-eighteenth century, it was on womanly wings, propelled by the promise of wholeness that could only be realized by contacting the femininity of the cosmos. For Rousseau, according to Felicia Miller Frank, it was 'his Aunt Suson's singing . . . (that he) remembers her by most vividly, and this memory of the voice of the woman who was mother to Rousseau organizes and suffuses his other memories of early childhood like a light or a science' (Miller Frank 1995: 17). For Goethe's Faust, Gretchen was a 'domestic angel' presiding over a 'place of Peace set apart from the contested spheres of historical time and public life.' Nowhere is this thematic more boldly advanced, according to Lawrence Kramer, than in Liszt's musical rendering of Faust, wherein one discovers a growing cultural conviction that music, first nurtured at the breast, fulfills the promise of its feminine provenance by affording the peace, integrity, and authenticity that were to be found nowhere else in the public world. As the post-religion of modernity, musical simplicities, such as the melodies hummed by Rousseau's Aunt Suson, began to generate a kind of cosmic eroticism, a passion generated in embracing the earth, in sinking into its warm and moist darkness, and in leaving behind the abstractions of light and the cold reasoning of the public day – these are the times that popularized notions such as 'mother nature' and 'mother tongue.'[6]

At mid-century, in Paris, Romantic bohemians retooled music to serve as a weapon in their war against the disciplines of the bourgeois life. Then and there, the power of music and of womanhood was attributed to forgotten pain and to the edgy and transgressive emotion that it generates. 'Promising pain,' that is what Wordsworth celebrated in the prostitute Alice Fell, as discussed by Sarah W. Goodwin (1994), and that too is what William Holman Hunt's original version of the painting 'The Awakening Consciousness' (1853) depicted in the face of the prostitute, Annie Miller, as discussed by Richard Leppert (1993). During that same period, scientists began registering the forgotten but promising pain of womanhood as if it were nothing short of the essence of the human essence. Focusing on symptoms of hysteria and multiple personality, they erected the disciplines that Ian Hacking suggests were forbears of psychology and anthropology, disciplines dedicated to the project of rewriting that of which science could not then speak, namely the human soul. Finally and closer to the present, Marianna Torgovnick has explored the inter-war period of the twentieth century, describing what might be called a 'feminoid primitivism' in music appreciation. Michael Leiris venerated jazz for its 'religious meaning,' its eroticism, and its power to bridge 'the gap that separates individuals from each other.' Through other media, sensitive males like Carl Jung and D.H. Lawrence and courageous females such as Isak Dinesen, Mary Kingsley, Beryl Markham, and Georgia O'Keefe created words and forms through which modern westerners could access a transcendent and oceanic cosmos . . . gendered feminine.[7]

Paradoxically but predictably, this celebration of oceanic femininity was carried aloft in the texts of mostly masculine seers, having been taken out of the hands of the women themselves. Though ordinary women might have been the models and targets of Romantic attentions, they were assumed to lack the verbal skills necessary for analyzing and registering that feminine soul. This was a man's job, and it required a man's well-disciplined form of language, as suggested by Judith Butler (1990). It was the male poet who transcribed and registered the movements of the female soul, and especially the female soul that sings. In the course of this process of transcription and registration, male voices gradually assimilated and then supplanted those of women. The woman's voice, the source of authenticity, was elided and usurped by the man's. Consequently, *his* voice began to sing at increasingly higher pitches – falsetto is a vocal technique for men only (Frith 1996: 194). After the invention of the microphone in 1925, the male singing voice turned whispery and warbly. Even the contemporary male voice in rock, according to John Shepherd, croons its tunes with head tones instead of singing it straight out from the chest – when it's not screaming outright misogyny.[8]

We see, in this foregoing thumbnail sketch, a picture of new musical styles riding a crest of popular interest created by the magnetic attractiveness of the introspected, marginal, exotic, oceanic, and feminine revelations, all of which had been appropriated and managed by men. As such and with these particular emphases, this sketch may be revealing, but it is also dangerously open to two forms of simplistic dichotomization. *First* and in the manner of Torgovnick, Root, or McClary, Romantic popular music could be said to be a royal road to the visions and powers that modern men have reappropriated from women. In other words, the history of popular music, could be – and in some cases has been – turned into a tug-of-war between men and women over access to enlightening emotion. On a *second* front, and in line with concepts of 'mass culture' and 'cultural imperialism,' one might counterpose commodified popular music to the purity, honesty, and authenticity of music in the counter-culture, contending that the former co-opts the latter. In other words, the history of popular music could be portrayed as a margino-centric struggle, a contest between the power-wielding bourgeois men at the social center and powerless bohemian women on the margins. As such, popular music seems to be a function of both gender struggle and class struggle. However, both these lines of argument, tantalizing though they might be, strike us as garden paths that, though invitingly clear, nevertheless lead to simplistic pictures of the processes at work.

For an antidote to these tempting oversimplfications, we could do worse than to consider the cases of 'Eliza' and 'Carmen', both of which scramble our easy dichotomies by showing that every instance of popular music operates from both the center and the margins at the same time, and from both the powerful and the powerless. Popular music is rarely an 'either-or' phenomenon, but almost always a 'both-and.' The fictional life of Eliza Gilbert and the real life of 'Carmen' will illustrate this contention.[9]

Eliza Gilbert was real enough as a person. Born around 1820, she passed her youth in India, married her mother's traveling companion, then left him, had a fling, was divorced, and returned to Ireland. Having lost both her honor and her income, Eliza sought to make do by acting and dancing. At twenty, she was too old to begin studying classical ballet, so she turned to national dance. As Bruce Seymour says, 'Spain and Spanish culture were then much in fashion,' so Eliza went to Seville where she studied dance for four months and then returned as Maria Dolores de Porris y Montez – or Lola Montez for short – the daughter of an ill-fated Spanish nobleman. Then and there in 1843, she was determined 'to be a figure of romance and fascination.' For a brief moment, her plan was successful. A critic of her first performance wrote that 'every gesture and attitude seems to be the impulse of passion acting on the proud and haughty mind of a beautiful Spaniard.' Other reviewers, however, were somewhat more discerning, wondering about this Spanish woman who seemed something less than fully Spanish. It was not long before her charade was exposed and she was identified in print as Eliza James Gilbert. She responded by publishing rebuttals in those same newspapers, refuting what she described as slanderous remarks, and reaffirming the absolute and unequivocal truth of her Spanish identity and emphasizing the authenticity of her dance. Having played her cards to the finish, she left London toured Germany and later Paris. There, her performances received consistently bad reviews, but still she flourished on the strength of her personal beauty, great charm, and indomitable spirit. One Parisian critic wrote that 'her debut at the Opera had been a fiasco.' Théophile Gautier captured the larger reality by noting that 'Mlle. Lola Montez has a small foot and pretty legs. As for the way she uses them, that's another matter . . . (She has) nothing Andalusian about her except a pair of magnificent black eyes.'

This case of Eliza Gilbert a.k.a Lola Montez sheds some new light on gender relations in the mid-nineteenth century, especially as those relations entered into the popular music scene. She eschewed feminine submissiveness – dramatically so when she took a riding whip to a Prussian gendarme who had tried to detain her for being literally out of line. She was, it seems, the Madonna of her age, a woman whose attitude was every bit as daunting as her physical being was attractive.

Now to the significance of Eliza as an embodiment of popular music and dance. She was on the fence with respect to gender, betwixt-and-between, both feminine and masculine. Bruce Seymour, Lola's biographer, labels her a 'social outlaw,' though he hastens to add that such a label is apt for any woman of the stage in the mid-nineteenth century – except perhaps the angelic Jenny Lind. 'Women of the theatre,' he writes, 'generally had exceptional status in society, but it was frequently that of a half-caste, of someone who did not deserve to be shamed by all decent persons but at the same time could not be received freely in their homes.' Eliza's shameless dissemblance along with her cigarette-smoking, flamenco-dancing, prince-loving, and globe-trotting practices were all tactical maneuvers that helped her to survive personally while also defining the boundaries of 'gender trouble' in mid-century Europe. Being neither on one side nor on the other, obviously not a man but not quite a woman either, she was a human harbinger of the social changes that were then afoot. The class and gender ambivalences that she embodied served to link these developing aspects of modern society to music, binding class, gender, music and dance together into one very beautiful but very volatile package.

Just as revealing as the fiction of Lola Montez is the reality of 'Carmen'. I refer here to Prosper Mérimée's novella of 1845, but also, by extension, to Bizet's opera of 1874, and recent films of that same name, especially Saura's *Carmen* of 1984. All three works of 'Carmen' are, of course, fictions. Carmen and Don José are imaginary and constructed characters rather than real people. As constructed symbols, however, they are condensations of some very real forces that were at work at the time that these 'Carmens' were composed and presented. When analyzed, the densely knotted symbols of Carmen and Don José afford insight into gender and class struggles through music from the beginning of modernity right up to the present.

Carmen is a person who stands for and lives out the bohemian lifestyle. She is free in spirit and unfettered in the expression of her intuitive gifts and heartfelt desires. She is brutally honest, and outwardly disdainful of bureaucrats, wage checks, and tightly furled umbrellas. She and her kind form living antitheses to the tight-lipped and socially responsible bourgeoisie of her day, rejecting all class, disavowing all social standing, kicking away the ladder, so to speak, and swimming in the free and passionate – but very smoky – air of an untrammeled spirit.

The cigarette symbolizes her spirit. Eliza Gilbert exploited that symbolism when she was photographed with cigarette in hand in 1851, possibly the first photo of its kind. In the same vein, as argued by Linda Hutcheon, Carmen used tobacco as a visual sign of her cultural resistance. Deval contends that a Carmen-like figure has graced packets of Gitanes cigarettes so as to remind every purchaser that smoking Gitanes is a metonym for the incendiary sensuality that is encountered in the bohemian lifestyle.[10]

Contrastively, the man in the Carmen narrative is a gentle and generally well-disciplined fellow. Don José was formerly a member of the security force at the tobacco factory where Carmen worked, but currently a bandit whose life was forfeit. He was doomed because of his brief flirtation with Carmen. His is a morality tale, a narrative of an Everyman who succumbed to the seductions of a bohemian woman.

Appearances, however, can be deceiving. Evlyn Gould (1996) suggests that Carmen, in the original tale and also in its adaptations and representations, is a complex figure whose symbolic opposition to Don José serves to define and objectify the bourgeois lifestyle, so much so as to make Carmen's very existence dependent upon her bourgeois foil. Like the reciprocally defined film characters of Larry Flynt and Jerry Falwell, Carmen and Don José are inextricably and unavoidably intertwined. Each presupposes the other.

Jerrold Seigel's history of bohemianism in nineteenth-century Paris reveals just how deeply this intertwined relationship runs (Seigel 1986). After 1850, 'bohemian' served as a cover label for events aimed at taking money from the bourgeoisie in return for the staging of musical and literary events that enabled them to participate vicariously in the lives of exotic libertines. Indeed, Emile Goudeau, inventor of the 'cabaret' in the 1870s, was a marketeer under whose guiding hand 'bohemia was turned into theatre, a site for acting out its estrangement from ordinary life, but also for masking it and channeling its energy to appeal to the bourgeoisie as patrons and consumers of literary and artistic work' (Seigel 1986: 225). In Spain, precisely the same dynamic opposition existed between Gitanos and the well-heeled (*señoritos*) in the context of the *cafés cantantes* popularized by Silverio Franconetti in the 1870s. There, the very image and identity of the Gitano was forged with an eye to its social foil, largely for the purpose of liberating the middle class from their money. Later, in Argentina, after the turn of the century, the same reciprocally defining relationship was replayed in the context of the new bohemianism of tango that reminded the bourgeoisie, as Savigliano has pointed out, of 'what they had lost and now could buy.' 'Exotics were there for the civilized to consume' and thus to overcome their lacks and limitations.

The cases of Eliza and Carmen serve to illustrate the social dynamics at work in early popular music and dance. These dynamics certainly do involve oppositions between male and female and highbrow and lowbrow, but never in any simple way or fixed fashion. Instead, early popular musical styles of flamenco and tango embody ambivalent and constantly shifting negotiations. As with the filmic characters of William Muni in the film *The Unforgiven* and Bernie LaPlante in the film *Hero*, all definitional lines are blurred. And as in *Blue Velvet*, apparent oppositions, so temptingly Manichean in their simplicity of contrast, cloak vacillations, shifts, and ambivalences that betray instability at the foundations of the modern social order.

Andalusian Flamenco

Flamenco music emerged out of the crowded and poverty stricken streets of southern Spain in the first half of the nineteenth century. The previous century had seen Andalusia's population double as immigrants flocked to the south in search of labor in ports of trade and in the tuna fisheries. But as the trade declined and the fisheries were exhausted, the only economic alternative for most persons was agricultural day-labor on the large tracts of land that were held by a few elite landowners. The hordes of landless Andalusians, including Gitanos, worked the fields – Romanichals elsewhere in Europe spurned agricultural labor – while some sought out interstitial occupations such as selling lottery tickets, trading horses, and working metal, these occupations being especially favored by Gitanos. Starvation and imprisonment were common correlates of lower-class life, as were the more proactive alternatives of prostitution, thievery, thuggery, and highway robbery.

Impoverished though they were, early-nineteenth-century Andalusians were also stalwart. During the War of Independence, 1808–1814, they joined forces with the British to drive Napoleon's forces back, thereby securing a laudatory chapter for themselves in the history books of later generations. Indeed, among expatriates returning to Spain in subsequent decades, a favorite pastime was the singing of ballads praising the bravery of Andalusians during the war.

The post-napoleonic era in Spain, as elsewhere in Europe, was rife with nationalism. Given that fact, it will not be surprising to discover, on one front, that Andalusians nurtured a love-hate relationship with Italian opera, at once rejecting it while also copying its vocal style. On a second front, they developed dance academies akin to those emerging elsewhere in Europe so that the middle classes could devote themselves with patriotic fervor to the study of their reinvigorated 'Andalusian folk dances,' practicing *boleros, fandangos,* and *jotas* as devotees of their new post-religion. As French Romantic influence gained strength, the interest in dance practice was replaced by a widespread embrace of the edgy passion of the Spanish soul, then as now, associated with a Gypsy life of transgression and suffering. The English and French were as eager to tap this passion as the Spanish themselves. George Borrow and Richard Ford from England and Théophile Gautier and Charles Davillier from France, in their several ways, sparked a mid-century fever for bohemian styles of flamenco all across Europe, so that by 1860, the word was out. Andalusia was the region to tour. For all those mid-century Europeans who, like Flaubert, found themselves suffocating on the stale air of European culture and who needed to get away, to breathe a spirit-revitalizing air, Andalusia was the place to go.[11]

Impresarios like Silverio Franconetti anticipated this wave of popularity. They created venues for commercialized song, the *cafés cantantes*. The Café de los Lombardos opened in 1842 in Seville, the first in a long and illustrious line of these establishments which, in the view of scholars like Blas Vega (1987), defined the flamenco 'golden age.' From 1860 until the turn of the century, these show-bars sprouted like mushrooms, catapulting artists – particularly Gitano singers and female dancers – to stardom, creating fortunes for the impresarios, and spawning a long and lively genre of debate amongst moralists, politicians and intellectuals most of whom took the *cafés cantantes* to be tangible signs of the moral decay of Spanish culture.

The rhetoric of moral outrage leaped to a new level of intensity after Spain lost the last remnants of her once vast empire in 1898. Xenophobics, Modernist cynics, and Romantics of both conservative and liberal stripes, all focused their fury on flamenco, accusing it of being symptomatic of Spain's decline. In the 1920s, Federico García Lorca, Manuel de Falla, and Andrés Segovia set out in search of the heart and soul of this quintessentially Andalusian style, hoping to peel away the depraved excrescences of the music that had been called flamenco so as to expose the inestimably valuable deep song that lay beneath. In other words, they set out in search of *cante jondo*.

Predictably perhaps, their search emphasized the male contribution to this musical style while downplaying the female's. These emphases were defended by appeal to Andalusian culture, from its roots in Roman times, through its heights in the middles ages when Jews, Muslims, Christians and, later, Gitanos had enjoyed unparalleled conviviality, and on through the sadnesses of the post-1492 period when Andalusia fell under the heavy-handed authority of Madrid. *Cante jondo*, they argued, was there through all these epochs as the music of men who gather in the parks, streets, and taverns. These public men carried forward this *jondo* style as they gathered together in public fraternity, tarrying with other men rather than returning to their woman-dominated houses. By sitting and chatting and drinking and eventually singing long into the night, they preserved the tradition. What's more, their songs became the banner of their masculinity, outward signs of manly control over the public sphere.

Their songs were shot through with painfully experienced, passionately introspected, and intensely expressed emotion. Like the British Romantics and Parisian bohemians, these Andalusian men drew on an allegedly feminine expressive style to mark out their distinctively masculine territory, while women were consigned to the margins and relegated to silence. An institution such as the *seccion feminina* (SF) embodied this gender paradox with surprising concreteness. Constituted on the assumption that womanhood was 'the fundamental guarantor of social stability,' the SF was Franco's program for using women to silence women and to return them to the confines of their homes where they were supposed to take up their proper duties of filtering and purifying the oral and musical traditions which that homelife should normally engender. As a result, 'Thousands of middle- and lower middle-class women were mobilized in its cadres to perform functions which signified the penetration of the private sphere by the state. In this way, middle-class women were being taken into the public domain and used to police other women – most overtly, the urban and rural poor' (Graham 1995). The SF became a major vehicle for censoring flamenco song and for bringing flamenco music into line with the cultural politics of the Franco regime.

The paradox that is evident in the operations of the SF is this: women exercised power so as to bring about their own disempowerment. SF women used their surveillance and censorship authorities in order to assure that women on the whole remain in positions of invisibility, silence, and powerlessness. Tarby (1991) wrestles with a variant of this same conundrum when he explores the male penchant for cante as a response to the largely 'feminine universe' in which men found themselves. Poor and marginalized men, Tarby argues, take up the feminized voice in such a way as to inventively co-opt that central, oceanic, cosmological power assigned by God to womanhood. They sing so as to stand tall in a universe that is not their own. Their cante defines for them a floor from which they can speak with some authority, albeit borrowed. As these men circle around one another after hours in the local bars, their passionate expressions effectively glue them together, creating for them an impregnable fraternity. Paradoxically but predictably, women are excluded from this fraternity. As one authority puts it, 'A woman's presence in the flamenco bars was not only demeaning for her, it made everyone involved uncomfortable and it interfered with the fluidity of the proceedings' (Pohren 1980).

Women do, however, find a place in that other dimension of flamenco performance, namely dance. Not in the dark and heavy bars where serious – though rarely sober – men sing, but in the bright and brassy atmosphere of fiestas and carnivals, provocatively dressed women dance, and have done so since the early nineteenth century. Curiously however, while the woman's dance attracts an audience's attention, the dancer herself is not the main event. Traditionally, she is the provocateuse, the temptress whose appearance and movements, so obviously but crassly reliant on the power of 'nature,' threaten to throw the 'cultured' man off balance. In the face of such dance, the singer and guitarist (*cantaor* and *tocaor*) – like the bullfighter facing a bull – reassert their cultural composure by taming the feminine animal force that they confront. The same word, *trastear*, is conventionally used to refer to a matador's 'taming' of the bull, to the guitarist's control over sound, and the man's domination of a woman. In all these domains, the man becomes the center of attention and the heroic main-event.

My own contributions to this collection reflect on contemporary struggles over this androcentric flamenco tradition. First, I offer an extended review of Carlos Saura's recent feature film, *Flamenco*, a film that is remarkable for its modernist cinematography and for its concerted effort to revise the clichés of flamenco that seem to have troubled Saura even from the time of his acclaimed film *Carmen*. My conclusion is that Saura's modernism, being itself high-handed, heroic, and arguably androcentric, is not yet prepared to fully reshape the flamenco tradition he addresses. Second, I reflect on flamenco dance, and specifically on the paradoxical hyper-masculinity of highly regarded male dancers. In line with Tobin's and Holst-Warhaft's essays here, I conclude that men dance for other men, and in doing so, they weave together movements that bespeak domination and collaboration, competition and homosocial desire.

In a third essay on the flamenco style, Timothy deWaal Malefyt has reflected on some contemporary tactical reinventions of flamenco history. He contends that a new wave of flamenco traditionalism is tapping into the currently powerful image of 'flamenco family' with all of the social solidity that that image connotes. 'Flamenco family' counterbalances the heavy emphasis given to flamenco-men-in-public by playing up the role of households, families, and especially their matriarchs in creating and preserving musical traditions. Towards this same end, flamenco clubs or *peñas* have sprung up in Andalusia and beyond since the early 1960s. Most of these imitate the 'close intimate community' that was said to prevail during the hermetic period when flamenco was allegedly celebrated in private circles and before it had burst onto the public scene in the *cafés cantantes*.

Argentine Tango

Our search for common trends and shared themes in popular music and dance has led to an emphasis on the role of music as a post-religious experience in the nineteenth century and to the nomination of anti-heroic, downtrodden, and allegedly feminine personae as post-priests. The history of Andalusian flamenco music, sketched here in broad strokes, illustrates these trends and themes with some clarity, making it apparent that flamenco was, and is, an elemental form of popular music that wrestles with the fundamental puzzles of modern social life without ever resolving them.

Because the forces and conditions that prompted the emergence of flamenco were general and distributed right across the board in the post-Enlightenment Western societies, popular musical styles of different hues and intensities emerged in parallel. Accordingly, British dance hall music and French *cafés concerts* music in the mid-nineteenth century were, like flamenco, perfused with strains of nationalism, bohemianism, and commercialism. While it is interesting to explore the parallel between processes of emergence in these styles, it is also interesting to consider the manner in which they were subsequently intermingled and hybridized in response to the orientalism and exoticism that pervaded Western societies in the late-nineteenth century. Both of these dimensions, parallel development and subsequent hybridization, can be profitably explored through considerations of tango, rebetika, and North American popular music.

The social historical context in which Argentine tango emerged in the 1890s had everything to do with the poor who were crushed into the urban poverty of Buenos Aires as a result of the implementation of economic policies by a development-minded government in the last half of the nineteenth century. In order to advance to the status of a first-rate industrial and political power, Argentina, it was argued, needed people, bodies, numbers more than anything else. A large population would, in and of itself, generate a vital economy and advance the national cause. To this end, immigration was not just encouraged but actively solicited and subsidized.

Culture figured into the plan as significantly as did economics. Specifically, the Argentine elite yearned to reconstruct a version of Europe on their American soil. Their immigration policies aimed to achieve this goal, in part, by overshadowing the non-European creole population, that is the indigenous and the African American populations, with newly immigrated Europeans, drawn especially from Italy.

The new immigrants, the pawns in these power plays, found themselves caught between old political rivals. They were rejected and controlled by both the Euro elites and their creole adversaries. Compounding their problems, was the fact that the infrastructure of cities like Buenos Aires was ill-prepared for the massive immigration that ballooned its population from 100,000 in 1880 to a million persons in 1910. A lumpen underclass developed, blending languages of Spanish-speaking, Italian-speaking and African American populations. The resulting hybrid 'lunfardo,' the cant of urban thieves and thugs, became a linguistic banner waved by the disenfranchized but defiant slum dwellers of Buenos Aires. In the 1890s a musical dance style emerged amongst these lunfardo-speakers, a dance that was, like the language, a blend of different traditions of music and movement. Various words were used to refer to this folk dance style, including *milonga* and tango. At the turn of the century a number of developments resulted in the popularization of this style, the most significant being the circulation of money as a result of the sale of sex in the very same social contexts where lunfardo and tango were strongly entrenched. The newly moneyed *compadritos* of this early period were passionate and allegedly ruthless dancers . . . and fashionable, paving the way to an era in which a Homburg and a smoking jacket were *de rigeur* for an up-and-coming tanguero.

Between 1900 and 1917, musical venues became more capacious. The accordion-like bandoneon replaced the less audible guitar as the instrument of choice. And tango grew to be famed and defamed as the tantalizing dance style of the passionate Porteño low-life. As if to co-opt some of the dangerous vitality of Buenos Aires, Americans and Europeans leaped into a tango frenzy. Vernon Castle, whose influence on American popular dance styles is charted in the essay by Susan Cook, helped to revise and disseminate a sanitized tango for widespread consumption. On the other side of the Atlantic, European artists and intellectuals raided the Argentine style for its transgressive energy. The soundtrack of Buñuel and Dali's surrealist film 'Chien Andalou' (1929) draws heavily on tango.

The period between 1917 and 1935 marks the heyday of tango song. The significance of the dance style was eclipsed by the energy and attention given to tango lyrics and tango singers, the most important of whom was Carlos Gardel. Lunfardo, never more than a functionally specific slang, was augmented and gentrified to become the *caló porteño* of the tango poets.

After a brief period of decline, following the untimely death of Carlos Gardel, tango was rekindled and revitalized during the regime of the strong-arm populists Juan Perón and Eva Duarte Perón and enjoyed widespread popularity as a musical symbol of national identity. Thereafter, tango has continued to rise and fall with political tides as much as with aesthetic interests, being distinctly out of favor during the rule of the military junta between 1976 and 1983 and then returned to favor with a vengeance thereafter, not only in Argentina but worldwide.

The parallels between flamenco and tango are strong and clear with respect to androcentrism. Donald Castro has identified a chronic strain of male-centeredness in both tango lyrics – working the same rich vein as Archetti (1994) – and in the persons of Carlos Gardel, Juan Perón and Eva Duarte Perón, all of whom he considers to be personifications of this style. He concludes from his analysis that tango is all about men suffering from love, sweeping up women to comfort and protect themselves, using them as crutches and as forms of insulation for their positions of passivity, or quietism, or for their general refusal to shoulder any sort of personal responsibility.

Jeffrey Tobin alludes to the androcentrism of male dancers, *tangueros*, and to the dominant theme of love as expressed in dance. But he diverges from the position taken by Castro, when he contends that the love experienced by tangueros is less a matter of heterosexual affection than 'the true passion of male friendship.' In Tobin's view, the woman (la tanguera) in this dance is not so much a love object as a medium and conduit for the transmission of affections between men. More disturbingly, a woman serves to enhance the status of her partner by the way she submits to his possession of, and control over her on the dance floor. According to Tobin, 'homosocial desire (in the tango dance) is expressed through the display of women.' The man 'leads the woman to perform very flashy figures while he himself moves as little as possible.' In this way the woman may well be the focus of visual attention in such events, but still in all 'the public watches the woman in order to talk about the man.'

Marta Savigliano's essay complements Tobin's by considering the dancing couple from the woman's point of view. For her, the tanguero is a carnivore, a creature who operates high on the food-chain of tango dance. Women, low on that chain, are used up and tossed aside, or worse, they are ignored entirely, falling out as wallflowers. Describing this scene from inside – herself a tanguera – Savigliano provides us with a sense of what it means to be a woman who is both threatened and muffled in the setting of the modern tango club, the milonga.

The tango tradition displays all of this androcentrism in parallel with flamenco, and to that degree, it deepens our understanding of modern popular post-religious musicality. Revealing as it is, however, too heavy an emphasis on male-centeredness poses the danger of oversimplifying the social history of tango. Tobin argues, for example, that a great deal more needs to be said about the gendering of tango besides the fact that it is 'androcentric.' Indeed, most of the delicious complexity of this musical style would remain untasted if commentators were to go no further than observing that tango encourages 'the true passion of male friendship.' For one thing, when considered up close, tangueros are rarely close to each other, hardly well-bonded as are flamenco men in Spain. In reality, the fraternity that they experience is marked by mutual suspicion and envy, and by repressed homosexuality. With comments that subvert the macho image of the dance, Tobin suggests that tangueros always operate 'across a leaky border that separates the straight and the gay.' Savigliano for her part, notes that tangueras, notwithstanding the threatening scene that they face, exercise manifold tactics to wrest control from their male partners on the dance floor: 'Women have never been just "docile bodies" or "passive objects" on the margins . . . In tango, the marginals are at the core.'[12] Obviously, relations on the dance floor are far more complicated than the image of androcentric tango would seem to suggest. Tangueros are caught up in complicated and repressed ties with each other, and the tangueras deploy self-empowering choreographic maneuvers while seeming to submit to their macho partners.

With these descriptions we can see that tango, like flamenco, is a site of significant gender performance. The boundaries dividing male and female are continually being breached and tested. A man who sings passionately to his confreres is not only reinforcing his ties to other men, he is also raising doubts about the very definition of the male identity that they share. And as the dominant classes draw on gender identity for their political capital – as they certainly have in both Spain and Argentina during the twentieth century – then such performances become politically significant.

Tango and flamenco performances challenge the conventions of gender at the same time that they rely on them. If gender, as Judith Butler has argued, 'is tenuously constituted in time, and instituted in an exterior space through a stylized repetition of acts' (1990: 140), then the homosocial practices of tangeros cannot but contribute to the reconstitution of gender. Theirs is an activity of border-breaching similar to Dennis Rodman's. By the same token, tangueras who deploy resistant maneuvers and choreographic powerplays on the dancefloor, are confusing and threatening, not unlike Madonna who, according to Susan McClary, is persistently invoking and then rejecting conventional gender identities, and thereby 'rewriting some very fundamental levels of Western thought' (1991: 148).

Rebetika

The Greek rebetika have their origins in the songs of the urban centers of nineteenth-century Asia Minor as well as in the sea ports of Greece. This geographical situation, in and of itself, should alert us to the possibility of fundamental differences between rebetika and its musical cousins that emerged farther to the west, flamenco, fado, and tango. Rebetika grew up, at the turn of the century, in societies whose roots stretch back to the Byzantine world rather than to western Rome and to eastern Orthodox Christianity rather than to Roman Catholicism. The implications of this cultural historical affiliation, explored here in an essay by Angela Shand, become particularly potent when one considers the human body and its role in song and dance. In contrast to the western Gnostic cosmology that gives warrant to mind over body, the kenoticism of eastern Orthodoxy celebrates the body and considers it as an equipollent player in salvation history. Hence, the music and dance, cultivated in those modern societies that are shadowed by Byzantium, respond to both the body-centeredness of the eastern world and to the mind-centeredness of Romanticism and Modernism in the west. As Shand suggests, the historical development of rebetika hints at the cosmological and theological tensions that rift it from within.

The centerpiece of rebetika is a solo song accompanied, in the Asia Minor style, by 'ud, santouri (dulcimer) and violin, and later by bouzouki, baglama and guitar. Such songs, as Gail Holst-Warhaft indicates, were often sung in a type of cafe called Cafe Aman. The generic name *amanes* was derived from standard song types that were called *amani* because singers, as they improvised, often fell back on long melismas over the exclamatory word *aman.*[13] Dance typically accompanied song, with rhythm marked by finger cymbals and tambourines after the fashion of Gypsies. *Zeibekiko* became the principle danced component of the rebetika style for males, with the female equivalent being *tsifte-teli.*

The rebetes themselves, that is, the adepts of this style, were denizens of their urban underworlds. These rebetes swaggered about defiantly, but also fashionably, not unlike the compadritos of Argentine lore. Their sartorial signature was a jacket worn with one sleeve left out. Their transgressive songs were replete with disparaging remarks about law and the police, and were drawn in part from a jail song tradition that had flourished during the oppressive years of the mid-nineteenth century.[14]

In 1922, the Greco-Turkish wars ended with a massive forced emigration of Christians – whether of Greek descent or not – from Turkish soil (see Eugenides 1998). Over a million persons, many of whom were Turkish and not Greek at all, were declared to be Greek and then sent back across the Aegean where they were crowded in Greek cities that subsequently fell deep into poverty, not unlike turn-of-the-century Buenos Aires. The streets of Athens and Piraeus overflowed with immigrants living amid the predictable circumstances of disenfranchisement and dislocation. The rebetes, always marginal and often poor, lived cheek by jowl with drug dens and houses of prostitution.

In the 1930s, as the impact of this demographic upheaval began to percolate through the society, a revised rebetika style appeared, one that reflected the Turkish roots of the new Greek urban dwellers. This Smyrna style was the foundation for what Holst-Warhaft has called classical rebetika.

As often occurs with 'classics', this rebetika style was coupled with political interests in subsequent decades. During the German occupation, and the Civil War that followed, the 'harsh and toughly humorous' lyrics of defiant rebetes were said by some to undermine working-class morale but by others to silently resist the regime. In the 1950s, the style bifurcated into easy-listening *laika* music and an 'art-popular' style that encompassed both explicitly political artistry and new-wave aesthetics. In 1960, the singer Theodorakis tapped the rebetika style to encourage opposition to the dominant and oppressive political regime, thereby generating what some described as 'a small civil war raging in the musical sector of our intellectual life.'

To make sense of this complex history, Gail Holst-Warhaft takes us back into the nineteenth century in order to witness a convergence of some distinct streams of cultural and musical practice. Western aesthetics was then bearing down on Greek nationalists and Romantics. However, Holst-Warhaft argues, these Western and Romantic influences never supplanted, but were instead joined together with age-old indigenous characteristics. Her history is, therefore, an exploration of cultural convergence. She demonstrates the presence in rebetika of the ancient female-centered tradition of lamentation, but she also considers newly emergent, largely Western, mainly male-centered forces that began to reshape rebetika in the 1930s, creating a new style that was to influence – if not haunt – subsequent periods of Greek cultural life.

North American Popular Music

During the half-century between 1880 and 1930, in the cities of Seville, Buenos Aires, and Athens, bohemian sounds jousted with bourgeois styles. In Seville, gitanized flamencos attracted hordes of middle-class 'wannabees' to the cafés cantantes. In Buenos Aires, street-wise tough guys shaped tangos that were promptly exported upward and outward to London and Paris. In Athens and Piraeus, the cafés amans gave way to an era of hookah smokers and their melismatic sounds, the dicey but tantalizing roots of rebetika. In each case, one finds a bohemian style, gendered female, pitted against a bourgeois highbrow lifestyle. The result of the contest was always the same. The lowbrow music was co-opted and sanitized by the highbrow, and as a result, the middle-class listener was given the wherewithal to imagine his nationhood.

This same process was repeated in North America, though, as Susan Cook contends, in significantly distinctive ways that should prompt our critical reflection. It was – and is – in North America that race served as a foil to both gender and nation, entering into and revising the tightly knotted complex of nation-gender-music that, as we have seen, undergirded modern Spanish, Argentine, and Greek cultural experience. In North America, race rewrote that triad. Racial identity, cognate of both national and gender identities, usurped the primacies of both, leaving modern popular culture in North America as much a race-music dyad as a nation-gender-music triad. The historical development of this race-music dyad has been distinctive but predictably revealing.

The Americas, at the turn of the century, were home to a massive and visible population of downtrodden and disenfranchized African Americans and indigenous people. Unlike Europeans who, it seems, had to be jolted into recognizing the moral bankruptcy of the bourgeois social order, Americans had lived with its moral scandal from the beginning. Unlike Europe, where it took remarkable events such as the Spanish debacle of 1898 and the Greek catastrophe of 1922, genocidal catastrophes were native to America, autochthonous, almost workaday. The United States was a systemically racist society with a lumpen class that had been present from its birth as a nation. And though the dominant population persistently repressed the moral paradox it sheltered, African Americans combatted that repression with just as much persistency. As a result, in the United States, bohemianism was not imaginatively constructed as it was in Paris. It did not need to be. The disenfranchized had been both present and resistant for a very long time.

That fact – coupled with predictably reactionary responses by the mainstream to new waves of immigration from Europe – helps to explain the prevalence of what Lawrence Levine has called 'the sacralization of culture' in the United States at the turn of the century. Unlike the Parisians and Sevillians who, at that time, were turning to bohemianism, New Yorkers were revitalizing their respect for respectability. Shakespeare, opera and symphonic performances were all resoundingly well received, though by audiences that were remarkably homogeneous in their unflagging thirst for edifying 'culture' and in their disdain for vulgarity of every sort. In the United States, would-be bohemians never got to enjoy their dirt before undergoing bourgeois sanitation. Bohemian initiatives were all thoroughly cleansed at their moments of birth (Levine 1988).

The contributions of Irene and Vernon Castle to American dance, described here by Susan Cook, tell this tale in concrete terms. Between 1913 and 1918 the Castles introduced tango and other forms of 'tough dancing' to the American public, but always with sanitations that blunted the intimations of feminine passion and lowbrow eroticism. Just as problematic as the Castles was the person of James Reese Europe, their bandleader. In Cook's account, Europe, an innovative African American musician, disavowed the value of the lowbrow dance style that his own music encouraged, therein playing out some of the same paradoxes that have continued to bedevil African American music right down to the present day. As Paul Gilroy notes, musicians, audiences and critics have been caught – really trapped – by the commonplace assumption that music springs from and speaks for the soul of a community (Gilroy 1993). Where such an assumption prevails, musical developments and hybrids – Jimi Hendrix, Miles Davis, Michael Jackson – are scorned. With such an assumption in hand, critics regularly ask how can innovative music continue to speak for the soul of the community? Evidently James Reese Europe thought it could not.

The perspective being developed here recommends that we defer answering poorly framed questions about music, authenticity, and identity. We argue that no music springs from, and speaks for, the soul of a community in any simple way. Despite essentialist views that persist in portraying popular music and dance as if they were an unchanging permanence through which a community realizes itself, they are better thought of, in Gilroy's terms, as 'a constantly changing same.' Music and dance are on the move. They are a ship rather than a house. They are route rather than a root. They are always hybridized, never not fractalized, and constantly becoming 'rhizomatized.' They serve social identificational functions but they do so as a flux. They are never staid, and therein lies its promise. Flux is what enables one to hope for a way out of the otherwise unresolveable contradictions of contemporary social relations. Music and dance, after all, are always about changing the world.

Existing commentaries on, and literature about, flamenco, tango, rebetika, and African American popular music are rife with debates about authenticity – Paco de Lucía and Camarón are said to have sold out flamenco, and don't even bother to mention the Gipsy Kings. However, from our vantage point, the developments that are so often accused of sinning against authenticity, may often be promising and still authentic in a manner of speaking. The fusions of flamenco with 'jazz' (here, a shorthand for the variegated popular styles spawned in North America), of 'jazz' with tango, of tango with flamenco (made clear in the border crossing films of Carlos Saura), of tango with rebetika, and of rebetika with 'jazz', may all be promises rather than problems. It is just such promise that we aim to explore here.

Notes

1. Works by Abbate (1991), Frith (1996a), Kramer (1990), Leppert (1993), McClary (1991), Shepherd (1987), and Silverman (1988), to name just a few have rocked musicology, and turned its ear towards feminism, performance theory, the new historicism, and Foucauldean criticism.
2. I have relied on histories of nineteenth-century bourgeois culture by Peter Gay (1996), Jeffrey Seigel (1986), Hacking (1995), and Andreas Huyssen (1986).
3. Over the past five years, flamenco scholars such as Steingress (1993), García Gómez (1993), Mitchell (1994), and tango scholars such as Castro (1991) and Savigliano (1995) have begun to explicate song and dance to reveal cultural patterns of and for social life, and rebetika scholars, notably Gail Holst-Warhaft (Holst 1977, 1979), have written works that prepare the way for our comparison and contrast of those patterns.
4. Paul Connerton (1989) and Richard Terdiman (1993).
5. Stoetzer (1996); Herzfeld (1987).
6. For more on Rousseau, see Felicia Miller Frank (1995). See Kramer (1990) for comments on Liszt's 'Faust.' See Kittler (1991) and Gill (1987) for comments on the nineteenth-century popularization of 'Mother Tongue' and 'Mother Earth.' These terms, it should be noted, date to periods considerably earlier than English Romanticism. The OED cites Chaucer's use of 'Nature' as feminine in 1374, Raynolde's use of 'Lady nature' in 1545, Herbert's use of 'Dame Nature' in 1634, and Milton's use of 'Mother Earth' in 1667. These citations noth-withstanding, the term 'Mother Nature' acquired a very special cachet in the nineteenth century.
7. See Goodwin (1994) for an analysis of Wordsworth's treatment, of Alice Fell and see Torgovnick (1997) for discussions of feminoid primitivism in the interwar period.
8. Judith Butler (1990) and Shepherd (1987).

9. Bruce Seymour (1995) has published a biography of Eliza Gilbert and Evlyn Gould has written about Carmen (1996).

10. Hutcheon (1996); Deval (1989).

11. It should be noted that the response of Europeans, particularly Anglo Europeans to this flamenco style was, and is, ambivalent. They persistently played off the animal magnetism of the style against the primitive and child-like culture of its Andalusian adepts, not only in their early writings, but also in later works by Havelock Ellis, Irving Brown, Waldo Frank, V.S. Pritchett. For an insightful discussion of the orientalism of Gustave Flaubert, see Terdiman (1985).

12. This quotation, from Savigliano's social history of tango (1995: 69) becomes especially significant when considered in conjunction with Jorge Zanada's film *Tango Nuestra Baile*, and specifically in association with the scene in which one hears the inner voices of a man and a woman as he approaches her for a turn on the dance floor. As the couple finally begin dancing, the narrator asks: 'Who was the first to give up dancing tango? She? He? Who began to think it was "machista?" He? She? Who wanted to equal the other? He? She? I?'

13. As such, *aman* parallels the flamenco *ayeo* in form and function. For an insightfully Romantic discussion of the *ayeo* in flamenco, see Rosales (1987).

14. Rooted in this prison experience, the rebetika style is parallel to the Andalusian flamenco style where one finds song forms entitled *carcelera* and *saeta carcelera*, together with a variety of lyrics referring to the prison experience, and numerous historical anecdotes that depict prison song in the most poignant terms.

Flamenco Song: Clean and Dirty
William Washabaugh

Part I

Clean is the word for Carlos Saura's latest feature film, *Flamenco*. Its voicing and imaging of flamenco artistry offer a squeaky clean restyling of the flamenco tradition. Its opening moments set the tone for the entire work. From behind the blackness of the screen, one hears some muted street noise that already, before any light is shed, promises a contemporaneity that will banish nostalgia and maudlin sentiment. This will be today's flamenco, music of the here-and-now, offered by men and women absolved of all debt to allegedly heartier yesteryears. This is the flamenco, Saura's flamenco, that prompts my reflections, laudatory for the most part, but not without reservations.

The first light, streaming brilliantly through the roof, presents the old Seville train station. Looking up from floor to girded structures overhead, the camera pans across the ironwork of the skylight with its sweeping Eiffel-esque design, and works its way down slowly and patiently to the floor, exposing to view what the silence of the place has made clear from the outset: it is colossally empty. Standing mirrors break the line of gaze, turning the emptiness of the place into something strangely fractured. Chairs – yes, they are traditional Andalusian straightbacks with reed-woven seats, but – freshly painted and utterly disembedded from all social context stand in an arc, stark on the polished wooden floor with a mono-chrome backscreen. This is the scene that prepares us for flamenco shorn right down to stubble, cut free from distracting detail, liberated from all visual sentimentality. This is the scene that prepares us for a squeaky clean take on flamenco, for a boot-camp bald representation that is every bit as fresh as the flamenco tradition itself is stale.

Then comes the cosmogony: the world is created. Initially, it is only a distorted reflection of humanity that is visible, shadowy figures reflected off the polished floor. But then the artists in full form enter the station, filing in column by column, filling its emptiness, populating its spaces, breathing into it life, relieving its dramatic stillness with banter, brightness, sassy laughter, and, in this thoroughly mythified moment, the only narration we will hear for the next hour:

Flamenco appears in Andalusia in the south of Spain in the mid-nineteenth century as a result of the confluence of communities, religions, and cultures that gave rise to a new style of music. The chorales of the Greeks, the sonnets of the Arabs, the chants of the Gregorians, the epic versus of Castile, the laments of the Jews, the sound of negritude, and the accent of the Gypsy community that came from far-off India to settle here, are mixed together to form the structure of the music called flamenco, a music expressed through song, dance and guitar.

At this point the lights come up on a group of about 25 artists seated in their Andalusian chairs. La Paquera strides forward to sing her trademark form, *bulerías*. Neither she, nor the guitarists, nor any of the other artists featured in the next nineteen performances are identified as they sing and play and dance. Viewers must wait until all twenty performances, strung one after the other, without comment, narrative, or revelatory context are over and done with. Then and only then can we discover who it is that has regaled us so with song and dance:

> *Bulerías* by La Paquera and Moraito Chico
> *Guajiras* by Merché Esmeralda
> *Alegrías* by Manolo Sanlucar
> *Farruca* by Joaquín Cortés
> *Martinete* by Manuel Moneo and Agujetas
> *Bulerías* by Mario Maya
> *Fandangos de Huelva* by Paco Toronjo
> *Soleá* by Fernanda de Utrera
> *Peternera* by José Menese
> *Siguiriya* by Enrique Morente
> Soleá by José Merce and Manuel Carrasco
> *Soleá* by Farruco, Chocolate, and Farruquito
> *Taranta* by Carmen Linares with Rafael Riqueni
> *Tango* by Juana de Revuelo, Remedios Amaya, Aurora Vargas and Quiqui Paredes
> *Villancicos* by La Macanita
> *Poema por Bulerías* by Lole and Manuel
> *Tangos* by Paco de Lucía and his sextet

Alegrías de Cádiz by Matilde Corral
Bulerías by Potito, Tomatito, Chano Labato, Rancapino, and Joaquín Grilo
Rumba by Manzanita and Ketama

Part II

From its very first moments of theatrical cosmogony, Saura began cutting away the old clichés of flamenco artistry. Indeed, it can be argued that his purpose in making this film is to perform some radical cultural surgery, to cast aside the banalities of flamenco, to dispense with the kitsch, and, perhaps most importantly, to excise the noxious gender politics that have clung like parasitic vines to the trunk of this style from its moment of sprouting, sucking it dry and threatening its vitality.

Viewers who understand flamenco's problematic gender politics in advance are in a better position to appreciate the brilliance of Saura's presentation. Accordingly, we will take a moment here to rehearse the dark and sorry aspects of flamenco, the better to appreciate what Saura has snipped away and carted off in this tree-trimming, house-cleaning film.

For most of the past hundred and fifty years, flamenco music has meant, first and foremost, flamenco song. Since 1850, rough-cut poetry has been sung to the accompaniment of percussive guitar during late-night gatherings of well-lubricated commoners sitting elbow-to-elbow with dreamy-eyed bourgeoisie in southern Spain. More often than not, the singers have been men. And men too were the ones who attended these events, applauding the performances in their distinctively macho manner. Their sung poetry – *cante* as it is called – has been the centerpiece of flamenco despite the fact that the passionate dances of wolf-eyed women are widely assumed to be the primary referent of the term 'flamenco.'

Over the past hundred and fifty years, artists and commentators have objectified cante as androcentric song. Their testiculatory efforts – at once man-centered and generative – have 'engendered' a bumper crop of excitement across Europe. Impresarios, café proprietors, and festival organizers have been harvesting the results and profiting handsomely ever since.

Flamenco men have generally come off as superordinately sensitive people. Like Byron's Don Juan, the cantaor has a heart that swells with passion and would, it seems, burst were it not held in check by his small-minded and priggish society. Such a singer, perpetually frustrated, lives out the gospel of the 'tragic sense of life' insofar as he penetrates the mysteries of death and transcendence yet still heels faithfully to the humbling constraints of the common life.

In all of this, women are said to play no great part. Most often, they are treated as an annoyance and a distraction. According to the authoritative voice of Donn Pohren in *A Way of Life*, 1980, 'A woman's presence in the flamenco bars was not only demeaning for her, it made everyone involved uncomfortable and it interfered with the fluidity of the proceedings. Women were, therefore, fated to be left out of much of the flamenco life of Andalusia.' Along this same line, the luminary-cantaor, Manolo Caracol, claimed that women are by nature bored by the seriousness of cante. He added maudlin emotion and cloying sentiment to his stage shows in Madrid in the 1950s in order to attract the feminine audiences that he thought were being driven away by pure cante.

Now, as Saura seems to recognize, one can easily overstate the case by dwelling on androcentric song. Women have also sung cante, and sung it well. Indeed, the woman's voice may well be the soul of flamenco. There is certainly abundant historical evidence that women were more than window dressing in nineteenth-century flamenco circles. Women were singing, as well as dancing, flamenco from very early in the nine-teenth century, according to Ortiz Nuevo's *Que se Sabe?*, 1992. Julio Romero de Torres, painting at the turn of the century, was fixated on women, portraying 'woman' in his *Cante Jondo* as nothing less than a god (Figure 2.1). García Lorca wrote phrases of lavish praise to honor the voice of Pastora Pavón 'La Niña de los Peines.' And Manuel and Antonio Machado in their play *Lola se va a los Puertos* (1929) apo-theosized the main character, Lola the cantaora. The puzzle surrounding such deifications is that they contrast so sharply with both the demeaning attitudes of most male flamencos – Pohren and Caracol above – and also with the flamenco role alloted to women in the twentieth century, namely that of 'sweater girl.'

The source and logic of the flamenca's tantalizing flirtatiousness is traceable if not altogether understandable. At fairs, and during carnivals, Andalusian women enjoyed rare opportunities to step out from the shadows of their domestic life. They donned bright, provocative, Gypsy clothing, and they danced the seductive dances attributed by some to Roman women of Cádiz, the *puellae gaditanae*. The objective of their performances was straightfoward: to unsettle men, to excite them, to tease them up to, but not beyond, the point that they lose control. In playing out this cultural script, women as much as men, portrayed femininity as a threat to cosmic orderliness. The man's job was to handle this threat

Figure 2.1 Cante Jondo by Julio Romero de Torres used with permission of the Ayuntamiento of Córdoba

and to reaffirm that order. The honorable man – consummately cool – gazed on the lovely bailaora, and, though lusting in his heart, disciplined his public self to appreciate only the aesthetic finesse of her dance. After a momentary encounter with her discomfiting femininity, he returned himself to his appointed state of unflappability, thereby reaffirming the stability of masculine public life in the face of threats embodied in women.

How can we make sense of this strange history of occasional deification and ubiquitous sexism in popular culture? The first thing to be said is that the sexism that infects traditional flamenco artistry is not new or uniquely modern. Spanish misogyny is as old as Spain itself, so much so as to be ironized in *La Celestina* at the beginning of the sixteenth century: *Who would tell you of their (women's) lies, their routines, their chatter, their superficiality, their tears, their brazenness, their dissemblances, their gossip, their tricks, their slips, their coldness, their ingratitude, their inconstancy, their . . .* and on and on. Like a stream polluted at its source, the current of misogyny runs forward through Spanish history tainting all its highs and lows, coming right down to the present day where it appears in the lyrics of flamenco song as illustrated by Génesis García Gómez in *Cante Flamenco, Cante Minero*, 1993:

> *Una mujer fue la causa*
> *de la perdición primera,*
> *que no hay mal en este mundo*
> *que de mujeres no venga*
> A woman was the source
> of the very first sin,
> and so nothing of evil in this world,
> come from ought but women.

That much having been said, however, it would be wrong and unfair to lay *all* the blame on Spain for the misogyny of the flamenco tradition. The fact is that Spanish misogyny was reinforced and rendered the more virulent by nineteenth-century German, British, and, later, French Romanticists whose writings were filled with double-edged commentary that both celebrated and demeaned womanhood.

We can best approach this dark dimension of Romanticism by considering the role of the 'inward turn.' English and German intellectuals – both exercised influence in Spain during the first half of the nineteenth century – directed popular attention to 'utopian longings, religious commitment, weariness with a world incurably corrupt, or the urge to flee to their chosen vocation,' all of which suggest an 'interiorization of vision.' Such interiorization gave new value to art, and above all, to music (Gay 1995).

The purchase of this inward turn was *understanding*, a deep, profound, whole-bodied appreciation of human beings in the world. Key, in this aesthetic, is the role of the concrete body as counterbalance to the Enlightenment celebrations of abstraction and the mind. Understanding is 'born of the recognition that the world of perception and experience cannot simply be derived from abstract universal laws, but demands its own appropriate discourse and displays its own inner, if inferior, logic . . . It is born,' says Eagleton (1990), 'as a woman, subordinate to man, but with her own humble, necessary tasks to perform.'

Woman is the source of this understanding, even as Eagleton's trope suggests, because a woman's being in the world involves her whole body rather than just her head. Her body, so clearly of the earth and its processes, bears within it a humic alliance with all other bodies in nature. Interestingly, this Romanticist association of woman with the dark earth harks back to classical Athenian legal practices wherein women, as beings of the earth, were held to be essentially unreliable witnesses. They were allowed, according to Page duBois (1991), to testify in court proceedings only after having been given over to a torturer who would, so to speak, shake the dirt out of their brains. However, for the Romantics, the humic mind of woman was a promise and a potentiality rather than a curse and a hobble. Thus, Wordsworth, in his poem, 'Michael,' celebrated the 'natural tune' of a baby at its mother's breast, a tune rendered perfect because it was mediated by woman, the ultimate mediatrix of Nature. A woman's voice, in its own right, was thought to spring from the depths of Nature and therefore to serve as a channel of transcendence, similar in its mediating powers to the Bible for twelfth-century Christians, not itself Nature, but that in which all of Nature was mysteriously inscribed.

This parallel is apt in one important respect. Just as the mute and muddled Bible had to be consumed by the holy men, the clerics, who were officially designated to interpret its mysteries, so too the woman's voice was assumed, by the Romantics, to be both confused and confusing so much so that it needed men, the poets, to properly inscribe its mystical resonance. Just as the Bible's voice was supplanted and then silenced by authoritative clerical interpretations in the twelfth century, so woman's voice was marginalized by the voices of the poets in the nineteenth.

Curiously, however, this marginalization of the female voice only enhanced its exotic power and mystical attractiveness. 'The very exclusion of women from offices,' says Wolfgang Kittler (1991), 'summoned women to their official capacity, as mothers, to elicit discourses generally and magically to transmute them into Nature . . . In Mother, the state found its Other, without whom it could not exist – as evidence, consider the passionate appeals to ministers, consistorial councilors, and schools inspectors to place the function of Motherhood above all political considerations.' 'Mother' thus acquired its powerful modern cachet as the site of the human essence and the source of all deep human understanding. My native English is not called my 'mother tongue' for nothing.

The Romantic conception of 'mother' rendered womanhood magically attractive. However, other aspects of Romanticism were nothing but conceptual minefields from the outset. I am speaking here of the Romanticist notion that passions-on-the-edge and a certain 'controlled de-control of emotion' were tell-tale signs of authenticity (Featherstone 1991). And, by their lights, no passion was riskier and no emotion more nearly unleashed as a woman's. Accordingly, femininity became synonymous with authenticity, as suggested in the writings of Andreas Huyssen (1986) and Mike Featherstone (1991). For the Romantics, feminine passion was a kind of tantalizing sentimentality that flouted the rules and deviated from prescribed paths for no other good reason than that it was close to the earth, to a warm and moist darkness that was impervious to cold reason and the abstractions of light.

The Romantic exploration of risky passion, forgotten pain, hysteria, multiple personalities and, generally speaking, of the subconscious life of women may well have been the critical component in late nineteenth-century efforts to rescue the Enlightenment project of representing the human essence. According to Ian Hacking (1995: 219), such explorations provided a 'forum for something of which science could not openly speak' namely the very essence of the human essence, the human soul . . . gendered feminine, of course, for purposes of transcription and analysis.

Pressing this logic further, Romantics contended that one could maximize the possibilities of accessing this dark and raging soul by searching out the riskiest passion and the most thoroughly forgotten pain. Their favored site for spiritual spelunking was, logically enough, the prostitute. This logic helps make sense of the long running Romantic concern with the prostitute's lament. Sarah Goodwin (1994) identifies the linkage of that cry with the poet's voice in the works of Wordsworth. Richard Leppert (1993) underscores that linkage in pictorial art, leading him to conclude that 'on woman were heaped the antagonisms and contradictions of masculinity. It was woman whose goodness harbored its radical opposite. It was man's duty to order the dialectic of woman within real women so as to articulate men's own identities and responsibilities.'

This Romantic misogyny so insightfully fingered by Goodwin and

Leppert goes a long way toward explaining the popularity of some passionate musical styles of the late-nineteenth century, such as flamenco, tango, and fado – if not rebetika – all of which were associated with the lamentational cry of the prostitute. It is not just that the middle-class men flocked to flamenco in order to satisfy base appetites, as Mitchell (1994) suggests. Less biased observers have been able to see that the gender complex associated with flamenco music is both less patent and more problematic than sodden sexuality. Neither is it the case that the lament-ational cry of the prostitute is a purely Gitano invention, a quirk of Gypsy life as García Gómez has suggested. Instead, we must credit the middle class with a benevolent but destructive spirituality that considered the prostitute's cry to be a kind of terminal heartache, the cry of a soul carried not so much by words, but by a moan (*el ayeo*) that is emitted before the words are even formed (Rosales 1987). For the middle-class listener, attending to this heartache is an act that makes space for a soul to stretch and breathe. To listen to this heartache is to live in fullness. So it happens that flamencas sing, and aficionados come away convinced that they have been involved in a truly and authentically HUMAN activity.

Now, as complicated as this history of gender in passionate song has become, we must add one more measure of complexity, at least with respect to flamenco music: Andalusian men usurped the voices of women. Not content to merely transcribe and celebrate the woman's voice – as in the case of Wordsworth and Alice Fell – they assumed primary responsibility for intoning Nature, for voicing the prostitute's cry, and for exercising the soul's essence. Men supplanted women and became the humic, whole-bodied adepts of Andalusian song. Not content with transcribing Nature's voice, they began producing it, using but also occluding the femininity that Romantics had long attributed to the woman's voice. Antonio Chacón, at the turn of the century, was singing in a high falsetto; Pepe Marchena in the 1950s, was murmuring his song and whispering his passion; Fernando Montor, in Granada in the 1970s, was performing the *soleá* of Juan Breva with long moans that built to crescendos of sobs and hiccoughs. Are these not female impersonations advanced during the very era when flamenco women were being turned into window dressing?

Just one viewing of *Flamenco* should be enough to convince any viewer that Carlos Saura aims to turn the tables on this paradoxical tradition. Like a double-edged sword, his film cuts a path forward towards a fresh future, while, on the backswing, it slashes away the outmoded past. True, he calls in all the usual suspects, the conventional forms, the hallowed singers, the acclaimed dancers, and the renowned guitarists.

But traditional flamenco artistry is here transformed in such a way as to throw every aficionado off balance. The transformation begins with the first light that hits the screen: Saura's flamenco performances are set in a train station.

To appreciate this setting, viewers must remember that while flamenco music has been celebrated in bars, on stages, in streets and in homes, it has rarely if ever been presented in a train station, and never with such visual elegance. Here, with a train station for a stage, Saura makes an end run around the clichés that have so bedeviled the flamenco tradition. Just enough remains to hint at what is absent, a quaint shawl draped around the shoulders of Manolo Sanlucar, the antique dress of Merché Esmeralda – 'renovators need to maintain alliances with traditionalists,' says Nestor García Canclini (1995). But, these vestiges of old flamenco are little more than retro clothing for the new flamenco body that Saura has constructed, a body, by the way, that appeals as much to the woman's eye as to the man's – Joaquin Cortés, stripped to the waist, certainly turned a few female heads. Saura's film, like the trains in his station, is poised for traveling out, for pursuing routes rather than roots and for shaking off the foul dust of the provincial past. Here, he conjures an upbeat future. By celebrating flamenco on polished floors in front of bright monochrome screens instead of on the time-worn cobbles of musty old taverns, he effectively does away with traditional flamenco while simultaneously ushering in a bold new world of possibilities. This is the best of modernism, not unlike Bill Watterson's renewal, managed with the help of a blanket of pure white snow, in his final offering of the Calvin and Hobbes cartoon series: 'Everything familiar has disappeared! . . . A fresh clean start! . . . A day full of possibilities! . . . Let's go exploring!'

Part III

Somewhere along the way, however, whether on the tracks or in the station, the train has faltered. Saura's effort to lift the flamenco artistry and imagery out of its cultural rut has fallen a bit short of its mark. Some commentators in Spain contend that Saura stumbled when he passed over such key singers as Juan El Lebrijano, Bernarda de Utrera, El Cabrillero, and El Cabrero, the dancer El Guïto, and such important guitarists Paco del Gastor, Pedro Peña, and Pedro Bacán, failing to make a place for them in his film. If only these artists had been included, Saura's synopsis would have been complete and he would have captured the fullness of this musical style.

For my part, I think that this criticism, regardless of the importance of the passed-over artists, fails to address a deeper problem in Saura's

Flamenco, the problem of gender. Saura's spare and minimalist film cleans up the old dirt of flamenco, but leaves viewers facing a new batch of problems, fresh piles of cultural rubbish.

We have seen that, traditionally, it is men who sing, often imitating the style of women. As if to break free of that tradition, Saura has La Paquera striding forward to begin the concert, a bold move that supplants man with woman. However the voice and style of La Paquera are ironically riddled with hints of masculinity, almost as if she were impersonating a man's impersonation of a woman. Her growling raspiness, *voz afillada*, and that of the grand matriarch of cante, La Fernanda de Utrera, put one in mind of Mae West, Marlene Dietrich, and Lauren Bacall, all husky in the voice (Silverman 1988: 61). Androgynous timbre dissembles their gender, and, in this film, muddles the effort to banish the old cultural politics.

The challenge of presenting flamenco women seems to have rattled Saura just a bit. Merché Esmeralda, dancing a beautiful *guajiras*, is lithe and winsome, but still somehow distant. Perhaps it is her invariant, almost frozen smile. La Fernanda is regal in her bearing, but perhaps overly so. Saura moderates her impact by editing in her impish query and child-like act of hushing herself at the end of her performance. Men, in contrast, seem to pose no problem at all. The heavyweights like Manuel Agujetas, whose lamentations bespeak nobility flirting with rage, and the lighter weights like Mario Maya, whose breezy *bulerías* helps keep the film afloat in the early going, stake out the domain and define clearly enough the territory of flamenco men. Might it not be the case that the woman's role in *Flamenco* remains problematic because the man's role is not?

Perhaps a part, if only a small part, of the problem of the handling of gender in *Flamenco* is attributable to Saura's modernist cinematography. His style, after all, calls for detachment, abstraction, rationality, and monologue, none of which are woman-friendly traits. True, his modernism enables him to dispense with incidentals and to focus all his attention on the sound and lighting, two standout features that set this project apart from all others of its ilk. But, on the downside, he disconnects viewers from the living art, and alienates the music from everyday life. Saura compensates for this alienation – while also drawing attention to it – with filmic fillips that satisfy one's need to flesh out the abstractions: Fernanda's post-performance antics mentioned above, and the post-performance footage of Joaquín Cortes as he pauses for six long seconds, exhales with a 'whew,' relaxes his posture, and then trudges off the screen. These moments break the monologue of sober and serious performance that prevails throughout the film. They point to life beyond art. They remind viewers that this documentary is just a bit too disembedded and perhaps a little too disciplined. But is that not how men would have it?

Saura's project is heroic. It searches out a position from which to appreciate the height and breadth and depth of flamenco spirituality while minimizing the dangers of contamination from the fast-talking, wine-swilling, loose-living folks who customarily play and listen. In the minds of many, his film must be chalked up as a resounding success, a gleaming, streamlined, lofty peak from which to see the whole world of flamenco at once. For the most part, I concur. But I cannot help wondering about the gender-trouble that lingers. It may be the case that women, so badly used in traditional flamenco practice, get good staging here. But, the stage, so clean and smooth and polished, still suggests the predominance of masculine desires. A jumpier, noisier production would have been more womanly . . . but maybe it would have been too dirty.

–3–

Fashioning Masculinity in Flamenco Dance

William Washabaugh

Introduction: Masculinity

In the flamenco tradition that has emerged with new vigor since the 1950s, men have typically done the singing while women have handled the dance. Moreover, the male-centered *cante* occupies the center of attention both in performances and in the literature while female-centered *baile* is given fairly short shrift, at least in Spain. Already, in such a division of labor, one can suspect the operation of some of the same gender politics described in the previous essay. The very fact that a verbal activity has been staked out by men whereas women have specialized in non-verbal movement, should be enough in itself to raise concern about exaggerated gender dimorphism in flamenco: Does flamenco collude with patriarchy? Is feminine power stunted by masculine co-optations of the voice? Can the expressivity of women, whether it is universal and grounded in the body as an 'écriture féminine' (Burt 1995: 68) or developed as a marginalized mode of communication in the course of socialization, ever break through the verbal limits imposed by the men who either sing or who interpret song with their intellectualizations (Dunn and Jones 1994)? Is the comfortable allocation of song but not dance to males a sign of an 'indefinite masculinity' that inconspicuously usurps pivotal practices as if such usurpation were natural, while simultaneously turning all attention to the supposedly more problematic practices of women (see Smith's discussion of 'indefinite masculinity' (1996) and Washabaugh's discussion of women's roles in *Flamenco* by Saura (p. 37)? Is flamenco not a site of 'abject masculinity,' where men repeatedly deny their identity with mother, and fashion an opposite identity for themselves, not just non-feminine, but the Manichean opposite of femininity, not unlike that described by Theweleit (see Gilmore 1990a: 40)? Some light can be shed on these questions by exploring the movements of flamenco men at dance.

It is true, after all, that men do dance flamenco. Some have even attained stardom and earned international reputations as exemplars of flamenco dance: Vicente Escudero, José Greco, Antonio, El Farruco, Rafael de Córdoba, Antonio Gades, El Güito, Joaquin Cortés, Joaquin Grilo, to name just a few. Given this fact, and also given that dance usually reflects the social context in which it occurs, it makes sense to consider male dancers with an eye to discerning in their movements some evidence for the collusion of flamenco dance with patriarchy.

An initial glance across the historical landscape of flamenco dance seems to suggest that the style and movement of male dancers is four-square supportive of Manichean gender relations, complicit with precisely the sort of suffocatingly patriarchal ideology outlined above. Gustave Doré's nineteenth-century ink drawing is symptomatic (see Figure 3.1). The male stands in defiant domination, here with arms outstretched over the body of a prostrate female. His pose is calculated to be aggressive. Is his icy stare directed squarely into the eyes of the spectators? Does it shoutdown the power of their gaze, more than compensating for the deep-seated fear associated with displaying the male body – a fear explored and exploited in the film *The Full Monty* (1997) (see also Burt 1995: 72)? Like the dance of a Greek *rebetis*, flamenco dance presents hyper-masculinity with a 'brusque swagger' that serves as the 'potent image of masculinity' (Cowan 1990: 177).[1]

The male dancer is aggressive and almost ferocious in his posture and movement. At the same time he is composed if not serene. Strange bedfellows, these qualities of ferocity and serenity. Stranger yet, these qualities inhabit the bodies of dancing men in precisely the same way they appear in a matador – literally, a killer – as he confronts a bull in the ring. The logic of this parallel has been explicated by Corbin and Corbin (1987). They argue that, amongst Andalusians, men are charged with the responsibility of guarding Culture and the orderliness of public life by fending off the chaos that is threatened by the forces of Nature. The bull, so massive, so strong, so fitful and violent, is a metonym for Nature, a piece of Nature whose very being bespeaks its dangers. Woman too, is a metonym for Nature, she with her alluring ways and her seductive powers. Accordingly, both the bull and the woman must be subdued in their separate venues by a male whose bodily style is at once powerful and aggressive enough to overcome Nature, but also composed enough to reaffirm the orderliness of Culture. Just so, the matador moves very little as he kills the beast, and the male dancer advances on spectators with steely ferocity, controlling, dominating, stopping them with succinct movement and eyes like a wolf. In every case, according to this argument,

Figure 3.1 El ole gaditano by Gustave Doré, used with permission of La Fundacion Machado, Seville

aggressive men joust with the powers of Nature in order to reaffirm the orderliness of Culture. Theirs is a noble masculinity, one that corresponds point for point with the North American 'civilized manliness' described by Bederman (1995) (see deWaal Malefyt, p. 54).

In flamenco dance, the aggressive behavior of males is said to reaffirm patriarchy. As in so many other styles (Burt 1995: 17), aggressive postures and angry gestures help to create an 'abject masculinity,' a male style that represses all the intimations of a feminine oceanic consciousness (see Torgovnick 1997). But unlike other dance styles, flamenco constructs this abject masculinity in response to an allegedly higher calling: to display the power of Culture over Nature. Through dance, a man defends the cultural public sphere against the threats of private Nature.[2]

It is only in the light of these central axioms of Andalusian culture that one can perhaps make sense of Donn Pohren's doctrinaire observation that 'The condition that men be men and women, women, or at least appear to be, is an absolute necessity in the baile flamenco if it is to be effective.' And, it is only such a higher calling that might enable one to tolerate, if not appreciate, the 'enormous macho ferocity' of Antonio Montoya Flores 'El Farruco' – *ejemplar de macho bravío abismal* (José Luis Ortiz Nuevo 1996: 96)

The case of Montoya is particularly revealing. His aura of ferocity was legendary. Flamenco lore is filled with anecdotes about his everyday life as well as about his dance. On stage, he was focused, deliberate, and given to frightening flashes of movement. He said that his distinctive style was of his own construction. He bowed to no higher authority in dance or in life. Says José Blas Vega, 'El Farruco is an angry courage a-dancing' *'Es El Farruco el coraje bailando'* (Blas Vega and Ríos Ruiz 1991: 290)

Interestingly, and as if to underscore the audaciousness of Montoya's machismo, he made the following pronouncement in 1996: 'When you mix the classical style with flamenco, what prevails is effeminate.' With a thinly veiled criticism of those who practice their steps in studios before mirrors, he claimed that 'Real flamencos (real men) don't need to practice' (Ortiz Nuevo 1996).

The figure of El Farruco, so full of macho bravado, is compelling partly because it is so exaggerated. In his comments, he talks a big macho game. And on stage, his movements were bold enough to match his words. In every way he personified Andalusian masculinity. In his dance, his macho movements seemed inseparable from the Andalusian gender complex that they represent. However, in this very way of describing El Farruco's style, we have tripped ourselves into a problem. To say that 'El

Farruco's dance *represents* Andalusian masculinity' is just too easy. The phrase rolls too trippingly off the tongue. The word 'representation' drops down onto the page too comfortably. To say that El Farruco's movements 'represent' Andalusian masculinity glosses over and conceals some of the most important aspects of his dance while at the same time unjustifiably directing attention to choreographic incidentals.

Metonymy

It is common enough nowadays to explore the contextual significance of dance. Though formalists in the preceding era had discouraged such explorations, contemporary intellectuals are increasingly prepared to accept the idea that '*representations* in dance are made up of discursive and affective symbols which are ideologically produced and historically and socially situated' (Burt 1995: 32). However, before we can move forward with this now widely accepted idea of 'representation,' we must specify and clarify the nature of the linkage between the dance and its context, as Burt himself acknowledges (Ibid.: 38–44).

In the past, the linkages between dance and context were assumed to be denotative (Ibid.: 39) and metaphorical (see Foster 1995: 4), resulting in danced representations that reveal the meanings of movements and the intentions of dancers. To borrow Wilshire's terms, dance 'is an essential and central metaphor for life . . . Here are the essential links – irreducibly metaphorical ones – between self and the world' (Wilshire 1982: 243). However in the current era, such links are being seen in a different light, more as 'inscriptions' on the dancer's body (Foster 1995: 5) resulting in movements that spring from repetitious drills (McNeill 1995), rather than as conceptualizations or metaphoric representations. Increasingly, dancers are said to exemplify and embody the world that has marked their bodies (Burt 1995: 40). In semiotic terminology, the open-sesame for appreciating the links between dance and its social context is metonymy.

A metonym is an expression whose semiotic operation depends on its being part of something else. In dance, a metonym is a movement and display that is a piece and part of some other dance or of some non-danced social practice. Just so, Desmond contends that 'Every dance exists in a complex network of relationships to other dances and other non-dance ways of using the body and can be analyzed along these two concurrent axes' (Desmond 1997: 31). Where metonymy reigns, a motion provokes meaning more than it can be said to 'have' meaning (contrast Hanna 1988: 14–15). Indeed, it is better when dealing with the metonyms, to say little or nothing at all about 'meaning,' such issues being best left to those who study kinetic metaphors. Instead, metonymic analyses spin out multiple and ramifying interconnections, some of which may be valuable, productive, edifying, some not. More than signs, metonyms are semiotic irritants; they deny our certainties by unmasking the world as an ambiguity (see Hutcheon 1994: 15). Their semiotic operations are internally unspecified because they are dependent on spectators' peculiar manners of attending. Different spectators can be expected to pursue the selfsame metonym in different directions.[3] For example, some have suggested that a boy scout's salute is a metonym for 'a healthy physique and character,' but others consider it to be a mark of proto-fascist anti-intellectualism (Boscagli 1996: 85). Here, one movement issues in contrastive interpretations, neither of which is true or authentic, because truth and authenticity lie outside the domain of metonymy.

Chastened by these constraints, and cognizant that metonymic analysis is suggestive but not definitive, I will undertake here an analysis of El Farruco's manner of incarnating an Andalusian gender ideology.

Men Weighing Their Hems

For purposes of this analysis, I will be focusing on the brief footage of El Farruco that is included in the BBC documentary film *An Andalusian Journey* (1989) and the very similar shots that are included in Carlos Saura's film *Flamenco* (1995). It goes without saying that these moments are fraught with metonymy, brimming with more linkages than we can even list, let alone analyze. El Farruco's posture, as he stands, walks, and turns, is redolent with exemplification of Andalusian culture. One might also claim that his posture 'denotes' machismo. To such a claim, I can make no response since I have no way of intuiting El Farruco's intentions. But denotation to the side, his posture certainly does succeed in directing my attention to what I have experienced in Andalusian social life, tapping my memories and summoning forth my own images of Andalusian men. Such is the impact of metonymy. Similarly, El Farruco's shabby old cordobesa hat points me to times past when such hats were more common than they are now. El Farruco's black pants, black vest, and white shirt – whatever they might denote – point me toward the colors that men typically wear, and, for me at least, they carry me back to Flugel's sartorial notion of the 'great male renunciation.' This is the way metonymy functions generating endlessly ramifying connections in the spectator's experience even as they spring from the endlessly repetitive and sedimented memories that constitute the person of the dancer.

One particular set of movements interests me in this footage of El Farruco. As he begins a spate of furious footwork, El Farruco reaches both hands, grabs the bottom hem of his vest, and hoists that hem vertically. In the BBC footage, this action of grabbing his leather vest occurs about eighteen seconds after he appears on camera. It follows a slow paseo section and immediately proceeds the escobilla section of the soleá that is being sung by El Chocolate. In Saura's film, El Farruco again dances to a soleá sung by El Chocolate. The paseo section lasts about two minutes before El Farruco weighs the hem of his vest and for fifteen seconds displays the rapid-fire footwork of his escobilla. Interestingly, his grandson Farruquito then steps in and dances for two minutes, displaying very similar moves, including that of grabbing the hem of his jacket.

Elsewhere in the displays of male dancers, this act of hoisting the hem of the jacket or vest is exceedingly common (Figure 3.2, Pedro Montoya). El Mono does it in the *bulería* that he dances in Saura's *Flamenco*. Felipe de Triana and Fernando Terremoto are shown doing it in the *Enciclopédico Diccionario Ilustrado del Flamenco* (Blas Vega and Ríos Ruiz 1991: 767; 747). This mannerism is repeatedly shown by a variety of different male dancers in the documentary film series *Rito y Geografía del Cante* and *Rito y Geografía del Baile* (Washabaugh 1996). Finally, in the informal gathering of singers and dancers that I attended at La Carbonería during June of 1997, Gitano male dancers persistently grabbed their T-shirts and guayabera shirts in precisely this way.

It may well be a kindred move that Joaquin Cortés displays in Saura's *Flamenco* when, just before beginning to dance his *farruca*, he takes his shirt off completely, and dances naked from the waist up. And, bolder still as associations go, we can turn to the observations recorded by Maria Papapavlou as she pursued anthropological research among flamencos in Jerez de la Frontera:

> During my field research in Jerez de la Frontera, I often had opportunities to take part in unofficial '*juergas*' organised by several peñas flamencas of the town. These meetings took place normally once in a week and were accompanied by drinks and some food (*tapitas*). All the members (*socios*) of the peña were invited, men, women, children and occasionally some friends.
>
> Such a meeting usually starts around 1:00 o'clock in the afternoon. The atmosphere soon gets relaxed with the help of a little wine (*copitas de Jerez*). After two or three hours, some people leave. Those who remain are mainly the men both young and elderly. They close the doors of the peña and a more private part of the juerga seems to start. Slowly they begin to sing flamenco. *Bulerías* '*pa escuchar*' and later *bulerías* '*pa bailar*.' The joyful rhythm of bulerías warms up the atmosphere. By now, most of the men are drunk or

Figure 3.2 Pedro Montoya, hoisting his vest; photo by Elke Stolzenberg, used with permission

nearly so. They create a good deal of noise with their 'jaleos,' shouted comments to the dancers. Some of the comments are :'*óle! Qué guapo! óle maricón! óle maricita!*' The word '*maricita*' (homosexual, gay) is used in a playful, joking manner, and so nobody gets offended. On the contrary, everybody laughs and has great fun. When one man sings or dances a good *bulería*, the rest of the men congratulate him by kissing him on both cheeks and hugging him warmly. The dancing style of *bulerías* sometimes display clear sexual reference. For example, when one man is just finishing his dance, another may accompany his final figures. At this moment, the two bodies of the male dancers are very close, the belly of the one is touching the back of the other. In this combination, they dance some more steps together, each moving his pelvis forward and backwards. This provocative movement generates even more jaleos from the spectators: '*olé, maricón! mira! mira! que maricitas*!!' Sometimes it happens that someone brings along a wig (*peluca*) in order to make more fun. He puts the long hair on and dances some steps of *bulerías*. At that moment, everybody is laughing and having great fun. The words '*maricón*' and '*maricita*' fall like a rain. This is the zenith of the excitement. The jaleo is getting very loud and all these commentaries about homosexuality multiply. Later, when they get tired of laughing and having fun, they go home. Usually it is already around six o'clock in the evening and their women are waiting at home. Sometimes, the women come themselves to the peña to search out their men. When this happens, such meetings come to an abrupt end.

The full puzzling and problematic irony of El Farruco's mannerism of lifting the hem of his vest may now be appreciated. By grabbing his vest and lifting its hem, El Farruco is performing a gender bender by presenting a metonym of feminine dance: his movement is similar to, and reminiscent of, the movement of bailaoras as they grab the hems of their dresses, hoisting them up to reveal their fancy footwork. As such, his hem-hoisting gesture runs squarely against the grain of the Manichean gender roles that his dance otherwise supports and confirms. In weighing his vest, El Farruco enters into moments of inconsistency and self-contradiction, and in so doing, he adds one more level of irony to the already rich ironic manifold called flamenco (Washabaugh 1996).

The Dilemma of Masculinity

What is the significance of El Farruco's gender bender? We can answer this question by exploring the kindred dance-style of men who harbor gender ideologies comparable to El Farruco's. Specifically, I contend that certain movements characteristic of male dancers in the rebetika tradition can help us to discover some of the underlying connections that are forged by El Farruco's gender bender.

As noted by Holst-Warhaft, Greek rebetes reproduce a sharply contrastive gender system, comparable in many respects to the Andalusian system described here. Commenting on aspects of their dances, Cowan has observed that for Greeks,

> A man's dancing can be sexual, and it can be provocative, but it is rarely provocative **because** it is sexual. However explicitly (in a sexual sense) men dance, and however they frame these performances (as serious parody, irony, burlesque), a man's performance of sexuality is not seen as a comment merely on itself. Rather, the poses a man assumes in the dance, whether they enact bodily control or the stylized performance of its absence (as in somatic representations of intoxication), are seen to allude primarily to this negotiation of power and prestige among men (Cowan 1990: 189).

In other words, men are dancing for other men. And often do so through sexual imagery, despite the fact that such imagery has nothing to do with sex. Just so, 'when a youth lies stretched out in dramatic gestures on the road, swooning . . . (his) gestures constitute a stylized performance of sexuality in which the prescribed sentiments and gestures together evoke the sexual encounter . . . in this play of gender, gender is a code of power' (Cowan 1990: 127). Not uncommonly, according to Angela Shand, a man will exclaim to another, 'I'll fuck you,' in this way threatening violent domination though nothing sexual in spite of the colorful detail that is sometimes used to embellish the threat.

Just how is it that, in the company of men, gestures such as lifting one's vest, removing one's shirt, dancing pelvis to pelvis, kissing, swooning are metonyms of power? We can turn to football – either the North American or the European variety will do – for an answer, focusing particular attention on the hugs and butt-pats that are taken for granted as part of this sport.

Using football to advance his argument, James Q. Wilson (1993: 165–90) has proposed the gender identity of a man is, generally speaking, ambivalent and fraught with self-contradictions in a way that the female's is not. Female identity, inextricably linked to the mother-child dyad, is defined in terms of bonding. Males, however, are either competitive predators and defenders of territory, where resources are scarce, or they are themselves collaborators and complicit with females in activities of bonding where resources are plentiful. In modern urban life – and in a variety of other common social circumstances – males find themselves challenged to create identities on both fronts, that is, to be fierce competitors and also to be compromising collaborators. In such circumstances, males frequently form cohorts in which both virtues are definitive. Accordingly, to play football is to engage in a kind of competitive collaboration, therein to take advantage of opportunities to enhance one's status by competition and also to rise above other's by displaying selfless collaboration. When a linebacker knocks an opponent senseless while playing football in the United States, he gains status on the scale of competitiveness. When the cornerback pats him on the fanny as a way of congratulating him on his 'hit,' he, the cornerback, gains status on the scale of male-male bonding.

A similarly bipolar account of masculinity emerges from Peter Wilson's study of Caribbean social organization (1973). Wilson finds that, on Providence Island, all men are at once driven to climb the social ladder of economic and political 'respectability,' climbing over others in the way crabs do as they try to scramble out of a basket. But every man also feels the need to rise above peers in a collaborative and bonding way, 'reputationally' in Wilson's terminology, by drinking, carousing, telling stories, and in other ways reinforcing the bonds between men in a 'crew.'

The activities of men engaged in dancing in Greece, football in the United States, and storytelling on Providence Island are suggestive in more ways than one. It seems that males often create venues within which to play out complex relations of competition *and* bonding as a way of resolving the ambiguities of their gender. Suddenly, in the light of these activities, El Farruco's hem-hoisting can be read as far more than just a quaint choreographic maneuver. It seems, instead, to be a socially relevant, intricately constructed gender tactic, a revealing variation on a widespread theme.

Conclusion

The flamenco dance that has been so much a part of Andalusian cultural life for the past century and a half, reveals linkages to its larger social context. Men compete at displaying their ferocious machismo, but at the same time, they enhance their standing vis-à-vis their peers by displaying acts of collaboration and bonding. In the light of this analysis, we can conclude that there is nothing so very strange about El Farruco's gesture. His movement is expectable. It is an action of a Hemingway weighing hem as he strides forward into the gaze of admiring male spectators. It is the choreographic counterpart of the social bet-hedging to which men are often driven.

Notes

1. In Spain the hyper-masculine dance style is not achieved, as it is in Greece, by the dancer's separating himself so completely from spectators as to turn the dance into 'a psychologically private act' (Cowan 1990: 177). Though inwardness or *ensimismo* is an important aesthetic dimension of flamenco dance, as Félix Grande (1992) suggests, it never floods the performance to the point of overshadowing the in-your-face, stare-to-the-soul performance style that has become its hallmark. Just so Antonio Gades, in *Carmen* yelled '*Look* at me! Look at *me!*' to Laura del Sol's Carmen as he tried to develop her wolf-like stare.

2. However deeply this ideology might seem to be installed in contemporary Andalusian culture, one should hesitate before calling it 'authentic.' On the one hand, one might well might claim it to be a human universal following (Ortner 1974) – though Gilmore (1990a: 223) raises doubts about such a claim. On the other hand, following Inman Fox (1997), one might argue this gender ideology to be the result of the deep penetration of Krausista liberalism into Spanish political life during the last half of the nineteenth century?

3. *Quidquid recipitur in modo recipientis recipitur* (Whatever is received, is received in the manner made possible by the receiver) is the watchword for this approach that considers spectators-readers to be active participants in the projects of constructing the meanings of the spectacles they witness (Iser 1974).

–4–

Gendering the Authentic in Spanish Flamenco
Timothy deWaal Malefyt

Spanish flamenco presents an apparent paradox to cultural understanding. On the one hand, to many travelers and visitors to Spain, flamenco evokes images of passionate dancers, clicking castanets, dramatic display, and colorful costumes. Images of the exotic dancer, whirling and gyrating in pounding rhythm, feed a growing public interest in flamenco as tourists fill theaters and night clubs in the big cities of Madrid, Barcelona, and Seville. Flamenco's current popularity is important economically to the nation's booming tourist industry, as Spain was reported second only to France last year in the total number of visitors to a nation.

However, cast in a different light, flamenco to many Andalusians represents a form of deep personal exchange and intimate communion that is said to inculcate traditional values of Andalusian community (Quintana and Floyd 1972: 68). Some claim flamenco song expresses the collective voice of the nameless Andalusian pueblo (Grande 1979). For Andalusian flamenco aficionados and artists who once gathered in pueblo patios and now in private *peña* clubs, flamenco apparently identifies a local tradition inconsistent with public commodification. Evidently, the former version of flamenco represents a form of commodity for public consumption in the expanding tourist market, while the latter version represents private cultural identity among Andalusian aficionados in secluded *peña* clubs.

Nevertheless, it is precisely this contrast of representations, juxtaposing one mode of performance with another, that stimulates a dynamic tension in flamenco today, and empowers the community of Andalusian flamenco aficionados locally against increasingly global and emergent forms of flamenco. In this chapter, I show how such complementary contrasts between popular and traditional notions of flamenco not only reflect a difference in aesthetic sensibilities, but reveal their *modus operandi* as central to gender ideology. In fact, the situation of complementarity is key to understanding flamenco today: Andalusian aficionados and artists direct aesthetic contrasts of private 'traditional' flamenco against the growing commodification of flamenco publicly. They further detail flamenco in the public realm as commercial and therefore 'inauthentic' in contrast to flamenco among themselves in private realms as 'authentic.' These contrasts of a private versus public sensibility in flamenco reflect a deeper understanding of performance complementarity based on formal concepts of gender symmetry of female and male. Aficionados evaluate flamenco, as good or bad, private or public, traditional or modern, overtly through performance sensibilities of authenticity, but indirectly they mediate an overall understanding of flamenco through complementary contrasts in gender schemes. Indeed, the symmetry of gender complementarity actually necessitates the public commodification of flamenco to substantiate the private.

To better understand how gender symmetry energizes flamenco conceptions, I first situate authenticity as a subsystem of gender schemes. As such, issues of authenticity like those of gender, reveal a flexible social construct about boundaries and complementary contrasts. Authenticity is an essentializing concept applied to an object, phenomena, or group that is often manifested in formations of 'tradition.' Authenticity is described as the symbolic, not factual, process by which the 'Other' is contrasted and compared, to the claims of the 'original' item or group (Handler and Linnekin 1984). In performance genres, issues of authenticity center on aesthetic contrasts that unite members as well as distinguish one group's practice from another. According to Bohlman, members of a particular group who claim a tradition, assign primacy to the aesthetic features of a musical genre they consider essential to its authenticity, which are then bolstered in ideology, acts, and practices against defilement by outside 'inauthentic' versions (1988: 10). The concept of authenticity thus implies an active, contrastive relationship between the putative original and other versions as the dialogic process vitally 'authenticates the original' (Geertz 1986: 380). Accordingly, comparisons in flamenco today are manifest in aficionados' formation of a flamenco tradition in private *peña* clubs, against which they contrast newer and more modern public versions. Moreover, it is precisely the contrasts of spatial domains and social relations found in gender ideology, sometimes expressed as aesthetic sensibilities of performance, which distinguish traditional flamenco from modern versions.

Complementarity in Gender Divisions

The complementarity of gender relations are at the center of popular and traditional conceptions of flamenco. Gender divisions reveal complementary contrasts of unity and division between male and female that are inextricably linked to social systems so as to be situated at the very core of a system's logic (Ortner and Whitehead 1981: 4–5). For individuals living within social systems, the 'logic' by which gendered contrasts are based appears utterly natural so as to be unquestionable, and create 'natural' or 'logical' boundaries of complementarity that call for gender-appropriate behavior in particular social realms. Such 'natural' divisions are ideological notions that offer a powerful means by which people articulate notions of unity and difference, and understand the world through concepts of public and private domains and corresponding notions of sociability.

Gender concepts of unity and difference also structure and explain the type of social relations within particular gender-specific domains. As such, sociability differs between, as well as among, spatial categories of male and female. Male relations in the public sphere are said to be competitive, where positioning and dominance over another male achieves social status. Masculinity is not given, but must be proven in actions, hence promoting 'vertical' relationships of competition, display, and inequality with other males. In contrast, females are united in private spheres, where sociability is sanctioned within domestic and familial domains. Women make decisions based on immediate and emotional concerns of others in the family so that females gain respect and status, not through challenge and defeat, but through constructing various personal 'horizontal' relationships with other women (Rosaldo 1974). While gender categories unite relations within their respective realm, they also divide relations between each other, limiting access from one to another. Thus, gender categories form a separate but complementary framework for social organization and spatial distinction through which men and women articulate notions of sociability.

In my study of flamenco, gender concepts create contrastive social categories of unity and division that lie at the heart of Spanish culture. They form a framework of complementarity in which all social relations can be understood. Categories of public and private profoundly influence notions of performance aesthetics, dividing performance styles into contrastive domains and forms of sociability as they would between genders. Brandes, Gilmore, and Uhl, among other scholars, have shown how gender systems in Spain are a powerful means by which Andalusians differentiate social reality between males and females in other areas besides performance. These authors describe modes of language and sociability as differentiating gender in forming complementary but contrastive systems of meaning.

In Spain, male forms of sociability in public realms are typically based on behavior that is competitive and exploitative, while females in private realms reveal behavior that is cooperative and constructive. Men compete in verbal duels of challenge and display to effect dominance of one male over another. Brandes finds that men in the town of Monteros perform jokes as hostile acts meant to trick, demean, or fool other men. To Brandes, men in the public sphere must constantly demonstrate their potential for aggression by placing other men in inferior positions relative to themselves (1980: 126). Similarly, Gilmore (1995) examines public display of Carnival in Fuenmayor, where men have to take 'the *broma*,' (the joke against them) even though it may sting, as men must show resilience to verbal challenge in front of other men in public spheres. In both studies, a show of emotion or intimacy in front of another reflects a failure as a man. Andalusian men are resigned to defensive posturing among each other in hostile acts which place other men around them as unequal.

In contrast, female communicative strategies in Spain show a very different pattern of social organization than that of men. Female relations are patterned to build rather than unmake intimacy among other females, and form a powerful force of unity against outside opposition. Studies show that female friendships in Andalusia forge deeper social bonds than those of men, since 'male friendships are founded as much on competition as cooperation' (Gilmore 1990b: 961). Feminine ties are the main social bond that persist in Spain when other male relations falter, writes Pescatello. She notes that unlike males, 'Females seem to cross kin, neighbor, and village lives quite easily, particularly in rural areas' (1976: 45). Moreover, female sociability is strongest within domestic realms in collective actions. Uhl (1991) observed that women peeling potatoes together discussed problems, showing a support system that strengthened their social bond, especially in times of stress. Inasmuch as females join with others to cooperate and exchange sentiments in domestic realms, males challenge and compete with each other in public realms. Domesticity and cooperative relations within, thus combine to make 'the feminine' and 'the private' a powerful and pervasive construct of group organization that complements but opposes perceived social inequality of 'the masculine' in the public realm. As gendered features of sociability join notions of public and private to form 'natural' complementary contrasts, we can examine how such ideological notions influence the way flamenco is divided into concepts and practices of traditional and modern.

Scholars show that categories of gender transcend individuals and their particular behavior to form an over-arching ideology of complementarity. Contrasts of public and private as reflective of male and female symmetry are important ideological components to notions of identity. Herzfeld (1986) demonstrates this in Greek culture, where two versions of Greek identity – one national and public (Hellenic) and the other private and local (Romeic) – form a system of complementarity analogous to notions of gender symmetry between male and female. Similarly, Gilmore (1996) shows how complementary gender relations of public and private are re-interpreted by Andalusians to express variable concepts of 'above and below.' This system of complementarity occurs as well in concepts of Spanish flamenco, and 'authenticates' a private local identity against public 'inauthentic' plurality created by national consumption. Sensibilities of flamenco as private or public reveal a basis for spatial distinction and socially appropriate behavior that model complementary notions of 'female' and 'male' in gender ideology. This over-arching ideology of gender complementarity in spatial domain and style of sociability leads the *peña* flamenco community to perform privately, holding their notion of tradition against the growing popularization of flamenco nationally in tourism.

Public Display and Social Inequality: The Masculine Realm

Spain is currently experiencing an incredible period of popularity in flamenco. Especially since the death of Franco in 1975, the experimentation and growth in flamenco has risen to such a national and international degree as to inspire terms of a new era (Caballero 1995). Another journalist has appropriately labeled its widespread popularity a 'flamenco boom' (Hooper 1987: 162).

Although flamenco originates in the South, it is probably most popular in the large cities of Madrid and Barcelona outside of Andalusia where it caters to an array of tourists in *tablaos* (nightclubs) and theater shows. Present-day commercial establishments encourage an openness to attract a wide public in flamenco. Public *tablaos* and theaters are situated in populated areas, such as in town centers, financial districts, tourist routes, or other zones accessible to visitors, travelers, and curious others. Moreover, these establishments are replete with signs, signals, and street markers that are frequently advertised in newspapers, magazines, and flyers as well as featured in visitor information and travel brochures freely distributed in tourist centers. Flamenco shows in the public realm not only display their open accessibility to strangers but compete for their attention. In this context of commodification, diverse people witness flamenco where social relations between artists and audience are based on commodity exchange and stranger-hood. Admonished by one flamencologist, foreigners pay money only to be entertained and 'prefer dance to song, and women dressed in "typical" attire of the Gypsy flamenco' (Ríos Ruiz 1972: 66). Historically as well, issues of popular display and tourism helped to develop flamenco as a public commodity.

Even before tourism took hold in Spain this century, flamenco had long been romanticized in popular culture. The sweeping romantic movement of Europe imagined the downtrodden lower-class Andalusian as exotic material for public display. Flamenco evolved from the urban ghettos of Andalusian cities during the nineteenth century around a time when Spanish and foreign elites exoticized the poor as the primitive ideal. Commercial enterprises quickly capitalized on moneyed interests and enlisted marginal Andalusians to perform flamenco in theaters, cafes, and night clubs before a diverse public body. Nevertheless, while the commercial market represented economic opportunity for many impoverished Andalusians, it also represented a classed system of competition, challenge, and inequality for struggling artists (Grande 1979: 344). Andalusians in cafes and clubs had to adapt performance styles to appease wealthy patrons' wishes, and often artists were exploited in these clubs for money or for prostitution. Artists competed for positions among themselves as pay was dependent upon popularity. Artist Antonio Mairena writes of this exploitation: 'They were difficult times, full of anguish and misery in a hallucinating ambiance of merry *señoritos*, militant rogues, and prostitutes in which occurred an endless number of things that today seems like a nightmare' (Ulecia 1976:45). Indeed, popular interest in flamenco exemplified a social relationship of display, competition, and inequality in the public realm for Andalusian performers. Such external social and economic conditions shaped an external orientation around concepts of public performance as well. Although modern Spain is no longer formally driven by a classed society, many aficionados still regard popular versions of flamenco as 'inauthentic' based on public display and competition, especially since flamenco currently drives a thriving tourist industry.

Nevertheless, according to our social schema, while aficionados may criticize the public consumption of flamenco, they also depend upon it to establish a private counterpart. Commercial establishments in the public domain of display, competition, and broad popular consumption offer fertile ground for contrasting flamenco as a domestic, local, and private 'tradition' in *peñas*. According to gender schemes of symmetry, flamenco in the 'masculine' public realm 'logically' reflects issues of inequality, display, and positioning. Indeed, flamenco in the public domain importantly constitutes a necessary gender complement for the emergence of a private flamenco, as well as for defining an orientation in social relations modeled on feminine sociability. As issues of tourist consumption conspicuously present grist for the traditionalist's mill, we can understand how the dialectic establishes a basis for gender complementarity. The current flamenco boom among tourists creates a public domain and type of circumspect sociability that is necessarily matched and equally met by an opposing sense of an intimate and private flamenco tradition.

Especially since the 1950s when Franco opened Spain to tourism, there has been a strong resurgence of flamenco as a private and local tradition, exclusive to Andalusian aficionados and artists in flamenco clubs called *peñas*. From within the private club system of *peñas,* flamenco takes on an inherently private and local sense that reveals aesthetic features of authenticity as based on gender conceptions (Malefyt 1997). *Peñas* represent a model of 'the female' in domestic appearance, spatial exclusivity, and egalitarian sociability, which complements but contrasts 'the male' in public realms of commercial establishments that are open to strangers. Tourists are not normally allowed in *peñas*. There are around 350 *peña* clubs in Spain mostly in Andalusia, each holding between 30 and 60 members, which began in the late 1950s with a 'mission', claims the preeminent dictionary, 'to uphold a flamenco tradition', to 'save', and 'conserve the art inside a pure line and positive evolution' (Blas Vega and Ríos Ruiz 1981: 587). Correspondingly, *peñas* have been called a last stronghold of 'true democracy' where differences of class and income meld into 'one cultural heritage' (Melgar Reina and Marín Rújula 1988: 27). Members regularly assemble in *peñas* to exchange lore, discuss, debate over, and practice traditional flamenco among themselves. Indeed, within an enclosed setting of social equality protecting purity from the outside, traditional flamenco assumes a quality of 'the feminine' guarding its essence from male predation, as female shame was once thought to be guarded from male defilement.

Domestic Enclosures and Intimate Relations: The Feminine

In a world of changing and competing public flamenco representations, aficionados tell me the 'best', 'purest', and most 'authentic' flamenco occurs among familiars within private settings, such as *peñas*. They tell me, in contrast, that flamenco in commercial settings is 'impure', 'trivialized', and performed in ways to trick you and take your money (*engañarse*). What they describe are aesthetic features of performance and locale, but what they symbolize by their reference to social familiarity in domestic-type domains highlights flamenco as a comparative construct of 'the female' in contrast to unfamiliar social relations in public establishments. The way their descriptions configure an inside orientation against outside incursion suggests how female domains and concomitant forms of sociability complement, yet contrast with, those of the male. Flamenco performed within the *peña* reconstructs social organization around private internal space, so that participation in the *peña* identifies close social relations within the gendered domain of the female. Accordingly, the domestic locale and 'female-type' friendship in the *peña* come to stand for notions of the 'authentic' in flamenco, as the public realm and 'male-type' social relations stand for the 'inauthentic.'

In contrast to the central accessibility of commercial establishments, flamenco *peñas* are most often situated geographically in particular, somewhat remote residential *barrios* where people work, live, play, and know each other for many generations. They are not commonly advertised nor highlighted for outsiders. *Peñas* are inherently local as they sponsor local flamenco festivals, hold song competitions in their clubs, and organize frequent meal gatherings; a few *peñas* have their own dance schools. Furthermore, *peñas* suggest a certain local exclusivity in their inconspicuous building design since their architectural features mostly lack adornment of signs, markers, or even front windows through which a curious passerby might peer inside. As structural features blend with local surroundings, *peñas* not only conceal activities from outsiders but symbolize a continued tradition within the neighborhood locale. Indeed, gender complementarity is revealed in building design and spatial reference, as *peña* buildings blend into the architectural traditions of their residential barrio while commercial establishments compete to stand out.

The coherence of *peñas* to their local surroundings extends even further once inside their structure. The inner realm of *peñas* is a highly domestic space, in appearance as well as in social function. The inside is replete with photographs of members, of members with artists, of featured artists, and of awards and plaques of recognition. One might compare the inside to a family den, caught up in the nostalgia of personal memorabilia and clan history. In addition, the performing stages of *peñas* are often modeled after Andalusian residential patios, adorned with depictions of fountains, latticework, colorful flowers, and songbirds. This vivid setting further creates an historical link to past Andalusian traditions, as painted idyllic scenes imagine a collective unity that once occurred among families harbored within the protective domains of the local patio. Spanish scholar Franca Carloni, reminds us that the patio historically signified a major form of group solidarity against an outside world of social inequality and hierarchy. Patios were small interactive worlds impermeable to the larger social environment as they represented 'centers of action for powerless people,' and distinguished '*los de patio*' from '*los de afuera*' (those inside the patio from those outside (1988: 128–9). Representative of an enclosed domestic environment, patios in the past and *peñas* today are vital social spaces that encourage local solidarity by the interaction of various familiars assembled within. As domestic space contrasts that of commercial establishments, the unity within the *peña* establishes a spatial context for intimacy that contrasts stranger relations outside.

Spatial distinctions between private and public further generate attitudes of difference in terms of sociability, where familiar social relations 'inside' a location contrast behavior and attitude 'outside.' In particular, activities that occur within residential domains provide the context for close social relations that enhance inner unity against outsiders. Gilmore explains that a natural affection and unity exist among people who share a common domain, which also creates a unity greater than with spatially dispersed, far off collaterals and affines (1980: 156–7). In *peñas*, domesticity within assumes an almost family-like status in modes of participation against outside, non-familiar social relations. As a domestic unit, flamenco aficionados regularly unite in *peñas* and often refer to their clubs as *casas* (homes). Spatial unity and social integrity within the domestic *peña* further accentuate a type of close-knit 'fictive kinship.' Frequent flamenco events not only amplify familiarity, but social gatherings in the *peña* enhance feelings of a residential kinship. Since members refer to their *peña* as a house, and act as a collective, they naturally share in similar experiences and in the cohesion of routines and activities within the *peña* '*casa*.' This unity adds to the mutual dependence and defensiveness, which is already created by friendship ties and is fortified by a shared private 'domestic' world inside the club. Through collective participation, members of *peñas* assert a status of inner domesticity against outside commodification.

During events in the *peña*, members participate in song and dance that generates feelings of domesticity as an egalitarian value of the female. After meals on select days of the week, members collectively participate in song and dance in the center space of the *peña*. They are encouraged to perform collectively by clapping and voicing rhythms in synchrony. They freely express their feelings because they are among familiars.

People participate in festive songs that inspire dance (*alegrías, bulerías*) and in somber 'deep' songs that inspire deep reflection (*soleares, siguirillas*). They clap hands, palm in counter-rhythm, sing, and move their bodies in unison. Even if one does not know all the intricate and complex song rhythms, within this ambiance everyone is included just from being present and attentive. Moreover, this level of involvement is expected from all those present in the *peña*. Members say that within this setting, 'true' (*el auténtico*) flamenco is transmitted, rather than being performed. Their coordinated skills make 'good' flamenco a shared event of the community in which outsiders cannot partake. Indeed, coordinating other's actions requires skill and timing and creates a precise assembly out of familiarity. Blending individual skills with collective action is a social activity that empowers local community, as 'it is understandable that collective dancing or singing, particularly spectacular cases of the synchronization of the homogeneous and the orchestration of the heterogeneous, are everywhere predisposed to symbolize group integration, and by symbolizing it, to strengthen it' (Bourdieu 1977: 232). Within the *peña*, enactment that is non-hierarchical and open to sentimental expression, not only reinforces an aesthetic sensibility of 'good' flamenco among its members, but also re-creates a social process of domestic cooperation by which they highlight themselves as the aesthetic standard of 'traditional' performance. Thus flamenco, performed among aficionados and artists is both reflective and reflexive of the domestic, of coordinated efforts, and of a 'pure' flamenco tradition they create for themselves.

Contrasts of context and sociability in flamenco, as exchanged within private locations of *peñas* versus performed for strangers in commercial establishments, extend beyond contextual and aesthetic differences to signal ideological gender differences between women and men. Flamenco in *peñas*, concealed among aficionados and artists does not merely create a boundary of private space or aesthetic difference against flamenco in public locations; rather, it invigorates a contrastive sense of gender sociability and gender domains through the collective action of flamenco performance. It is not so much that these things occur absolutely in one domain or another, but that they are perceived to and described as dividing and re-orienting flamenco socially.

Flamenco in *peñas* models features of female solidarity and domesticity as a natural division against outside public forms of flamenco. Like formal gender schemes in Spanish society, they divide flamenco representations into mutually contrastive social categories. Members of the *peña* flamenco community identify themselves in the forms of intimate sociability and private contexts which they articulate to discriminate themselves from others. Aesthetic sensibilities, such as a local flamenco tradition, are employed by aficionados to construct social boundaries of unity and difference, as difference is an essential feature of identity and boundary making in the particular manner in which 'the Other' is contrasted or compared, either in the way they are, or wish not to be (Cohen 1985: 12). In promoting self-signifying expressions, 'authentic' flamenco is then a powerful unifying and dividing concept for engaging a much larger world of complex social and economic forces. Thus, unity and privacy in performance practice and social orientation create an 'authentic' flamenco that is genuine to them insofar as it is contrasted to public 'inauthentic' versions.

It is in this sense that intimate communion in private realms becomes authentic as a system of complementarity meaning and a system of resistance to larger cultural appropriation by tourism. Relational divisions are significant as the female domain counters the public popular male domain, and gender divisions in gender ideology support contrast through flamenco representations.

Gender conceptions are important to understanding how flamenco popularity becomes redefined by the *peña* community through familiar systems of meaning. Gender ideologies reveal how individuals and groups construct certain understandings within 'natural' systems to deal with conflict and tension in their lives. In a world increasingly inundated with experimental, commercial, and popular versions of flamenco, gender-specific ideology of a private and familiar flamenco complements but counters popular representations in the public sphere. Flamenco, organized through gender-specific notions of female interaction and within natural kinship domains, identifies and unifies aficionados under concepts of a local tradition as well as separates them from change in public systems. Gender notions thus authenticate flamenco as a natural and stable extension of the Andalusian flamenco aficionado and artist community.

These considerations reveal how gender constructs influence performance constructs of popular music to empower a local community against larger systems of change. Female equality in the domestic realm becomes increasingly important to the *peña* community as a model of inner unity, stability, and empowerment that complements but contrasts flamenco in the public 'masculine' realm of Spanish society. Even if women and domesticity are not directly implicated by *peña* members, the female system of social integration in the domestic realm leads an ideology and practice of group formation that effectively unites members against public commercial forms of flamenco, analogous to the masculine domain. As a means of differentiating themselves and elevating flamenco in private performances of *peñas*, the female construct of social unity and cooperation is a powerful model for sociability and of group support that competitive male-oriented public representations lack. The domestic, the private, and women thus form an effective model of identity that leads flamenco concepts and practices among aficionados, and strengthens their unity against the increasingly divergent and competitive world of outside flamenco representations.

5

Carlos Gardel and the Argentine Tango: The Lyric of Social Irresponsibility and Male Inadequacy

Donald Castro

> Yo también soy Juan Tango cuando sueño,
> cuando digo mi amor, cuando trabajo,
> *!porque yo, con Juan Tango, soy el Pueblo!*[1]
> (I too am Juan Tango when I dream
> When I say my love, when I work,
> Because I am, with Juan Tango, the People.)

Premise

The lyric of the Argentine tango is the mirror of the Argentine soul. It serves as the painful expression of Argentine male loneliness, betrayal, and unrequited love. The protagonist is always the victim and as such is not responsible for the failure of the relationship. Only the protection and intercession of the saintly mother figure can save the male from destruction. The aggressive dance is characterized by passive male-oriented lyrics where the victim only reacts. Thus, the tango lyric is a commentary on personal irresponsibility. This chapter will show that, when this view of the world (as expressed in the lyric) is expanded into broader social, political, and economic interactions, the message given is that the individual, or the body politique, each of which is largely defined as being male and child-like, needs protection from the outside world. While the protection and comfort needed in the tango is that of the adoring mother, the socio-political need for protection takes the form of *caudillos* such as Hipólito Yrigoyen and Juan Domingo Perón or from the adoring saintly mother of the Eva (Evita) Perón persona. Yet, while the tango lyric is a social document, it is not one that calls for revolutionary or proactive social action. It is one of isolated introverted versus collective altruistic action. This explains why such a socially charged vehicle has very few politically motivated lyrics because they would call for collective action not possible in a society composed of isolated and insulated people. Since Carlos Gardel is the arch male symbol in Argentina, and in him the tango and male symbols combine, he will be used as the focal point of this study.

Introduction

The major period in the evolution of the tango is the Golden Age (1917–1935). This is the era dominated by the symbol of the tango, Carlos Gardel, who died tragically in 1935. The last period of the tango is the modern one in which we now live (post 1935). This is the era in which the political and cultural symbols of Juan Perón and Carlos Gardel merged into one. This chapter will focus on the period after 1917, the date given as the time of origin of the tango-canción, where the lyric played a more important role than in the earlier and later forms of the tango-danza where the music and the dance step had more significance, and on Carlos Gardel, who is still considered the chief interpreter of the tango canción. After the scandal of the white slavery ring Zwi Migdal, even protectors of prostitution such as Alberto Barceló, a close friend and political patron of Carlos Gardel and mayor of Avellaneda, had to check their activities.[2] This new morality no doubt cut deeply into the cabaret and popular theater attendance even by those who could afford it. Even Gardel, when he was at the height of his career, suffered falling attendance in what would be his last porteño appearance in 1933. Perhaps this, and falling record sales, led Gardel to seek better prospects in the expanding film industry in Europe and in the United States because he left his beloved Buenos Aires in 1933.

The factor that stands beyond all others in warranting the claim that tango is integral to porteño – and by extension Argentine – culture was that of the leaders of Peronism themselves, Juan and Evita Perón. They were tango. The theme of their government and political mission was tango. Perón's image as the comrade to the workers, coatless among the multitude, while at the same time champion of the industrialist, dressed in a smoking jacket, conjures up the image of Carlos Gardel. The rags to riches story of Perón's success from a poor boy in the provinces to President is Gardelian in its scope.[3] Evita's tragic life, beautiful on the outside and cancerous on the inside could easily have been a theme for a Discépolo tango. Further, even while dying, her good works for the poor and the sick were symbols of her sacrifice. When she described herself as the bridge of love between Perón and the people was she not the same as the self-sacrificing mother of the tangos of Celedonio Flores? This image was cultivated by both Eva and Juan when she lived. After her death, Perón encouraged the people to call for beatification because her sacrifice was apparently comparable to that of a Madonna. Was not this idea tangoesque? Clearly Perón realized the political potential of the tango and through it the possibility of control of the loyal tango audiences. While it is not possible to document the determination of the Peróns to use the tango and the tango-related images including Carlos Gardel for political purposes, circumstantial evidence points to that logical conclusion.

Gardel as the epitome of the porteño was, and probably will always be, the symbol of Buenos Aires in human form. If, as maintained by Blás Matamoro in his important study (1969: 179), the political base for Perón was also the cultural base for the tango, then it follows that Perón would not long miss the significance of Carlos Gardel as a useful symbol. It is telling that the state-controlled film industry made three full-length feature films about Gardel during the Perón Era (*Se Llamaba Carlos Gardel*, 1949; *La Guitarra de Gardel*, 1949; and *El Morocho del Abasto*, 1950). The internal migrant from the *tierra adentro* had, after some ten years of porteño existence, come to be identified with the tango. This is clearly shown in the reliance on the Gardel symbol and in the continued use of the tango in sports clubs dances, carnival dances and dance festivals in the porteño sports arena of Luna Park. The big band sound of Hugo del Carril in the late 1930s and early 1940s was continued under the baton of Alberto Castillo, who became the most famous of the *tango masivo* conductors (large-scale ballroom tango dances).[4] The tango as such was now more of a vehicle for the feet and the body than for the ear and the mind. The evolution of the tango from dance to song (tango-danza to tango-canción) had now reversed itself. Therefore, the offensive lyric of the old tango in terms of language and then of content was of no matter. The tango was now more for dance. This was the tango of the Perón Era. When the lyric became important it was a nostalgic lyric pruned of any social content.

Carlos Gardel: Man and Symbol

The Argentine elite, by rejecting its own past in its attempt to create a Europe in America through massive immigration and capital importation, created the basis for the marginality of the creole and later the immigrant masses that was exacerbated by the depression. While it is true there have been popular or mass leaders in Argentina – Rosas, Yrigoyen and Perón – after the fall of each the masses were left amputated from the body politique as if thrown out to wait for a new cause, a new way, a new master or leader.[5] In recent times Gardel has become a cultural symbol to fill a political leadership vacuum. His image rose after the fall of Yrigoyen and after the fall of Perón and in the recent troubled times of the 1970s and 1980s. In some ways he represented a cultural security blanket to an isolated and insecure population.

On the fiftieth anniversary of Gardel's death, the mass distribution porteño daily *Clarín* (The Bugle) devoted a special Sunday supplement to Carlos Gardel (June 24, 1985). Under the front page banner headline *Carlos Gardel: Medio siglo a cuenta de la eternidad* ('Carlos Gardel: A Half-Century of Eternal Greatness'), the dead artist was described as the creator and defender of a purely Argentine national cultural form. Not like pre-Gardel Argentine culture, which was nothing more than a sub-product of Europe, the tango was purely Argentine and Gardel as a defender of Argentineness became the symbol of the nation. The *Clarín* lead article also explained the reason for the greatness of Gardel which was to be found in the fact that he most personified the dreams and aspirations of the Argentine people. This was his power and his magic (Gardel has been called *el mago*, The Magician).

The same theme of Gardel as the defender of Argentine culture and as the symbol of the Argentine people was expressed in an earlier official government publication celebrating the fortieth anniversary of his death in 1975. Gardel is described as the archetype of the tango, which in turn is defined as an authentic national expression and as an Argentine passion.[6] It is significant that this work (published by the Argentine Senate and dedicated by then president María Isabella de Perón) invoked the image of the leader of the Argentine masses, Lieutenant General Juan Domingo Perón. Further in the work, Perón is described as: *Conductor de un pueblo, líder de movimiento de justicia social de liberación hombre de paz, destino de maestro de multitudes ... Perón también sabía de tango.*[7] (Leader of a people, leader of a movement of social justice, of liberation, a man of peace, with a destiny of being a teacher of the masses ... Perón also knew tango ...)

If Gardel is tango, Perón is tango, and ... *el ser Argentino, en general, vive la expresión tango,* (... the Argentine essence, in general, lives through tango), Gardel and Perón are *el ser Argentino* (the Argentine essence).[8] A further refinement of this concept of Gardel (Perón) as the archetype Argentine, is that he is the symbol of Buenos Aires (so well demonstrated in the murals in the popular pizzerias *Los Inmortales* (The

Immortals) in Buenos Aires). Gardel is god-like and this is shown in the way his photograph is displayed in homes, buses and cars along with the Virgin of Lujan. One Argentine author has suggested that only through Gardel can Buenos Aires be truly understood and another has called Gardel the true historian of Buenos Aires (Couselo and Chierico 1964: 12; see also Manzi 1947). There could never have been a better source for a porteño legend or folk hero than Carlos Gardel. His very beginnings were, for a period of time, an enigma that evidently was fostered by Gardel himself. It is reported that early in his career he claimed to be a native Argentine and later an Uruguayan (see Escardó 1966: 87). Perhaps this was critical in his early career as a singer because he sang creole songs and how could a French immigrant – though he was only three when he came – sing creole songs? Perhaps this was also why he changed his name from Gardés to Gardel. His tragic death adds to the heroic, and that he was a rags to riches phenomenon only expands this, and that his private life was just that, leads to more conjecture and mystery.

Recognizing the number of homages paid to Carlos Gardel and the continued success of his recordings (number of re-emissions of records, and so on), it is clear that he is considered a true folk-hero of Buenos Aires. In a survey carried out by a leading porteño tango journal *Estudios de Tango* (August 1972), he was voted the number one favorite as the best interpreter of all times of the tango.[9] In a multi-volume history of the tango, *La Historia del Tango*, one whole volume is dedicated to Carlos Gardel. Gardel's life has also been the source for numerous feature and short message films, the earliest of which was made only four years after his death (using the starting date of production).[10] Such tribute is not paid to any other singer except on a very limited basis for Ignacio Corsini. Another fact that clearly marks Gardel as a hero or folk myth is that he and his image are sacred and inviolable. In fact, those who criticize Gardel . . . *ayudan a socavar los cimientos de nuestra cultura de la que es Gardel pilar valioso y fundamental* (. . . aid in undermining the foundations of our culture of which Gardel is a valued and fundamental pillar) (Meregazo 1971: 210).

Another example of Carlos Gardel's contemporary popularity is the public outpouring of grief during his funeral in Buenos Aires. After the crash in Medellín, which made headlines in all the porteño newspapers and entertainment magazines, his body was sent to New York for shipment back to Argentina. It finally arrived at the end of 1935 and a special funeral and wake were arranged in the sports center Luna Park (similar to Madison Square Garden) for February 1936. A special commission was established to organize the funeral and it included many tango stars of the period such as Francisco Lomoto, José Razzano, Armando Delfino, Azucena Mazani, Charlo, Libertad Lamarque, and Ignacio Corsini as well as theater and radio owners/producers such as Jaime Yankelevich.[11] The procession of the cortège went from Luna Park (foot of Corrientes Avenue) to Chacarita Cemetery. One contemporary of Gardel, Francisco García Jiménez, a noted tango composer himself, writing in 1976 described the procession saying that 'the people on the street who mourned him became mixed with the funeral cortège, yet no one supposed that they carried a dead body, but only a recently born enchanted myth.' Therefore, Carlos Gardel did not die, his body and spirit were transformed into an enchanted myth.[12]

While it is almost impossible to document what might be the essential elements for the creation of a porteño idol or folk myth, the following elements are given as the basic necessary building ingredients for such a male figure: must be a macho, must demonstrate fidelity and loyalty, must be successful materially, must demonstrate a sense of alienation/vulnerability, and must exude an air of smugness and superiority. Carlos Gardel meets all of these. In fact Gardel even sang and thereby made famous a tango that outlined the qualities necessary to be admired in porteño male dominated society: *El Malevo* (The Bad Dude) (Maria Luisa Carnelli) *Lo tengo que decir: Muñeca pa tallar y labia pa engrupir nunca te va a falter porque sos el mejor reo de la ciudad, canchero, arrastrador ...! te sobra autoridad!* (I must say it: You will never lack women to toy with and fools to sweet talk because you are the best man who lives by his wits, you are always in control, always able to lead the pack ... You ooze authority and power!)

Since *El Malevo* has been described as the tango in which ... *los valores que admira (el porteño) en el líder* (... the leadership qualities most admired by porteños in their leaders) are defined, an analysis of these leader/hero traits is useful for the understanding of the Gardel man/myth (Mascia 1970: 295). The key personality words in this tango immortalized by Gardel are: *mejor reo, canchero, arrastrador*, and *sobrar autoridad*.

A man described as a *reo* is a person who has no known source of income yet lives well. Such a person lives off women, is a thief, is a con artist, or whatever it takes to be successful as long as it is not through regular employment. The critical component to being a *reo* is to survive by one's wits. Not only was the person in the tango a *reo*, but the best one in the whole city. Furthermore, he was a *canchero* (from *cancha,* soccer field, e.g., one who dominates the playing field/controls the ball well). A *canchero* is an individual who is always in control – not only of himself but as well of all situations in which he finds himself. In addition, other people, in the situations along with the *canchero*, are also under his control. If these traits were not sufficient to define this dominant male, he is also an *arrastrador*, or a person who is able to influence and bring along other people to his way of thinking and acting, or to do his bidding. In summation, the tango lyric concludes that *te sobra autoridad*. This expression means that the *malevo* of the tango embodies all of the necessary masculine leadership qualities to such an extent that he has a surplus. This is a super male who even has more – if that is humanly possible – a golden tongue to sweet talk his way into or out of any and all situations (*labia*). This was, and is, the porteño ideal man, either as a leader or as a hero. This was Carlos Gardel.

Numerous Argentine and non-Argentine social scientists have tried to define what exactly is the Argentine porteño character.[13] Most seem to agree with the great Spanish philosopher, José Ortega y Gasset's 1928 assessment that the porteño is *un hombre a la defensa* (a man always on guard).[14] This is very evident in the air or *pinta* (ego image or impression in an external sense) that a porteño tries to project. This too has a porteño descriptor – *el aire sobrador*. As shown in the tango *El Malevo*, this air is one of surplus male characteristics. However, there is also a degree of ambivalence in this display of maleness – is this air due to an overabundance of confidence, or is it due to a need to cover a weakness? (López-Peña 1965: 90). The porteño covers his vulnerability by adopting an air of petulant, aggressive masculinity. Hence the Ortega y Gassett reference to the porteño's defensive nature. The porteño is most vulnerable in his dealings with women. It is therefore ironic, and appropriate, that this tango glorifying maleness was written by a woman who by virtue of her sex knew full well the weaknesses of the porteño male and need for masculine display. Gardel could be the hero because he had the *pinta de macho*, because he was *un hombre canchero*, and because he had *sobra autoridad*. He was also vulnerable. In this Janus-view of the porteño male, Gardel combined petulant masculinity with timidity towards women, a sense of control combined with a sense of helplessness in the face of destiny, and above all he had the golden tongue to charm the masses – one of his nick-names was *el zonsal* which is a bird of the pampa noted for its sweet song. He was the *malevo* of the tango.

Perhaps the most controversial of all of the elements is Gardel as a *macho*. This is the role he projected in his films as a leading man. He was always conscious of his image and was throughout his career concerned about his weight and its impact on his image as a ladies' man (Morena 1983: 51). This preoccupation is also further evidence of the importance of women as integral to the tango audience and the visual impact of film on a broad cross class base.[15] The element of love was important. In his songs he projected the porteño ideal of love and the relation of a man to women. In a careful analysis of Gardel's tangos, Dario Canton in *Gardel, ¿A quien le cantas?* (Gardel: To Whom Do You Sing?) (1972) studied ninety-nine Gardel recorded tangos in terms of content and image. Fifty-four percent of these tangos are about love.

Love in tangos, and the love that Gardel sang about is not the simple boy meets girl, they fall in love, and live happily ever after. In fact, the Gardel tangos tell of a man who suffers from love and in most cases the love affair ends because of the female's infidelity (*tración*) and the abandonment of her lover (see the tangos *Nunca más* and *La cumparsita*). The love affairs are all irregular (e.g., outside of marriage) and there is no mention of the traditional ideal of husband-wife relationship with home and children. In some cases where the love affair is closed because of the woman's action, the man expresses relief and is thankful for the return to liberty as a cover for male ego loss due to abandonment (see the tango *¿Te fuiste? !Ja, Ja!*). While these themes do not fit the classic definition of *machismo*, they do seem to fit the opposite – castration. The tango has been described as a song of male defeat. For an example of this type of love tango, consider *Nunca más* (1922) (Never More) (Oscar Lomuto): *Yo que te quise por buena y en tus dulces labios, nena, me quemaste el corazón* . . . (I who thought you to be good and in your sweet lips, girl you burned my heart). Also, *¿Te Fuiste? !Ja, Ja!* (1924) (You've Gone? Ha, Ha!) (Juan Baustista Abad Reyes): *Mi bulín está mucho más linda, más aireao, ventilada y compadre con las pilches por el suelo, todo bien desarreglao. Ya no tengo nadie que me bronque ni pichicho que me muerde o ladre te agradezco, mina otaria de que me hayas amurao.* (My room is so much nicer now, airier, better ventilated and homey with the dust devils on the floor a complete mess . . . Now I have no one to yell at me nor a little dog to bite and bark at me, I thank you little foolish girl for having left me.) Also, *La cumparsita* (Si supieras) (1924) (If You Only Knew) Pascal Contursi: *Desde el día que te fuiste siento angustias en mi pecho; decí percanta, qué has hecho con mi pobre corazón. Al cotorro abandonado ya ni el sol de la mañana asoma por la ventana como cuando estabas vos.* (From the day you left me I feel pains in my chest; Tell me dear girl what have you done with my poor heart. Our abandoned love nest no longer gets the morning sun peeking through the window as it did when you were here.)

When Gardel recorded *La cumparsita*, he changed the words of Contursi to suit his feelings relative to the situation described in the song.

Gardel personalized the tango. His lyric interpretation of tangos was his great power. While the modifications made in *La cumparsita* were not major, he was able to capture Contursi's intent and thereby better present the tango poet to the listener. This personalization of tangos – in the form of the lyric and through his voice modulation – made Gardel the favored tango interpreter to both the tango poet and to his audience. In the tango *La gayola* (The Jail Cell), his changes clearly showed Gardel's interpretive skill, his understanding of his audience and his own character. He made substantive changes to this tango by Armando José Tagini (1906–62). Gardel recorded the tango in 1927.

The changes in the lyric made the verses stronger in this unusual tango, unusual because of its theme and content. Unlike most tangos of male defeat, this one is predicated on actual – versus symbolic – violence. It is about a man who has killed his rival, the one with whom his love betrayed him. While betrayal is a common theme in the love tango, murder is not. This tango is about a violent crime of passion. The changes Gardel made make this message clear. In the original lyric, the act of murder is impersonal, and through the use of the reflexive verb the knife killed and not the man. *Pero me jugaste sucio . . . y, sediento de venganza, un cuchillo, en un mal rato, envainó en corazón* (You played me dirty . . . and, thirsty for revenge, the knife, in an ill moment, unsheathed in a heart.) Gardel changed this verse to show the protagonist's active and passionate role. *Pero me jugaste sucio . . . y, sediento de venganza, mi cuchillo, alcé una noche, y lo llevé hasta un corazón* (You played me dirty . . . and, thirsty for revenge, my knife, one night I raised, and I carried it to a heart.)

The betrayal was so cutting that in the heat of the moment the tango's protagonist killed. He was the one who killed and not his knife (and not any knife as in the original, but his knife). The act of murder was an act of passion, one in which the man could not have been a passive on-looker. Gardel sensed the passion and clearly changed the wording to convey this message. This active voice is very rare in tangos and very rare in Gardel's interpretation of love tangos where the man is for the most part a passive agent carried along by an uncontrollable event called love. Given the theme and the conclusion of the tango, Gardel may have felt it was necessary to make the message clear that the murder was in fact an act of passion and, therefore, pardonable because in the tango the protagonist is pardoned and set free after serving a long term in prison.

Other major changes made by Gardel in the lyric relate to the role of mother and to the countryside (*el campo*). These are also significant changes because the Gardel audience of the 1920s was still made up of many immigrants, and in particular *Las golondrinas* (the Swallows), the migrant Italian immigrants who came in the Argentine spring and left after working the crops in the Argentine winter. In the original version the image of the protagonist's mother comes to him in a dream he has in his cell. She is described as *tierna madrecita* (little mother of tenderness), this Gardel changed to *querida madrecita* (beloved little mother). In another part of the tango, the mother is described as *la pobre* (the unfortunate) and this Gardel changed to *santa* (saintly). These changes are far more appropriate. The image of a mother who is self-sacrificing was so dear to porteño males who came from single parent families held together by mothers. Such circumstances Gardel could identify with directly – true as well for many tango stars such as Corsini and Maizini. The mother in this tango also parallels the Madonna image of other tangos in that she intercedes on behalf of her son for his own betterment. The changes made by Gardel further enforce this image.

Once pardoned and freed from his cell the protagonist has dim prospects in the outside world. He faces the indifference of a world in which he has no place. He has no earthly love not even that of his mother who is now at the side of God. He wanders the streets begging for a bowl of soup and living the life of a lost soul. His only option is to go far away to find work. In the original version he will go *a trabajar muy lejos* (to work far away). This is too imprecise. Gardel changed this to *voy al campo a laburar* (I will go to the countryside to work). The use of the word *laburar* instead of the standard Spanish verb *trabajar* seems to show Gardel's recognition of the *golondrinas* because *laburar* in Argentina is of Italian origin (*laburare*) and often means to work as an agricultural laborer.[16] Through these changes Gardel made *La gayola* more understandable to his audience, more forceful and direct in its content, and above all more personal. These are factors that made Gardel the interpreter of tangos and as well of his audience.[17]

The tango as both a dance and as a song is filled with latent sexuality. Perhaps this exists as a confirmation of virility even in defeat. Even after the entry of women as an important part of the tango audience, they are drawn as a *mal necesario* (necessary evil) in the gardelian tango. They are needed however. The lonely man who has been repeatedly rejected still needs female companionship even if it is illusory.[18] It is almost as if the male needed protection from the cruel world and this could only come through a painful search for the right woman who would be like the ever sacrificing and protecting mother. *Sentencia* (1923) (Sentence) (Celedonio Esteban Flores): *El cariño de mi madre, mi viejecita adorada, que por santa merecia, señor juéz, ser venerada, en la calle de mi vida fué como luz de farol.* (The love of my mother, my adored little old lady who as a saint, Mister Judge, should be venerated, because in the dark street of my life she was like the light of a beacon.)

In another famous tango of Carlos Gardel *Madre hay una sola* (There Is Only One Mother), the theme is that in this life of betrayal and adversity there is one good that transcends all and that is one's mother (Gobello and Bossio 1979: 85). She helps the hapless male overcome all evil and heartache in this life. This tango theme of female goodness in the form of mother is an appropriate one for Carlos Gardel because Gardel's only lasting relationship with a woman was with his mother, Doña Bertra – *una mujer sacrificada* (a sacrificing woman). He never married.[19] While it is true his main audiences were women, his love affairs, if they ever existed, were rarely publicized. Only one was ever revealed and, even then, it was still one of rumor and mystery (the relationship with the Baroness who was in fact the American socialite Mrs. Sadie Baron Wakefield). When close friends and associates were asked about Gardel's love life they were also quick to report he was a man of honor and did not speak about such things to them. They do imply that *como un hombre* (as a man) he did have such relations.[20] This is another example of Gardel as a man of mystery. The conclusion that is drawn, however, is that as a man, and as a porteño, he *had* to have had relations with women. Therefore, he did.

Gardel's relationship with friends and in particular his relationship with his mother are more clear cut. He was a man of loyalty and was faithful in his duty as a son. He took care of his mother and friends. He bought his mother a home and maintained her and his other relatives in Argentina. In Gardel's tangos there is a strong influence of the incomplete family (i.e., *hijo natural* or illegitimate son). This theme was one with which many in the lower classes could identify because of the instability of the family due to poverty and due to the Argentine immigration phenomenon of the seasonal immigrants who often established casual relationships.[21] Children of such unions often formed a very strong protective bond with their mothers. Therefore, Gardel the man fits well within the essential myth element of loyalty/fidelity.

Gardel was an important entertainment figure. He was successful financially and lived very well. Too well sometimes, because he complained of his constant need to work to maintain his image.[22] He dressed well, ate well and for all outward appearances had money to burn. There are many stories about his gifts of money to those less fortunate. In one case he met a young man in the streets and gave him enough money to completely clothe himself in fashionable attire.[23] Further, Gardel was an active turfman. He owned a race horse, Lunático, and frequented Palermo race track. He was a friend of jockeys and trainers and was a close friend of Leguísamo the noted jockey of the 1920s. He was also a heavy better and lost a great deal of money on the *burros* (the dogs) of Palermo (García Jiménez 1976: 240–54). Gardel recorded numerous tangos with the theme of the Sport of Kings and in one the theme of betrayed love is joined with horse racing. In the tango *Por una cabeza* (1935) (By a Head) the lyrics were written by Gardel's close associate and friend Alfredo Le Pera – the music was by Gardel – love is like a lost horse race in which the man has no real control. Love is a game of chance where fate rules.[24] As a devotee of the Sport of Kings, this reputation added to his *pinta* (a special air) as a man of substance. He won the admiration of those who aspired to *hacer la América* (to get rich) in Argentina. He demonstrated that one could go from rags to riches. If Gardel could do it so could any porteño. In this case man and myth merge.

It should be noted that the respect for wealth was a love/hate relationship. Those who had wealth were envied and ridiculed while those who were poor and made it were looked upon with more acceptance by the urban poor. The tango *¿Qué Vachaché?* (What are You Going to Do?) by Enrique Santos Discépolo (1926) is a clear demonstration of the corrupting effect of money: *Lo que hace falta es empacar mucha plata, vender el alma, rifar el corazón* (What is needed is to collect a lot of money, sell your soul, raffle off your heart) (Gobello and Bossio 1979: 62). Yet, in the more humble theaters of *revistas* and *sainete*, the cabaret life was portrayed as something to be desired and to be emulated. The symbolic use of the dinner jacket to show wealth and social acceptance is a clear example of this emulation. For example, this is very much the theme in Corsini's tango *Patolero sentimental* (The Sentimental Guy), in his theatre production *El rey del cabaret* (The King of Cabaret) in 1923, and in his 1924 production of *Un programa de cabaret* (A Cabaret Program), as well as in his 1926 production of *Cabaret, tango y anexos* (Cabaret, Tango and Other Things).[25]

The last essential element for the construction of a heroic/myth of Carlos Gardel is a sense of alienation and vulnerability. An important theme in Gardel's tangos was inescapable fate. Destiny is omnipotent and omnipresent. The orientation of many of his tangos is *la de un hombre sin futuro, encerrado en el presente, inclinado sobre su pasado* (that of a man without a future, imprisoned by the present, inclined towards his past) (Canton 1972: 44).

Fifty-two of Gardel's tangos deal only with the present and of these thirty-eight express a negative view. Thirty-eight tangos have a perspective of looking back from the present to a past, that, in twenty-nine cases, was also negative. Man is caught in a time frame of past, present, and future over which one had no control (Ibid.). Gardel's life was one where he was born out of wedlock, had no family, no wife no children and that ended tragically. Given the porteño world-view, Gardel was an ideal figure. It is obvious from an analysis of tango lyrics that the tango as a human expression is ego oriented. As a result it is not a musical form dedicated to the well-being of others. Very few tangos can be called socially oriented. Instead, the music separates and isolates each individual from others within society and adds to a sense of alienation. Tangos that *can* be considered political are: *Los radicales* (pertains to the middle-class political party Unión Cívica Radical or simply The Radical Party), Hipólito Yrigoyen, Barceló (ward boss of Avellaneda), don Nalalio (editor of the popular newspaper *Crónica),* and *Viva la Patria* (Long Live The Fatherland, a gloss of the September 6, 1930 coup). Tangos that dealt with social issues are even fewer; they are *Guiseppe el zapatero* (Guiseppe The Shoemaker), *Buenos Aires*, *Pan* (Bread), and *Sentencia* (The Jail Sentence). Tangos that deal with labor/strikes are even fewer; they are *Al pie de la Santa Cruz* (At The Foot of The Holy Cross) and *Varsena* (refers to the Semana Tràgica of 1919). Gardel recorded *Buenos Aires* in 1922 (*Odeón* #18071) and in 1934 (*Odeón* #18919). *Guiseppe el zapatero* was recorded in 1930 (*Odeón* #18836) and *Al pie de la Santa Cruz* was recorded in 1933 (*Odeón* #18896).[26] The fact that Gardel recorded such tangos also adds to the view that he cared for his audience. In an ironic way the porteño admires those who care about the well-being of others e.g., Evita Perón, self-sacrificing mother, Yrigoyen and Perón as *Padres de los pobres* (fathers to the poor). At the same time porteños as individuals do not seem to have much extroverted sense.

Carlos Gardel does not seem to have been identified with any political grouping. He was known to frequently have coffee with the socialist Alfredo Palaciuos, was seen in the company of the conservative politician Juan Ruggiero (Ruggierito), and sought the political protection of Alberto Barceló who was the conservative charismatic ward boss of Avellaneda. When the Uriburu coup of September 1930 occurred, Gardel expressed his opposition to the overthrow of Yrigoyen by giving a special show on stage in face of a ban on such activities due to the declared state-of-siege. Yet shortly thereafter (nineteen days later), he recorded *Viva la patria* (Long Live the Fatherland) written by Francisco García Jiménez. In November of 1933, Gardel flew to Montevideo to show his support for the rightist coup of Gabriel Terra, which had occurred earlier (March 31, 1933). This action had a negative impact on some of Gardel's more liberal friends, such as the newspaperman Samuel Blixen Rámirez who broke with him (Zubillaga 1976: 43). One Peronista friend commented to me that if Gardel were alive today he would be a Peronista. As noted earlier, this is a point that the Peronistas are trying to make as part of party propaganda. They have added a further refinement of equating Perón with Gardel and Gardel with Perón so that the myths of these two men have merged. It is probably more accurate to say of Gardel that he was politically naïve and probably sought out conservative political leaders and causes as a means of gaining social acceptance. While it is true he was of working-class background, he adopted a life style that emulated the idle rich and was often portrayed in his publicity photographs dressed in a smoking jacket. Gardel escaped from his lower-class origins through his success in the tango – it gave him wealth and a sense of upper-class status. Through him his audiences also escaped. These porteño qualities listed above are also those of a personified tango; that is, the tango became for the porteño, in terms of its lyric and its rhythm, his soul exposed. This is well expressed in the tango definition: *Tango – eres un estado de alma de la multitud* (Tango – you are the soulful condition of the masses).[27] Carlos Gardel was the personification of the tango – he was tango and the tango was he.

Conclusions

From the time of its inception as *tango canción*, the tango lyrics as social and political documents are significant more in what they do not say than perhaps in what they say. The tone of the tango lyric message is also very telling evidence of the passivity (and therefore accepting) of the tango audience. They are not called to any great action even though they may be suffering. The lyric catalogs suffering, yet it offers no solutions. One is to suffer and accept that suffering as a normal part of life. Salvation, if it comes, comes in the form of escape through the projecting of self through others, Carlos Gardel for example, or through drink, or through prayer to one's Mother. The tango offered the Argentine no solace and left him alone, very alone. Even the tango-hero Carlos Gardel represented qualities which when analyzed coldly leave one to wonder what kind of role model or hero he did represent. He obviously was a vulnerable, indecisive, gender-uncertain male persona. Yet he clearly represented the male ideal and as such still serves as the epitome of Argentine masculinity. The close identification of Juan Perón with the Gardelian figure served the Peronista movement well into the 1970s as a vehicle for political adulation and popular support. The sense of personal isolation of Argentines, particularly in Argentine males, also served the Peronistas well because they promised protection from the cruelties of the modern world. Evita also served as part of the tango pantheon when she adopted the adoring and protecting mother figure. Male passivity combined with the paternalism and materialism of the Peronista movement and forged a bond through which the Argentine could give up personal responsibility for protection and security.

Notes

1. José Portogalo (1957: 51).
2. Blás Matamoro (1969: 149). See also Norberto Folino (1983). The Zwi Migdal was purportedly a Jewish benevolent society which in an investigation carried out in 1930 turned out to be a white slavery ring.
3. For the impact of Gardel on Argentine culture, see República Argentina, Senado de la Nación (1975).
4. The continual use of the photo of Gardel in homes, cars, buses, shops, and so on, as if it were a photo of a saint (along with The Virgin of Luján) signifies the great importance of Gardel to the common people of Buenos Aires.
5. For an interesting discussion of the city of Buenos Aires and its masses in terms of heros see Ezequiel Martínez Estrada (1957: 152ff.)
6. República Argentina, Senado de la Nación (1975: 3).
7. Ibid.: 70.
8. Ibid.: 3,4.
9. El *ranking* del tango (El Instituto Argentino de Studios 1972: 508–12). Male soloists were ranked as follows: Carlos Gardel, Augustín Magaldi, Ignacio Corsini, and Roberto Díaz.
10. Volume nine of the series. The first feature film was *La vida de Carlos Gardel* (1939), a production of Argentine Sono Films.
11. See Miguel Angel Morena (1983: 216); and also in the memoirs of tango great Francisco Canaro (1957: 150–1). Canaro considered Gardel to be *el astro máximo de la canción popular* (Ibid. p. 168).
12. Francisco García Jiménez (1976: 313). See also Moreno (1983: 230) for a detailed description of the funeral.
13. Probably the most interesting of the Argentine authors are Julio Mafud and Ezeiquel Mártinez Estrada.

14. José Ortega y Gasset, complete works (1964: 349f.).
15. For a discussion of the role of women in the world of the tango, see Donald S. Castro (1994: 66–76).
16. The term had by the time of Gardel become part of *caló porteño* and was interchangeable with *trabajar*. It could also mean to rob.
17. For the tangos cited, see Idea Vilariño (1981: 46, 56, 76) and José Gobello and Jorge A. Bossio (1979: 186f.) See also Roberto Puertas Cruse (1959: 49) which presents an interesting interpretation of the Gardelian tangos.
18. Ibid.
19. Gardel's mother is so described in Senado de la Nación (1975: 104).
20. This issue is of such importance that García Jiménez devoted a chapter to the subject (1976: 308–11). See also *Revista Gente,* special edition on Carlos Gardel (6-2-77), pp. 36–7. The television homage to Gardel, on the Spanish International Network, *Homenaje a Gardel,* also devoted time to an interview with Isabel del Valle, reputed lover of Gardel. She was very circumspect. Another tango star on the program, and a contemporary of Gardel, Mona Mares stated Gardel was . . . *muy tímido con las mujeres.* Simon Collier discusses this issue as well in his study (1986: 176).
21. For a discussion of the 'swallows' as an immigration factor in Argentina, see Donald S. Castro (1982: 50–62)
22. Also see Morena (1983: 189f.).
23. Julio De Caro (1957) as quoted in Jorge Miguel Couselo and Orisis Chierico (1964: 26)
24. For a discussion of the tango and its relation to horse racing see Jorge Larroca (1981).
25. See Ignacio Corsini, (hijo) (1959: 24) and Gaspar J. Astarita (1981: 131). The tango *Seguí mi consejo* by Eduardo Trongé (1893–1946) is also in this vein. Advice of this 1928 tango is to live by night because that is what the rich people do (*vivila siempre de noche porque eso es de gente bien*) (José Gobello and Jorge A. Bossio 1979: 196). *Patolero* is a person who hangs around the streets in a neighborhood, and he and his fellows form a band of fun seekers.
26. Analysis made from discographic notes in a commemorative record album produced in honor of the 28th anniversary of Gardel's death. Odeón-Buenos Aires, Serie Coleccionista (OLP 311) 1964.
27. See Tomás de Lara and Inés Leonilda Roncitti de Panti (1961: 116).

6

Tango and the Scandal of Homosocial Desire[1]

Jeffrey Tobin

Tango's Primal Scenes

In recent years several Broadway-style tango shows – such as 'Tango Argentino' and 'Forever Tango' – have had successful runs on the stages of Europe, Japan, and the United States. In Buenos Aires, similarly grand-scale shows, directed at Argentine audiences – such as 'Tango X 2' and 'Gotán' – have had great success in downtown theaters, while more modest shows aimed at tourists have enjoyed long runs at nightclubs such as El Viejo Almacén and Casa Blanca in the old neighborhood of San Telmo. The shows tend to be quite similar. Indeed, dancers, musicians, and singers routinely move from one show to another without significantly altering their performances. For example, the tango-dance couple Carlos and Alicia moved directly from 'Forever Tango' in Los Angeles to Casa Blanca, and they danced some of the very same choreographies in both venues.

It is perhaps de rigeur for all such tango shows to begin with a history lesson, educating audiences about tango's origins. Two images inevitably dominate these primal tango scenes. One image is of a brothel in Buenos Aires. Extravagantly-dressed men dance tango with barely-dressed women. A fight breaks out over one of the women, leading two of the men to perform a choreographed knife fight. Jorge Luis Borges is probably more responsible than anyone else for the association of tango-dance with knife fighting. In *Evaristo Carriego* (1930), he writes, 'I would say that tango and that milongas directly express something that poets, many times, have wanted to say with words: the conviction that to fight can be a fiesta' (Borges 1989: I: 161), and in a poem entitled 'El Tango' (1964), he writes 'Tango creates a disturbed / Unreal past that in some way is certain, / The impossible memory of having died / Fighting, on a suburban corner' (Borges 1989: II: 267; see also Borges 1989: II: 349, and Taylor

1976: 281). In each case, the context makes clear that by 'fighting,' Borges means 'with a knife.'

The other image that dominates tango's primal scenes is of a street corner in Buenos Aires, on which men dance with one another, playfully competing to display the fanciest steps. No women are present. Note that each primal scene features a competitive choreography performed by two men. In both popular and scholarly discourse such same-sex dancing is routinely chalked up to the relative scarcity of women in the early-twentieth century Rio de la Plata region. It is supposed that if two men danced with one another – or otherwise embraced – it was because there were no women available (see Figure 6.1). José Gobello writes that 'The compadritos launched masculine couples only when tango's rhythm put ants in their pants and they did not find a female companion at hand' (Gobello 1995: 'El Compadrito'), and Julie Taylor writes that tango-men's 'defensive attitudes toward woman are recognized to have been fostered by the low percentage of females relative to males in the foreign-born population' (Taylor 1976: 274 and 284; see also Chinarro 1965: 27).[2] As the sex ratio was straightened out, this story goes, so was the dance, and the culture.

'This is Tango'

The film *Tango Bar*[3] includes a typical Argentine tango show, called 'This is Tango' (*Esto es Tango*) and the show, of course, includes the obligatory dance between the two male protagonists: Ricardo Padín, played by the Puerto Rican actor Raúl Julia, and Antonio Estévez, played by the Argentine tango-singer and bandoneon player Ruben Juárez. Ricardo is a Puerto Rican who has immigrated to Buenos Aires, where he works as a tango-lyricist and piano player. Antonio is an Argentine tango performer returning from exile following the so-called 'Dirty War.' Ricardo and Antonio's dance itself is quite brief. What is most noteworthy is the dialogue that precedes and follows the dance:

> *Ricardo:* Don't fool yourselves, *señores*. The ruffians (*malevos*) knew how to be friends. Friendship for a *tanguero* is funda-mental. They were capable of dying for a friend, of putting their life on the line. Loyalty toward a friend, señores, *this* was what had value for a ruffian.
>
> *Antonio:* Loyalty toward a friend and tango. All of that was in the heart of the ruffian, but there was also something else. They were consumed by a passion for . . . broads (*minas*).

Ricardo:	Broads.
Antonio:	Broads. The *compadritos* liked broads so much that they practiced tango with one another. Ricardo, please . . . (They dance together, first touching only foreheads, then fully embracing. The audience laughs. The two pause, cheek to cheek, and turn to the audience and smile. The audience applauds enthusiastically.)
Antonio:	(To audience:) As I was saying. (Aside, to Ricardo:) Thank you.
Ricardo:	You're welcome.
Antonio:	The *compadritos* liked broads so much that they practiced tango with one another so that later they would know how to lead dancing with women. How are you going to pick up a broad if you don't dance tango well?
1st man in audience:	What? The men danced tango with one another?
Antonio:	Hold it right there, friend, I said they *practiced*.
2nd man in audience:	But, with one another?
Antonio:	But what's wrong with that, brother? What's wrong with what Ricardo and I were just doing?
1st man in audience:	Well, I don't know, but it seems to me . . .
Ricardo:	It seems to me that what the gentleman wants to know is if the *tangueros* were *machos*.
Antonio:	Why don't you just ask, *che*? Is it that you want to dance with me? I'm sorry, you're not my type.
Ricardo:	Listen. The broads danced with one another, too. For the taste of the forbidden. Because tango is this: the underworld, the forbidden, the sinful. To sum it up, men danced with one another thinking about broads, and broads, thinking about men. The broads, ladies and gentlemen, were always essential for the *tangueros*. Because without broads, there is no tango. (Enthusiastic applause.)

In actual tango shows, there is very little talking beyond the introducing of singers, musicians, and dancers. I do not believe that many Argentines would sit still for a show in which the performers presumed to lecture on the history of tango. Most Argentine men – or at least those who would go to a tango show – present themselves as experts on tango's history, and they are much more comfortable talking about what tango really was or is than listening to others talk about it. Moreover, it is especially difficult to believe that an audience full of Argentine men would accept listening to a Puerto Rican lecture on the history of tango. Indeed, the only tango expert more objectionable than a foreigner is a woman. Thus, the spoken narrative of the 'This is Tango' show seems contrived. Nevertheless, the dialogue surrounding Ricardo and Antonio's dance is worth exploring because it calls attention to the dominant themes in the Argentine discourse of male-male tango dancing.

Roots of Male Desire

Did tango begin as a predominantly male-male dance? Borges is one of many to argue that in tango's early years, 'on street corners, pairs of men danced it, because the neighborhood women did not want to participate in a brothel dance' (Borges 1989 I: 160). The question, then, is whether tango was primarily danced by men on street corners, or whether, as Antonio in *Tango Bar* asks, 'the *compadritos* liked broads so much that they practiced tango with one another so that later they would know how to lead dancing with women'? What if a man practiced tango with other men one hour for every five minutes he danced with a woman? Is it a question of how much time he spent practicing tango with other men and how much with women, or is it a question of his motives for dancing with men? Or, as Ricardo in *Tango Bar* asserts, is it a question of whether or not while dancing with other men, a man is 'thinking about broads'?

José Gobello is one of the most adamant defenders of tango's heterosexual stability, arguing that 'from its earliest days, tango was danced by women.' Gobello interprets the Bates brothers' comment that a certain club in San Telmo 'was one of the first places where tango was danced among *just men*' (Bates and Bates 1936: 36) to mean that male-male dancing – at least in clubs – was a secondary development, and that tango was originally danced by heterosexual couples (Gobello 1995). Gobello adds that 'In any case, we are dealing with an exception, because if there was one thing the compadrito did not have even a hint of it was misogyny.' Horacio Salas makes the same argument (Salas 1986: 38), but Savigliano observes that he thereby 'equates misogyny with the lack of interest in women and not with the shape and nature of that interest' (Savigliano 1995: 244–5). The absence of misogyny obviously does not confirm a man as straight any more than the presence of misogyny confirms him as gay. Eduardo Archetti follows Gobello in asserting that 'It has been erroneously assumed that originally the tango was mostly danced by male couples', adding that 'the importance of the "dancing academies" as meeting places for men and "waitresses" or for couples cannot be overlooked' (Archetti 1994: 100). Or, as Ricardo in *Tango Bar* asserts, 'without broads, there is no tango.'

Jorge Salessi presents the strongest version of the argument that tango was originally a predominantly homoerotic, male-male dance. He observes that some of the prostitutes on whom Gobello and others rely to constitute early tango-dance as heterosexual were men in drag, and that even those prostitutes who were women were categorized by contemporary hygienists as 'masculine' (Salessi 1997: 161). I would even argue that dancing tango itself made any woman seem masculine, since the tango couple is composed of two masculine subjects, even if one – or both – of them happens to be a woman. Thus, Felix Weingartner wrote in the 1920s, 'The majority of women who dance tango do so quite badly, while the men are almost all excellent dancers' (quoted by Tomas de Lara 1961, quoted by Taylor 1976: 289), and Julie Taylor reports being told by an informant in the 1960s that 'It was difficult to find women who danced well. I practiced with my sisters and my cousins but the girls did it badly' (Taylor 1976: 289). I believe women are thought to dance tango badly because tango-dance retains something of the homosocial sparring evident in its primal scenes: men trading fancy figures or dancerly swipes of the blade. As Salessi – drawing on statements by Salas and others – argues, 'In its stage of being prohibited music, tango has a choreography in general executed by pairs of men' (Salessi 1991: 47). Salessi merges this argument with Gobello's observation that 'tango is a lascivious dance . . . and the total representation is an erotic simulacra' (Gobello quoted in Salessi 1991: 47) to conclude that tango is homoerotic. According to Martínez Estrada, also, tango 'is the sexual act itself, devoid of fiction, no innocence, without neurosis' (Martínez Estrada quoted in Savigliano 1995: 43). Note, however, that Gobello denies that tango was ever much danced by men with men, and that when he and Martínez Estrada assert that tango-dance simulates the sexual act, it is clear that they mean the *heterosexual* act. Salessi's argument, though, is that repressed or forbidden homoeroticism at least adds to the titillation that even straight couples find in the tango-dance. I venture that the original tango, repeatedly described by the historians of Argentine music as a simulation or a choreographic representation of sexual intercourse, is a cultural expression with significant homoerotic and homosexual connotations that today are deeply embedded in the imagined national identity of the large Argentine middle class (Salessi 1997: 140). Or, as Ricardo in *Tango Bar* observes, 'The broads danced with one another too, for the taste of the forbidden, because tango is this: the underworld, the forbidden, the sinful.' Thus, contemporary tango-dance continues to be marked by forbidden homosocial desire. The contemporary tango couple dances its way back and forth, over the fortified and leaky border separating the straight and the gay. After decades of traveling across marital, class, and national boundaries, it is possibly tango's nightly trip across this sexual boundary that continues to be its dangerous and forbidden passion.

Why is This Man Smiling?

Carlos Gardel is far and away the most important figure in tango's history. Writing in 1976, Taylor observed, 'Gardel's smiling face is an integral part of the Argentine scene, beaming down at the public from the place of honor in the front of buses and taxis given to decals of his portrait' (Taylor 1976: 285; see Figure 6.2). Despite claims that Maradona's image has displaced Gardel's from at least some Buenos Aires buses (Libertad Berkoweiz in Moreno Chá 1995: 64), Gardel remains on the center stage of the Argentine popular imagination, even if nowadays he has to share that stage with Eva Perón and Diego Maradona. As the popular expression goes, *cada dia canta mejor* (he sings better every day), which among other things means that his fame and importance do not diminish, but grow with time. Gardel and his smile are almost invariably described as enigmatic. Gobello argues that Gardel's famous smile was a mask that hid more than it revealed:

> Surely the smiling and superior Gardel, bon vivant and somewhat cynical, was nothing but the mask of an artist, the mask of a pain, of an anguish that came from far away, that came from his own social condition, or from something deeper still, from the social solidarity that from his subconscious put that choke in his throat that even a yankee could see, when here (in Argentina), they saw only, perhaps, his toothpaste smile (Gobello 1995: 'Otra Vision de Gardel').

Thus, Gobello suggests that despite the ubiquity of Gardel's smiling image, Argentines do not usually see beyond the superficial grin. In fact, scholars in Argentina – and Uruguay – endlessly debate the date and

Figure 6.1 Juan Manuel Fangio dancing Tango. Used with permission

Figure 6.2 Carlos Gardel. Used with permission

place of his birth, his popularity and his politics, and the circumstances of his death. Was he born in Toulouse, France or in Tacuarembó, Uruguay? On 10 or 11 December 1890? Or 1887? Was his popularity in Argentina declining at the time of his death? Did he join the oligarchy in celebrating the fall of Hipólito Yrigoyen in 1930? Was his death really an accident? These are just some of the well-known debates that I will not enter.

In addition, Norberto Chab mentions some other Gardelian themes that are not debated so openly: 'His loves, his relation with his mother, his virility, his presumed juvenile delinquency, his heritage, his fortune, his descendants, they are the recurring themes that are raised to darken his career' (Chab 1995: 37). Taylor tactfully alludes to some of the same dark rumors, writing, 'Nor could any account, imaginary or real, of his talent, generosity, *machismo,* or filial devotion ever be effectively disproven' (Taylor 1976: 286). Chab with his mention of virility and Taylor with her mention of *machismo* are each hinting at a forbidden but ubiquitous debate. As Ricardo in *Tango Bar* observes, 'It seems to me that what the gentleman wants to know is if the *tangueros* were *machos.*' Or, in this case, if the *tanguero* par excellence was straight. That the debate about Gardel's sexuality is forbidden is evidenced by the fact that Argentina's National Academy of Tango expelled a member for speaking about Gardel's rumored homosexuality in public. Nevertheless, conducting fieldwork in the tango scenes in Buenos Aires and Montevideo, I found that such rumors were easy to come by in casual, not-for-attribution conversations. For example, a professional tango dancer in Montevideo acknowledged that the rumors were rather common and that he could see the merit of the argument that Gardel was gay. His own thoughtful theory, however, was that Gardel's apparent lack of interest in women was a sign not of homosexuality, but of asexuality. A more irreverent tango-dance teacher in Buenos Aires jokingly more than concurred, suggesting that Gardel was a natural-born castrato. (The film *Farinelli* was showing in Buenos Aires theaters at the time). As evidence he called attention to Gardel's chubbiness and his ability to hit high notes.

The debate about Gardel's sexuality is complicated by the fact that many clues that are read to mark a man as manly are also read to mark him a *marica* (fag). Thus, Gardel's suspect sexuality can be attributed to his apparent non-interest in women, or that same apparent non-interest can mark Gardel as a man's man, who did not waste time on feminine 'things.' As Savigliano observes, 'Any interest in either love or sex (with a woman) would corrupt the macho picture' (Savigliano 1995: 43). Alternately, Gardel's rumored homosexuality can be traced to his role as the first hero of romantic tango, as opposed to the more robust, ruffianesque tango that preceded it, or that same romantic role can mark Gardel as a ladies' man, who proved his manliness by turning tango into a tool of seduction.

Borges explores such paradoxes of Argentine masculinity in his story 'La Intrusa' (The Female Intruder). Commenting on the story, Borges observes that 'Really there are only two characters – the two brothers,' Cristián and Eduardo (Borges 1970: 278). Thus, Juliana – the 'intrusa' of the title – is, significantly, a non-character, 'a thing' (Borges 1989 II: 404). Cristián brings Juliana to the home that he and Eduardo share. When Eduardo also falls in love with her, the neighbors happily anticipate the fight to come. Instead, Cristián arranges to leave Juliana and Eduardo at home together, and before departing, he says to his brother, 'There you have Juliana: if you want her, use her' (Ibid.: 404). For a while the brothers share Juliana, but they find that they cannot contain their latent rivalry because they are in love. 'In the hard suburb, a man did not say, nor was it said, that a woman could matter to him, beyond desire and possession, but the two were in love. This, in some way, humiliated them' (Ibid.). Though the obvious reading is that 'the two were in love with Juliana,' it is quite possible to read the line as 'the two were in love with each other.' Accordingly, what each brother objects to may be that Juliana has another lover, or it may be that his brother has another lover. It is also possible to attribute their humiliation to being in love with a woman or to being in love with each other. There is evidence that the brothers are more jealous of Juliana than they are of each other – that is to say, that what bothers the brothers is sharing each other, not sharing Juliana. Thus, at one point in the story, they sell her to a far-off brother, so that they can return to 'their old life of men among men' (Ibid.: 405), but that plan fails when Cristián finds Eduardo at the brothel, 'waiting his turn' to be with Juliana. The brothers are not bothered by sharing Juliana with other clients at the brothel. What bothers each of them is finding his brother among those clients.

Homoerotic allusions mount as Borges explains that 'The woman attended to the two with bestial submission' (Ibid.: 405). Bestiality is not sodomy, but as Suárez-Orozco observes, the two are sometimes mingled in the discourse of Argentine sexual insults (Suárez-Orozco 1982: 22–3). Eventually, Cristián kills her, explaining to Eduardo, 'She will no longer do any damage' (Borges 1989 II: 406). The story ends with the brothers embracing, 'almost crying. Now another link bound them: the woman sadly sacrificed and the obligation to forget her' (Ibid.: 406). Daniel Balderston concludes that 'as the story makes clear, woman here is the token that allows the functioning of homosexual desire, even though

– in the perverse world of the story – that desire requires the death of the woman' (Balderston 1995: 35). Borges, commenting on the story explains it came out of a conversation in the late 1920s with his friend Nicolas Paredes. 'Commenting on the decadence of tango lyrics, which even then went in for "loud self-pity" among sentimental *compadritos* betrayed by their wenches, Paredes remarked dryly "Any man who thinks five minutes straight about a woman is no man – he's a queer (*marica*)." Love among such people was obviously ruled out; I knew that their real passion would be friendship' (Borges 1970: 278; see also Borges 1989 II: 414–5 and Savigliano 1995: 45). Borges does not need to specify that Gardel was one of the foremost 'sentimental *compadritos*,' who sang tango lyrics that went in for 'loud self-pity.' For example, the song that in 1917 launched both the romantic *tango-canción* genre and Gardel's career was *Mi Noche Triste* (My Sad Night), with lyrics by Pascual Contursi and music by Samuel Castriota (Romano 1990: 53–4).

> *Percanta que me amuraste*
> *en lo mejor de mi vida*
> *dejándome el alma herida*
> *y espina en el corazón.*
> *Para mi ya no hay consuelo*
> *y por eso me encurdelo*
> *pa' olvidarme de tu amor.*
> (Broad, you who abandoned me
> at the height of my life
> leaving my soul wounded
> and a thorn in my heart.
> For me there is no long comfort
> and so I get drunk
> in order to forget your love.)

And in 1928, just at the time of Borges's conversation with Paredes, Gardel recorded *Malevaje* (Gang of Ruffians), with lyrics by Enrique Discépolo and music by Juan de D. Filiberto (Romano 1990: 151–2).

> *No me has dejao ni el pucho en la*
> *oreja*
> *de aquel pasao malevo y feroz.*
> *Ya no me falta pa' completar*
> *más que ir a misa e hincarme a rezar*
> *Ayer, de miedo a matar*

en vez de pelear
me puse a correr...
Me vi a la sombra o finao,
pensé en no verse y temblé.
Si yo que nunca aflojé
de noche angustiao
me encierro a yorar.
You have not left me even the cigarette
behind my ear
from that ruffian and ferocious past.
Now I don't lack anything to complete the
picture
but to go to church and get down on my
knees to pray
Yesterday, afraid to kill
instead of fighting
I ran away
I saw myself imprisoned or dead,
I thought of not seeing you and I trembled.
If I who never went soft
anguished at night
I shut myself in to cry.

The character Gardel performs in *Malevaje* confirms that the sentimental compadrito can not coexist with the *malevo* (ruffian) of yore. His
obsession with a woman has made him, like the tango, lose his 'ruffian
and ferocious past.' Thus, he now flees from the fight that epitomized
the earlier tango culture, because he is afraid to kill the other man. The
price to recover the ruffian past he has lost is to give up seeing the woman,
but neither he nor his new tango can pay it. They have gone soft, turned
inward, and taken to crying.

Thus, the *malevo,* who shuns all things female, and the sentimental
compadrito, who suffers women obsessively, are both of suspect sexuality.
Gardel, as the transitional figure, never quite lost his ruffian edge despite
his status as a romantic icon. That is to say, though he performed the role
of the sentimental compadrito, he was never caught off stage pining away
for any woman. Is his sexuality suspect because he remained immersed
in the all-male *malevo* world? Or is it suspect because he left that world
for the softer, more feminine world that succeeded it? Alternatively, are
Argentines fascinated by Gardel because his life affords subversive
readings, or despite such readings, or because his life affords different

readings by different audiences? Similarly, does the almost obligatory speculation about the homosexuality of any 'sex symbol' indicate that being queer makes one seem sexy? Or, does it indicate that being sexy makes one seem queer? Or, is there pleasure to be derived from the delicately maintained ambiguity regarding a sex symbol's true desire?

Phallic Displays

The primary relation in tango is not between the heterosexual dance partners, but is between the man who dances with a woman and the other men who watch. A tango exhibition that I witnessed at a Buenos Aires milonga[4] is typical of the homocentrism of the Buenos Aires tango-scene. One of the club's organizers announced that there was going to be an exhibition of 'five authentic milongueros.' In fact ten dancers, not five, took the floor: five men in their sixties or seventies with their partners, who were women ranging from about eighteen to twenty-five years of age. As the couples danced, men in the audience shouted out words of encouragement and praise to the men on the dance floor. At the conclusion of the exhibition, one of the male dancers rushed over to the man with whom I was sitting, asking, 'Did you see the *nena* (chick) I was dancing with? Did you see her?' The *nena* in question did not strike me or my friend as a particularly good dancer, but she was pretty and young – only about twenty years old – and she was wearing a short skirt and blouse that left her belly-button exposed. I read the *milonguero*'s 'Did you see the *nena* I was dancing with?' as evidence of a homosocial relationship between the two men. Here, I follow Sedgwick in using the concept of homosociality to mark a heterosexual formation (Sedgwick 1985). In tango, however, I find that homosocial desire is not expressed through the *exchange* of women – as Sedgwick theorizes in her reading of English literature – but that it is expressed through the *display* of women. Or, as Savigliano argues, 'Tangos are male because their intimate confessions are mediated through the *exposure* of female bodies'(Savigliano 1995: 61, my emphasis). For example, it is commonly asserted that 'the man's role in dancing tango is to make the woman look good.' Similarly, in 1931 Waldo Frank wrote that 'Man is the creator of the tango dance because he conceives it on the woman's body' (Frank 1969: 350).

Thus, in the Buenos Aires milonga circuit especially – more than in European or North American tango – there is a minimalist style of leading. The man's goal is apparently to lead the woman to perform very flashy figures while he himself moves as little as possible. Many men explain that it is an effeminate vanity in a man to put too much effort into his own steps. His job is to shuffle along inconspicuously, moving only as much as is necessary to stay in the proper position relative to the woman. Here, I find Susan Foster's reading of gender relations in classical European ballet useful. Like the male and female dancers in tango, the male and female dancers in ballet, according to Foster, 'do not enjoy equal visibility.'

> *She*, like a divining rod, trembling, erect, responsive, which *he* handles, also channels the energy of all the eyes focused upon *her*, yet even as she commands the audience's gaze, *she* achieves no tangible or enduring identity. *Her* personhood is eclipsed by the attention *she* receives, by the need for her to dance in front of everyone. Just as *he* conveys her, *she* conveys desire. *She* exists as a demonstration of that which is desired but is not real. *Her* body flames the charged wantings of so many eyes, yet like a flame it has no substance. *She* is, in a word, the phallus, and *he* embodies the forces that pursue, guide, and manipulate it (Foster 1996: 2–3).

Similarly, in tango-dance, the woman is the focus of visual attention. Her's, not the man's, is the body that is exposed and displayed. In the discourse about the dance, however, 'women are, so to speak, the exhibited signifiers' (Savigliano 1995: 46). The milonga public watches the woman in order to talk about man. In Lacanian terms, the male lead in tango *has* the phallus while the female follower *is* the phallus. Thus, he is a subject of desire and she, an object. This is why five *milongueros* were announced, even though there were ten dancers. It is customary in Buenos Aires, to give a man most, if not all, the credit for a tango performance. The tango-dancing woman – again, in Lacanian terms – does not exist, except as a symptom of the tango-dancing man. She is not herself a desiring subject, but is the phallic display of his desire (Lacan 1985: 84,48).

When Dancing is Not

Fieldwork in the contemporary Buenos Aires tango scene reveals that many men continue to spend much of their time on the dance floor in the arms of other men despite the availability of female partners. Taylor reports that 'In 1966 a porteño told me that he as a boy in the 1940s had learned tango when he and a group of boys became interested in the subject together. They all learned by practicing with each other' (Taylor 1976: 289). Savigliano reports hearing similar stories thirty years later. Older milongueros, in particular, recount that they began by learning the woman's part exclusively for a couple of years, typically with an older relative or neighbor dancing the part of the man (Savigliano, personal communication, 1996). To this day, most tango-dance instructors are men, and they routinely give private classes to other men. In one extreme case, a professional male dancer reported giving private classes to a male student from Japan four hours a day, seven days a week, for a month. The teacher would demonstrate a new step by performing the man's role with the student performing the woman's. Then the student would practice the new step performing the man's role with the teacher performing the woman's. In the evenings, the two went to the teacher's stage show and then to dance clubs, where the teacher danced with women, but the student only watched. Thus, the student returned to Japan having danced over a hundred hours with his male instructor, and not once with an Argentine woman. Moreover, the teacher, during that month, spent more time dancing with the Japanese man and other male students than he spent dancing with women, including his stage-tango partner. Several teachers reported that Argentine, Japanese, and European men readily learn by dancing with their male teachers, but that it is necessary to provide a female partner when teaching a North American male student.

My own experience was mixed. An older (sixty-ish) male tango instructor – Pedro Monteleone – had his daughter perform the woman's role in his classes with me, but he did not have her present for classes with male Argentine students. In private lessons I took with two younger (forty-ish) male tango instructors – Carlos Rivarola and Carlos Gómez – there was no woman present. Gómez, however, was one of those who told me he usually did hire a female assistant for teaching North Americans. He explained that he saw me as an exception since we had gone to the *cancha* (soccer stadium) together. I noticed that Rivarola danced the woman's role with great flare and, apparently, gusto, but when I complimented him, or asked how he learned to dance the woman's role so well, he would invariably respond with false modesty, denying that he was in fact *dancing* the woman's role, or that he had actually ever learned how to do so. Similarly, Gómez, despite executing particularly flashy figure eights, claimed, 'I don't really dance the woman's part; it is just for teaching.' Like other men, he simultaneously showed off with his feet and downplayed with words his ability to dance the woman's part.

As a rule, Argentine men do not refer to what they do with other men as 'dancing.' Just like Antonio in *Tango Bar*, they insist on the word 'practicing' to label spins around the dance floor in the arms of another man.

Ist man in audience: What? The men danced tango with one another?
Antonio: Hold it right there, friend, I said they *practiced*.

I put this observation to the test in a group class taught by Monteleone. Since there were many more men than women in class that day, Monteleone assigned me and an Argentine man to practice the tango-walk with one another. The man, who is a physician, told me that he was uncomfortable dancing with another man. I do not know if my being a North American contributed to his discomfort, or if his discomfort meant that he was 'americanized' – a trait not unusual among thirty-something doctors in Buenos Aires. Falling back on what I had heard from other Argentines, I assured him that we were not 'dancing,' we were 'practicing' and he appeared to accept this distinction with genuine relief.

Argentine men routinely teach one another how to dance in tango dance classes, and they often practice and even show-off dancing together in tango *prácticas*, but in the milongas of Buenos Aires and Montevideo men never dance together. A few women, too, practice with one another in tango *prácticas*, but they are often met with disapproval. The common explanation is that a man must learn the woman's part in order to lead a woman, but that a woman does not have to learn the man's part to follow a man. Many men even warn that once a woman has learned to lead, she is ruined as a follower. Thus, if a woman in a *práctica* dances the man's role with another woman, she is unlikely to be asked to dance by any of the men who are present. The stigma of having danced the man's part may even follow her from the *práctica* to the milonga, where she is still less likely to be asked to dance, and if she does dance, her dancing of the woman's role is likely to be judged harshly and to be held up as an example of the damage done by dancing the man's role. Conversely, a man who dances the woman's part at a *práctica* is not stigmatized in any way. Occasionally, at *prácticas* or very informal milongas, or near the end of the evening, a couple will play at inverting their roles – the woman leading and the man following – but this arrangement rarely lasts for an entire song, and it is always accompanied by joking on the part of the man who is dancing or on the part of other men who are witnessing the spectacle. In sum, it has been commonplace for men to dance with one another in tango's primal scenes and in its contemporary practice, but one way or another this same-sex dancing is dismissed as incidental to the heterosexual dance. Men are said to dance with other men only because no women are available, in order to learn how to dance with women, or as a 'passing' joke.

Choreographies of Gender

The continuing ambiguity of tanguero sexuality is evident in the tango dance. Dance reconstructions indicate that the embrace in early, homo-social tango was very loose and that the relationship between 'leading' and 'following' was not fixed. The dancers only nominally 'led' and 'followed' one another. By contrast, in European social dance, the embrace was and is more rigid than in early tango, and the couple is more stably sexually dimorphic, composed of a man who leads and a woman who follows. Savigliano documents the disciplinization of tango by social dance masters in England and France (Savigliano 1995: 95–100). European dance masters endeavored to take a couple-dance that was neither bourgeois nor heterosexual and to make it conform to the established mechanics of European, bourgeois, heterosexist social dance, in which a dominant man leads and a docile woman follows. The English dance masters were both more and less successful in this endeavor than their continental counterparts. They were more successful because they created a dance that conforms completely to heterosexist, European social dance conventions. They were less successful because the dance they created is hardly recognizable as tango. Outside of the highly-disciplined, enclosed world of 'Ballroom Dancing', the tango created by English dance masters is not considered tango. As Savigliano observes, in Japan and the United States, Ballroom Tango and Tango Argentino are two distinct dances, practiced by two nearly distinct communities.

Tango Argentino is itself increasingly divided among, for example, European and Argentine, stage-oriented and salon-oriented dance masters (Marta Savigliano, personal communication, 1996). Salon-oriented tango-dance in Argentina displays elements of both its homosocial roots and its European disciplinization. For example, a common saying in the Buenos Aires tango-scene expresses the relationship of leader and follower as *el hombre propone y la mujer dispone* (the man proposes and the woman decides). Thus, Ezequiel Martínez Estrada, an early critic of tango, chose to attack tango-dance precisely because the man's role is so weak. 'It is a humiliating dance for women, having given themselves to a man who does not lead them, who does not require them to keep alert to his whims nor to give up her will. It is humiliating in that the man is as passive as she is' (Martínez Estrada, quoted in Savigliano 1995: 44). This view of tango-dance is a long way from the practice Taylor has found in her excursions in the Buenos Aires tango-scene. She argues that 'the overwhelming choreographic statement of the central theme of the dance (is) the relationship of man and woman seen as an encounter between the active, powerful, and completely dominant male and the passive, docile, and completely submissive female' (Taylor 1976: 281; see also Taylor 1992: 381). I can confirm that there are men and women in Buenos Aires who dance tango as Taylor describes it, but theirs is by no means the only tango-dance style. Many if not most couples in Buenos Aires continue to dance a tango in which neither male dominance nor female submission is complete.

There is, in fact a great deal of variation within the Buenos Aires dance scene. For example, some of the most obvious differences, even at a glance, include whether the dancers dance with their heads facing the same direction or in opposite directions, and whether a woman places her left hand lightly on her partner's right forearm or drapes her left arm over his right shoulder. Older milongueros report that those differences and many more used to correspond with particular neighborhoods. They claim that they could easily tell what neighborhood a partner was from by the way he or she danced. Nowadays, the milongueros report, tango-dance styles are not associated with neighborhoods so much as with teachers. Thus, they claim that now they can often tell what teacher a partner has studied with by the way he or she embraces and dances. My own impression – from taking classes and attending *prácticas* with many different tango instructors around Buenos Aires, and from dancing with women who learned with instructors I never even met – is that the heterosexualized dance style described by Taylor corresponds, for example, with the tango-dance taught by Zoraida at La Ideal and by Carmona on Calle Moreno. The tango-dance taught, for example, by Bocha at the Commercial Workers' Union or by Juan Carlos at an Unidad Basica near Avenida Cordoba, is quite different. One difference is that a woman taught by Zoraida or Carmona will not perform a *gancho* unless her partner specifically calls for her to do so, while a woman taught by Bocha or Juan Carlos will decide for herself whether or not to perform a gancho when the opportunity arises. In the first case, the man decides what his partner will and will not do. In this tango-dance style, a good male dancer marks his decisions clearly and somewhat forcefully, while a good female dancer understands and performs her partner's marks. In the second case, the man proposes, but the woman decides what she will and will not do. In this tango-dance style a good male dancer adjusts his marks in response to his partner's decisions, while a good female dancer improvises her steps in a responsible and productive way.

Differences between the two broad styles I have been describing may also have much to do with a dancer's experience. A woman generally learns how to submissively follow a man's mark before she learns how to improvise within and around that mark, and a man generally learns how to mark a step for his partner before he learns how to respond to her improvisations. Thus, Savigliano catalogues many of the non-submissive tactics available to experienced female tango-dancers.

> Milonguitas could challenge their male partners with the thrust and energy invested in the walks; manipulate their axis of balance by changing the distance between the bodies, the points of contact, and the strength of the embrace; play with diverse qualities of 'roundness' in their steps; modify the 'front' given to their partners, choosing to 'face' them in misaligned angles of torso and hips; disrupt the cadence sought by their partners by not converting their trampling cortes at the proper musical time (thus imposing a need for skillful syncopation in order to keep up with the music); and add unexpectedly fancy ornamentations (*adornos*) of their own to the figures 'marked' by their partners (modifying the height to which a leg should be raised in order to complete a certain figure, adding small stompings in between each step, lacing one leg around the back or front of the other before engaging in a conversion), complicating the timing of the conversions, creating anxiety, and even causing their male partners to modify their plans for upcoming steps (Savigliano 1995: 60).

Clearly, few if any of these tactics are available to the beginning dancer – at least not at an intentional level. Nevertheless, in both its older and more expert forms, tango-dance is not marked by complete dominance and submission. Rather, the tango-dance couple remains composed of two subjects who evoke tango's primal scenes of men competing with steps or knives.

Playing Whorehouse

Fans and devotees seldom if ever attribute tango's famous scandalousness to same-sex dancing or homosociality. Rather, the scandal of tango is supposed to come from the dance's early association with brothels. There, male johns and female prostitutes transgressed marital, class, and racial boundaries to the rhythm of tango. Salessi and Savigliano each argues that the prototypical tango pimp and prostitute are gender transgressive: he is a feminine man, overly concerned with his dandyesque appearance and financially dependent on his woman, while she is a masculine woman, who earns her living in the public sphere and is capable of defending herself with a dagger (Salessi 1991; Savigliano 1995). Savigliano also observes that tango is class transgressive. For example, in *El Dia Que Me Quieras*, Carlos Gardel's upper-class character woos a lower-class, professional dancer, and in *The Four Horsemen of the Apocalypse*, Rudolfo Valentino plays an upper-class Argentine who learns to dance slumming it in La Boca, and later earns a living as a gigolo in Paris, dancing tango with the wives of wealthy men. Thus, it is said that through tango the aristocratic, the bourgeois, and the lumpen came together in brothels, as did the European, the African, and the Creole. Even after tango moved up into respectable, European society, it retained the taint, and the glint, of the brothel. The real and imagined world of the Buenos Aires brothel was mythologized, for example, in the lyrics of tango's Golden Age so that to this day, the international tango scene is populated by dancers posing as *muñecas bravas* and *cafishios milongueros* (wild dolls and tango-dancing pimps).

In North America – not surprisingly – it is sexual transgression that dominates the tango scene. Here, tango is almost synonymous with extramarital sex. Thus, Woody Allen draws on a long-standing Hollywood tradition in his film *Alice* when he uses *La Cumparsita* to musically accompany Alice's thoughts as she first contemplates infidelity. Similarly, dancing tango gives apparently monogamous, heterosexual couples a venue for playing at being promiscuous. In December 1995, Marta and I attended a dance in San Francisco for which 'tango attire' was requested. Most of the men and women were dressed according to their ideas of how early tango pimps and prostitutes dressed. To me, the dancers looked like the cast of 'Guys and Dolls' – gangsters and chorus girls – tangoized by the addition of a silk scarf here or a slitted skirt there. This being the 1990s and San Francisco, some of the women were crossdressed in gangster attire, but none of the men were dolled up. A few geographically-challenged women were dressed as 'Carmens': Spanish señoritas, complete with peinetas in their pulled-back hair and mantillas draped over their shoulders. These women were examples of what Savigliano, following Edward Said, calls 'Hispanolism' (Savigliano 1995: 96): a stereotypical, colonizing representation in which the near-Other Spanish female stands in for extended Latin American hordes, much as in Orient-alism, the near-Other Arab female stands in for extended Asiatic hordes (Said 1979). In Buenos Aires, there is a stricter division between *tango de espectáculo* and *tango de salón* (stage-tango and salon-tango). Thus, when the Argentine cast of 'Forever Tango' arrived at the dance in San Francisco, they had changed out of the old-fashioned, pimp-and-prostitute costumes they had worn on stage – which would have fit in beautifully – and into outfits typical of the Buenos Aires milonga circuit.

The Buenos Aires tango-scene is not as stylized in terms of clothing as the corresponding scene in San Francisco. Milonguero men do not wear much that is peculiarly tangoesque except for their dance shoes and an occasional silk scarf, tied à la Gardel, but they do engage in their fair share of tango posturing. For example, a tango-dance teacher in Buenos Aires explained to me the importance of maintaining a low center of gravity by saying that 'dancing tango is like knife-fighting.' I am certain, however, that the teacher, no more than I, has never been in a knife fight. He was no doubt repeating what another non-knife-wielding teacher had told him, or perhaps he had read Borges. Thus, he was inviting me to join him in performing the role of a compadrito, an underclass, tango ruffian from the *suburbios* of turn-of-the-century Buenos Aires. Compadrito performativity is facilitated by the milonga custom of never talking about such mundane matters as the existence of wives, children, and day-time jobs. So long as the milonguero does not mention (and is never asked) if he earns his daily bread working as an usher or a jeweler, it is possible to maintain the fragile illusion that he is a compadrito who derives his income from intimidating other men with a knife or from seducing women with a *firulete* (a tango-dance embellishment). Many of the younger milongueras (female tango-dancers) in Buenos Aires do wear special tango attire, apparently aimed at attracting the attention of professional male dancers. Ironically, in early 1996, when Madonna was in town dressing like one particular, famous Argentine woman of the 1940s, many Argentine women were dressing like Madonna of the 1980s. Typically, one of these women wore a see-through blouse that stopped above the navel and a skirt that began below, a black brassiere and fishnet stockings, high heels, and a belt of leather, chain, or silk hanging on the hips. This fashion may or may not have come directly from Madonna videos, but it certainly owed something to the 'whore look' that Madonna was instrumental in popularizing (Schulze, White, and Brown 1993). In sum, all of these dramatic personae – the throw-back Guys and Dolls (and Carmens) of San Francisco and the updated pimps and prostitutes of Buenos Aires – evoke transgression, but it is a transgression that is kept safely straight – and white.

A Sad Thought

Most tango-practitioners and tango-scholars are more or less open to reading tango as transgressive in terms of gender, class, race or morals, but the costuming and posturing practices of the international tango scene usually remain safely heterosexual. Meanwhile, homosocial tango-dancing – common at tango's primal scenes and in its contemporary practice – is studiously disassociated from the famous eroticism of tango. Salessi, however, suggests that tango's homoerotic roots continue to inform tango's paradoxical passion. 'Considered from the present moment, in the context of this history of the tango, is not this sense of loss, this yearning for a "legendary skill", this "mournful cry for that which is lost and gone" a nostalgia for homosexual desire lost in the sanitization of a forbidden dance?' (Salessi 1997: 168). Much as Salessi recognizes in tango, a 'mournful cry for that which is lost and gone', Savigliano recognizes that 'Machismo is a cult of "authentic virility" fed by a sense of loss' (Savigliano 1995: 43).

Judith Butler argues that a sense of loss is endemic to heterosexuality, which is marked by 'a mourning for unlived possibilities' (Butler 1995: 27). Butler is referring to the heterosexual's unlived possibilities of homosexual love. It would, for example, be possible to interpret Borges's reference to 'a disturbed / Unreal past that in some way is certain, / The impossible memory of having died / Fighting', as the expression of a related feeling: the feeling of losing what one could never have had. For Butler, Borges's 'impossible memory' would be symptomatic of heterosexuality, since it is always 'haunted by the love it cannot grieve' (Ibid.: 26). The straight man can not grieve the forfeiture of homosexual love because he can not acknowledge ever having wanted homosexual love. Developing Freud's reflections on mourning and melancholia, Butler coins the term 'gender melancholy' to refer to the straight man's incomplete mourning for the gay man he might have been. 'When the prohibition against homosexuality is culturally pervasive, then the "loss" of homosexual love is precipitated through a prohibition which is repeated and ritualized throughout the culture. What ensues is a culture of gender melancholy in which masculinity and femininity emerge as the traces of an ungrieved and ungrievable love' (Ibid.: 28). In other words, 'The straight man *becomes* (mimes, cites, appropriates, assumes the status of) the man he "never" loved and "never" grieved' (Ibid.: 34). Straight gender identities, according to Butler, are attempts to compensate for the forfeiture of homosexual desire. Butler theorizes identification and desire as two sides of the same coin. Her argument is that a straight man's masculine identification is a compensation for not being able to desire other men. The identification is melancholic because the lost attraction is not acknowledged, and therefore can not be properly mourned. According to Butler, straight people's hyperbolic gender displays – such as the pimps and whores performed by tangueros in San Francisco – result from the denial of same-sex desire.

Thus, following Butler, it could be argued that tango's repressed homoeroticism is a driving force behind tango's hyperbolic displays of masculinity and femininity. The tip-off that the straight gender identities are built on forbidden homoerotic desires would be the pervasive melancholy of the tango scene. Anyone wishing to make this argument would, no doubt, call attention to the most widely quoted description of tango: *'El tango es un sentimento triste que se puede bailar'* (Tango is a sad thought that can be danced)' (commonly attributed to Enrique Santos Discépolo). Tango's unnamed sad thought, the argument would go, is the homosexual desire that is forbidden and, what is more, perforce forgotten. I admire the logic of Butler's argument about the 'culture of heterosexual melancholy,' and I see how the argument could be deployed to make sense of tango's paradoxical sexual formations. There is, for example, something similar about Borges's riddle that 'Any man who thinks five minutes straight about a woman is a marica' and Butler's that 'the "truest" gay male melancholic is the strictly straight man' (Ibid.: 33). I also recognize and share some of the political motives for producing a queer reading of tango in general and of tango-dance in particular. Nevertheless, I am reluctant to apply Butler's argument wholeheartedly, in part because it reminds me of an observation from the introduction to Soren Kierkegaard's dissertation:

> If we say that the substantial aspect of Socrates's existence was irony (this is indeed a contradiction, but also meant as one), and, if we postulate further, that irony is a negative concept, then one easily sees how difficult it becomes to secure an image of him, yes, that it seems impossible, or at least as baffling as trying to depict an elf wearing a hat that makes him invisible (Kierkegaard 1968: 50).

I find Butler's reading of 'the strictly straight man' similarly baffling. Like Kierkegaard's elf, he wears a hat – in this case one that makes his homosexuality invisible. Butler proceeds to depict for us what his invisible desire would look like if it were not invisible. I recognize that Butler's discourse is thereby reminiscent of Freud's descriptions of what the unconscious contains. Butler's discourse is, in fact, a mirror image of Freud's – an inversion – to the extent that Butler deploys Freudian rhetoric to stand Freud on his head. Now I have no objection to upsetting Freud. Indeed, I find de Lauretis's similarly inverted reading of Freud's theorization of the phallus and the fetish quite compelling (de Lauretis 1994: 228 *et passim*). De Lauretis, however, draws on accounts of lesbian experience to correct Freudian theory. Her argument, like Freud's, partakes of the authority of case studies, such as the passage by Joan Nestle she offers in support of her retheorization of the fetish. Butler, by contrast, is going on pure logic. Much as Vincent Crapanzano (1986: 75) observes that there is not *a* Balinese cockfight in Geertz's analysis of *the* Balinese cockfight, I observe that there is no straight man in Butler's analysis of 'the strictly straight man.'

Note that Freud, too, was at his least compelling when he set his considerable logical faculties loose from the analytic situation. We anthropologists must be especially aware of the brilliant but utterly groundless argument he put forth in *Totem and Taboo* – which Kroeber did well to call a 'just-so story,' as in, 'the elf is dressed just-so.' As an anthropologist, I look for indications that buried beneath my informants' masculine displays is the ungrievable loss of homosexual desire. I try out reading tango's sad thought as heterosexual melancholia, but the elf's clothes don't fit. The straightest men in my sample show no particular signs of grieving for unacknowledgeable loves lost. Rather, I find that most of the strictly straight Argentine men I know are quite playful about their hyperbolic displays of masculinity, and that they are also quite comfortable talking about latent homoeroticism. Perhaps Butler's 'just-so story' fits middle-class, White, North American culture better than it does the working- and middle-class cultures I have studied in Buenos Aires. The one great limit I find in her analysis is that it does not admit even the possibility of such cultural and class differences. So far as I know, Butler has nowhere addressed differences associated with culture, class, or race, except in the most perfunctory manner (e.g., Butler 1993: 226–30). Lacking openness to cultural and class differences, Butler, like Freud, unwittingly universalizes insights gained from the study of an unmarked – un-remarked-upon – bourgeois Western society. If I single out Butler, it is not to suggest that her brand of queer theory is worse than others. Indeed, I have found her work extremely valuable and provocative. Moreover, Butler's work is no less sensitive to cultural and class difference than, for example, that of Sedgwick. I would also observe that in general queer theorists are not any less aware of cross-cultural theories than anthropologists are of queer theories. Thus, what is lacking is a theorization of sexualities that partakes of the sophistication of queer theories and the cross-cultural awareness of ethnographic research.

Notes

1. I thank Marta Savigliano, my wife, whose influence on my work on tango is boundless. Living and dancing with Savigliano might have inhibited me from writing about tango-dance, since she is among the foremost experts in the field, but she encouraged my ethnographic incursion into Buenos Aires's tango-dance scene, and in her discussion of tango and masculine sexuality, I found an invitation to step onto the theoretical dance floor. 'Machismo is a cult of maleness and, as such, perhaps should be left in the hands of its devotees. This has been the position of most women interested in tango. And I see the point. There has been so much macho pride (and so much macho history) invested in these misogynistic remarks that one is tempted to leave machismo to die on its own' (Savigliano 1995: 46). Savigliano does not leave machismo to die entirely on its own, but she does refrain from delving too deeply into 'where it hurts the most: women and homosexuality' (Ibid.: 44). By contrast, being a man and an outsider, I plod right in.

2. I leave compadrito untranslated. The diminutive of *compadre*, compadrito is a word peculiar to Rioplatense Spanish, indicating a 'popular guy' (Real Academia Española 1992) in the sense of 'vulgar', or 'low-class.' More often than not, the word is used with reference to tango or tangoesque manners. Gobello explains that the compadrito 'is a gaucho who enters, because of the nature of his employment, into contact with urban civilization' (Gobello 1995: *El Compadrito*).

3. There are actually two films with the title 'Tango Bar.' The first, and justifiably more famous, was released by Paramount in 1935. It was directed by John Reinhardt and starred Carlos Gardel. The second, which is the one I discuss here, was released by Castle Hill in 1987 and was directed by Marcos Zurinaga.

4. 'Milonga' could be translated as 'tango dance club,' but Savigliano explains more precisely that a milonga is 'a space and time when and where tango bodies get together to produce *tanguidad* (tanguity, tango-ness)' (Savigliano 1997). Thus, early in the evening a space might contain a *práctica* (practice session), whereas later in the evening, the same space can contain a milonga. Milonga also refers to a category of tango dance and music.

7

From Wallflowers to Femmes Fatales: Tango and the Performance of Passionate Femininity

Marta E. Savigliano

In the milongas (tango clubs) of contemporary Buenos Aires tango is referred to as a drug and the practice of tango, as an addiction. Tango, however, does not fall into the category of intoxicating products, the simple consumption of which generates an altered state of consciousness. Access to the tango ecstasy requires much preparation and much practice; a carefully crafted road that involves highly developed skills on the part of its practitioners. The tango 'high' – and this is a rather bad choice of a word for reasons I will soon explicate – comes, takes hold of the tango dancers somewhat like a trance, a state of possession that is achieved with much effort and usually not at all. The tango 'trance' is, thus, a promise, nurtured by the milongueros/as' memory of past experiences or by the memories passed down to them by other, more experienced tango dancers.

For lack of a better word, this special tango 'state' is referred to as passion. And I emphasize the imprecise nature of the 'passion' word/ concept as ascribed to the tango in an attempt to echo that moment of hesitation, that searching of the mind's archives and of the taste of words in the mouth that takes place whenever I ask tango dancers to explain what is it that they are looking for, night after night, in the milongas. Passion, they repeat, as in taking hold of something somewhat recogniz-able, open and ambiguous enough to accommodate a wealth of feelings, both positive and negative, regarding what it takes to get there, to live with it, and to survive the consequences.

For, let me remind you, tango dancers pursue passion, the sparkle of the passionate event in their lives, as addicts, as if against their will, as if they could not help but search for it. Performing tango steps, they cultivate passion, passionately. The passion is already there, in the attempt, and yet it is displaced to that fortuitous moment of condensation, consecration – that moment at which a particular, stabilized, experience of passion is achieved. That moment, that event, is what I have improperly termed the tango 'high.' Improperly, because it is not euphoric, bubbly or happy, supernaturally transcendent or otherworldly. It is calm and fluid, comforting, as when things finally fall into place, difficulties are left behind and the reward is pure serenity, fully in control without effort, a fix of 'natural-ness.'

This is the state sought in and through the dance, when two bodies communicate perfectly (and look perfectly and beautifully matched). Absentmindedly, tightly embraced, their torsos tilt toward each other in a delicate balance, their legs tracing sinuous paths on the dance floor, muscles fully alert to the doing and undoing of mutually provoked entanglements. Their improvised steps surprise each other, and yet the music – the rhythm and the melody, they insist – hold them together, prompting the smooth continuity of the conversation between these distinctly gendered bodies. It is a dialogue that in order to be perfect prescribes the absence of words, avoids the verbal pollution of the passionate event, the awakening of intellectual sources that, inevitably, reproduce miscommunication.

The tango 'high' is a paradoxical state of abandonment and full control, of bodily awareness and mental disengagement. The feet seem to be doing all the thinking, and to be making all the necessary decisions. 'Naturalness' in the tango dance is not the avoidance of tension, but rather its comfortable manipulation. And it is not an innate ability, but rather a skill painfully gained through experience. Experience in dancing tango, experience in the tango world, experience in the world at large: streetwiseness. It is a very ambitious state, no doubt, given the precarious material and emotional conditions under which most Argentine tango practitioners live.

'Away from the milonga, out there, there is only solitude,' the milongueros/as say, but they also repeatedly proclaim that 'there are no friends in the milonga.' There is no secure, restful place either outside or inside the milonga world. Despite the fact that the milonga, the site in which the tango passion comes to life, evokes images of a strange cult in which dance and music invoke Tango, the god, who would descend or arise, choosing well-disposed victims of possession, and despite the proliferation of ritualistic practices and codes, the tango cult does not amount to a tango 'community' or to states of 'communitas.'

In the milonga scene, everyone is there for themselves. Associations and demonstrated interests are vested interests. These entirely personal interests, moreover, are legitimate and assumed. There is no pretense and no expectation of communal feelings beyond the common interest of maintaining the milonga scene, that is, keeping the tango dance halls open and running, and reproducing committed tango dancers. There is no real commitment either to a particular tango dance hall nor to an established social group of tango dancers. The milongueros and milongueras are nomadic, and enjoy moving to a different milonga every day of the week. Sometimes they even make incursions into several milongas on the same night, looking for the most suitable and compatible partners.

Belonging to the milonga scene is also an unstable status. The environment is cool, not hostile but rather loosely interested in anyone's particular presence, and the relationships established in the course of any one night carry on rather dimly into the next. Being a part of the milonga scene must be constantly re-enacted. Having met, done small talk, or danced enraptured with someone does not warranty in any way that you will be greeted, addressed, or that you will dance with this same person ever again. There is no social contract beyond that ephemeral incident of a one-night encounter. The milonga is cherished as a place of fortuitous and fleeting relationships, with no established loyalties or commitments, where you risk again and again the open possibility of fate putting some sweetness in your path. And you should be free and ready to take it. In entering the milonga, tango dancers step on a highly competitive stage ruled by the laws of naked seduction.

The dance starts way before the actual dancing. The foreplay requires a considerable amount of plotting. Rules, codes, and the dance technique must be mastered. Every move is informed and conducive to seduction – a seduction that is not restricted to any one particular purpose but that is open to a multiplicity of possible gains, rewards, and pleasures, from the most innocent to the most vicious. Nothing and nobody should be trusted. In the milonga everything means something else, and everyone pretends to be somebody else. Thus, everything is under scrutiny, and everyone, under suspicion. This nightmarish situation could be interpreted as collective paranoia if it were not for the wide use of experientially established 'tables of conversion and decodification' shared among the nocturnal milonga habitués.

Every new arrival is observed, carefully pondered, discreetly discussed, casually engaged in conversation when necessary, and, eventually, trotted around the dance floor. Every look, exchange, and invitation to dance (whether given or received) is a test. More precisely, it is a placement test in a complex and hierarchical chain of milonga initiates. It is a living chain, organized on the basis of time (marked by one's persistence in attending tango clubs and endurance at practicing the dance technique), seniority (marked by one's knowledge of the different tango styles and experience in the tango world), public recognition (such as that of professional tango dancers, renowned amateurs, or simple practitioners), age (divided according to young and old, and new and established tango dancers), nationality (Argentine, Uruguayan, or foreigner), class and gender.

In addition, the 'nature' of the interest in tango is a fundamental placement datum: Are you a professional tango dancer seeking to practice traditional, milonguero, tango styles? Promoting yourself and/or looking for tango students? Stealing new tango steps for your next show? Or are you an aspiring professional tango dancer trying to be noticed and selected? Are you really interested in tango, that is, a legitimate addict, or are your interests purely 'professional,' that is, financial? Do you understand the tango world or are you simply looking for excitement? Are you seeking an exotic experience (outside your class or culture), an affair perhaps, a simple squeeze, or do you really care about the perpetuation of the tango tradition?

The list of trick questions continues. The slots in the chain are there, ready to accommodate each and every one. The questions are never open and direct. The string usually starts by: 'I haven't seen you before. How long have you been dancing? What brought you here? Where do you go dancing? Where did you use to go? How did you learn? Where do you live?', and so forth. A night or two at the milonga is usually sufficient for experts to complete the questionnaire. You've entered the milonga food chain.

In 1996, the milonga food chain in the downtown tango-dance circuit of Buenos Aires – I must be specific here for the chain is fluid and changing – was headed by two or three professional, male, tango dancers, who upon entering the milonga, are quickly surrounded by a group of aspiring professional, male dancers. These aspiring professionals follow the established ones in hopes of being included in a future tango production, and they do the work of trying out new aspiring professional female dancers. These established and aspiring professionals (that is, stage tango dancers) also attend the milongas in order to catch the eye of spectacle impresarios, foreign and national TV and film crews, and to attract tango students of both genders.

Foreign female dancers are especially sought after, since they provide the necessary contacts for touring and teaching abroad. In addition, foreign tango students are a rich vein of cash, not because they are necessarily wealthy (as a matter of fact, wealthy visitors to the contemporary milongas are rare) but because they come to Buenos Aires with a certain amount of cash to be spent in tango training over a short span of time. To get hold of them from the beginning is essential. The most appealing foreign dancers are the ones who arrive independently, as opposed to those large groups who come in so-called 'tango tours' with contacts and classes pre-arranged by foreign organizers or Argentine organizers who live abroad. Foreign tango students, in turn, are given the opportunity to learn 'authentic' Argentine tango styles, to mingle with 'real' milongueros, to get the flair of the milonga world. If they are professional dancers themselves, especially tango teachers, the milonga experience and the rubbing of elbows with renowned tango dancers adds prestige to their credentials and, hence, increases their enrollments back home.

(You might wonder at this point about the professionally established Argentine tango female dancers, the ones who form the renowned tango couples of the staged tango. These women rarely appear on the milonga scene. Their male dance (and, frequently, romantic) partners venture into the milongas on their own.)

Old, experienced, traditional male milongueros (frequently including the owners or organizers of the milongas) come next to the professional tango male dancers and their courts in the hierarchical chain – and they often resent it. These men have often been the informal masters of the younger professional dancers, the ones who generously taught the younger men the core of what they know. (The special dance embellishments, suitable for the stage, are taught by old professional male dancers who rarely appear in the milongas.) The experienced milongueros, who frequently can be found sitting in groups of two or three at the edge of the dance floor in visually strategic, well-located tables, are the heart of the milonga. They have seen all, and they know all, and their interest in the continuity of the tango tradition is beyond dispute. They are the figures of authority of the milonga as popular culture.

These older milongueros own most of the shares of tango's cultural capital but they have little access to tango's accumulation or circulation of economic capital. Experienced milongueros rarely conduct formal tango classes or participate in tango shows for the stage. Old milongueros are or were great dancers, which in tango means that they made original contributions to the dance vocabulary through improvisation, that they are able to master the conundrums of tango's syncopated rhythms, and most importantly, that they know how to 'walk' the tango (considered to be a greater accomplishment than any flashy, complicated tango 'figure'). In addition, by participating over the years in the milonga scene, they know all the secrets to the female tango dancer's body. But they are old,

old-fashioned, slick in an unfashionable way, and frequently with a lower level of education and/or sophistication than the young professionals. Consequently, their ability to seduce is based solely on their dancing skills. But then, it is dancing, more than anything else, that determines one's placement in the milonga food chain. Who these old milongueros dance with determines their rank, and frequently enough, they get to dance with the youngest and loveliest women of the milonga.

These women, regardless of their dancing abilities, are their trophies of the milonga night, and they make sure that the younger male dancers know it. In the strong, male homosocial bonding of the milonga, the competition over spring-chicks is all-important. If the chicks are good or promising dancers, of course, it's better. This is, however, a statement based on my observations. In formal interviews, experienced and aspiring milongueros will insist that in the tango world looks don't matter; what counts is the skill at dancing. And they add with a smile, 'good looks, of course, don't bother.'

Young and middle-aged female amateurs, then, make up the next link of the milonga food chain, followed, in turn, by middle-aged male amateurs and some foreign male dancers, who are themselves followed by older, female, experienced milongueras, and, finally, a group of tango couples of diverse ages and origins who participate only sporadically in the chain's avatars. Couples attending the milonga as dancing couples are less 'mobile' than individual male or female tango dancers, in part because they are usually taken for romantic couples as well. Thus, presenting themselves in public as 'a couple,' they sort of freeze their status as players in the games of seduction. But only for the night; the situation is re-assessed nightly. The milonga is definitely about dancing tango, 'but if you can top the night by taking someone to bed, it won't hurt,' I was chuckingly taught by Juan Carlos, an old milonguero. The milonga is about dancing, picking up, and pick-pocketing of diverse and variable kinds.

Let's return, now, to those older, experienced milongueras, sitting in groups of two or three, staring at the dance floor, waiting to be asked to dance. In a way, they set the tone for the female presence at the milongas, and their position condenses both the fears and the expectations of the milonga's heterosexual plays of gendered syncopation. The presence of the old milongueras is a testimony to tango's addictive powers. In their particular case, tango is beyond all doubts a passion. They just want to dance. Few women accede to this position. In the milonga world, males usually endure much longer than females. It is said that women, after a while, fall in love – inside or outside the tango milieu – and either their jobs and domestic obligations or their lover's jealousy prevent them from coming back. Others add that for men tango dancing is more taxing and time-consuming than for women, either because men are worse 'natural' dancers than women or because the male part in tango is harder. For whatever combination of reasons and beliefs, old milongueras sit there, witnessing the milonga changes with few complaints – as opposed to their male counterparts. They know what they are doing. Their alert sitting confirms that they are aware of their position in the food chain, and they are willing to pay the price: Tango is worth wallflowering for.

As a matter of fact, all women who approach the milonga scene must learn, sooner or later, that every time they enter a milonga, they will do so as a wallflower. A woman's wallflower position will be tested every single night at the milonga, no matter how good a dancer she is. The events of the night, some of which are easier to predict than others, will bring her, more or less successfully, out of this position and closer to its opposite, the one of the dancing femme fatale. Dancing makes the difference. The wallflower becomes the femme fatale by dancing a sufficient quantity and quality of dances. But at the beginning of the night, unless she arrives with her set dancing partner, every woman wallflowers – and to a certain extent, so do men. Nobody enjoys it, and some are better at it than others.

In order to move out of the wallflower position, you must become an object of desire, more precisely, of tango dancing desire. An object of a doubly interwoven desire that includes the promise of becoming a potential vehicle for attaining the passionate tango state – that ephemeral sense of being bodily connected against all odds – as well as of generating desire on the part of those who watch the possibly sublime tango take place. For these are the femme fatale's witnesses and her future dance partners. In their arms, tango after tango, the milonguera – or aspiring milonguera – will move from wallflower to goddess of the milonga.

To conclude, the fatale-ness of this woman needs some explication. She might or might not be beautiful, but she is necessarily smart. Her threatening fascination resides in how she combines intelligence and dancing skills (mind and body). She is the master of her own body's seductive powers. She is fatal in that she has made herself vulnerable by accepting a subservient wallflower position to begin with – which is taken as a sign of admirable courage – and in that she has succeeded in making herself an object of collective, tango dancing desire – a sure sign of possessing a highly competitive gift for intelligent manipulation. In addition, she is capable of exerting discrimination, either by refusing to dance or by measuring how much of her dancing talent she gives out to each of her desiring male dance partners. Sweet revenge, murmurs the femme fatale of the night, knowing – if she is wise enough not to be tricked back – that she will fall back into wallflowering as soon as she steps into the next milonga.

8

Rebetika: The Double-descended Deep Songs of Greece

Gail Holst-Warhaft

What has the double-descended modern Greek taken from his father, what from his mother? . . . He is clever and shallow, with no metaphysical anxieties, and yet, when he begins to sing, a universal grieving leaps up from his Oriental bowels and breaks the crust of Greek logic.

Nikos Kazantzakis, *Journey to the Morea*

The scene opens with two men dancing on a Cretan beach. Neither one is Greek and both are lousy dancers. The Mexican-Irish-American with a day's growth of beard is playing the quintessential working-class Greek. The Englishman in the white suit is playing a western-educated Greek intellectual. The working-class Greek says: 'Boss, I never loved a man as much as you!' and the music speeds up so that the *rebetiko* rhythm of *hasapiko* becomes a *hasaposerviko* and the *syrtaki* is born. The Greek intellectual knows nothing of the rebetika, of his earthy companion's ability to lose himself in the bodily pleasure of the dance, but is aware of his insufficiency. Zorba, the true Greek male, can teach him about wine, women, song and dance. What fascinates the Kazantzakis/Alan Bates character about Zorba is what made the film so popular. The ability of a man to dance with another man in a spirit of uninhibited camaraderie, throwing pain and care into a passionate dance, is something lost to the sophisticated European. It may be a romantic and distorted vision of what the working-class *rebetis* – the term is used both for people who played the music and lived the lifestyle described in the songs – offered the Greek intellectuals, but it may have something to do with why the rebetika songs have been so enthusiastically revived since the 1960s. It may also be what attracted foreign scholars to the genre. As Anthony Quinn said in a recent interview, the moment on the Cretan beach is what stands out for him from his whole film career. The fiction of the scene is of a world where men could express ecstasy, sure of their manhood. This is a world as exotic to the Greek intellectual as to the European or American.

In discussing the rebetika, the 'Zorba factor' cannot be discounted. Like many other styles of popular music, including tango, fado, blues and flamenco, the rebetika are commercially successful popular songs. However much they are, or once were, the expression of a marginalized group, they are listened to, exploited and analyzed by people who are not part of that group. The reason they are listened to has as much to do with non-musical as musical factors. An important element in their reception, in Greece as in other countries, has been the perception that these early urban popular songs represented something 'deep' or, as Washabaugh refers to it, 'elemental.' As distinct from rural folk music, urban popular music that becomes pan-Spanish, pan-Argentine or pan-Greek is usually an invention, a cobbling together of musical styles to suit a mood of nostalgia for an unrecoverable rural past. Whereas regional folk music is intimately tied to a landscape and a population that has inhabited it for centuries, city music is the music of immigrants. In addition to the fact that the city dwellers, at least those of the first generation, have broken their ties with a particular landscape and its local customs, they are often cut off from the bonds of family, especially from women family members. In such circumstances it is not surprising to find songs that speak of the pain and hardship of exile, of mean streets, heartless women, drugs, drink and male camaraderie. More difficult to explain are the non-verbal elements that are assembled to form the basis of popular music, including the dances that inevitably accompany the songs. Just how and why a certain instrument, dance, or rhythm becomes a touchstone for a generation of Greeks or Argentines is not easy to analyze. It may be a co-optation of the exotic, as Washabaugh suggests for flamenco, but it is successful to the extent that it is sufficiently grounded in the familiar musical elements of a culture to become a symbolic vehicle for a passionate identification. Initially, the identification may be of the disenfranchised; later it is packaged and sold to a broader audience.

It is in the nature of such popular musical styles that they tend to be viewed in isolation. Regarded from within the culture as quintessentially Spanish, Argentinian or Portuguese, they are often thought to be incomprehensible to the outsider. They attract passionate disciples who pride themselves on their 'true' understanding of the music, their participation in a small, virtually impenetrable circle of practitioners and afficionados. Part of the mystique of the marginalized is its uniqueness and inaccessibility. The essays in this collection make clear, however, that there are strong parallels between the development, success and commodification of such styles as tango, flamenco and rebetika. An awareness of the similarities in the development, reception and dissemination of these styles should not blind us to the particular circumstances of 1920s Greece, Argentina or Spain, but it may help us link the music to the broader social and artistic movements of the period. It also offers us a comparative context for a discussion of what has been traditionally neglected in accounts of the music: the question of how gender is constructed and reflected, not only in song-lyrics, but in vocal style, dance and instrumentation.

The Oriental Bowels

I have argued elsewhere (Holst-Warhaft, 1992: 130–51) that the feminine and the Oriental were linked in the Greek or at least Athenian consciousness as early as the fifth century B.C. There is evidence to suggest that female dirge-singers were regarded as the mistresses of their craft in the classical period and were employed to lament with passionate gestures and voices by the inhabitants of the Greek mainland. That Kazantzakis should situate grieving in the Oriental bowels' of modern Greece, and that this grieving should be attributed to maternal inheritance, may reflect a long tradition of Greek beliefs about the Orient, but its immediate associations are closer to contemporary Greek reality.

In the closing decades of the nineteenth century, debates arose among the intellectuals of Athens about the true Greek nature of their popular music. The discussion was occasioned by the appearance in Athens of two new musical venues: the European-style *café chantant* and the oriental *café-aman*. Champions of the oriental style, including the most famous poet of the day, Kostis Palamas, regarded it as more 'dignified' than the decadent and light-hearted European style. Precisely what the repertoire of the cafe-aman was at the time, we cannot be sure, but that a major part of the repertoire consisted of stylized laments or *amanethes* is evidenced by the criticism levelled at the oriental music and by the name of the establishments in which it was performed. Western-leaning Greek intellectuals championed the *café chantant*, and appear to have been more in tune with public taste, for the oriental-style music seems gradually to have slowly died out. As Gauntlett (1989) has suggested, the debate over the merits of the oriental-style music of the *café-aman* and the occidental *café chantant* can be viewed as the earliest of a series of debates about Greek popular music. It precedes the designation of any of the popular music as rebetika, but it rehearses some of the themes that would resurface in later debates about those songs. Had it not been for a disastrous event in Greek history, the 'oriental'-style songs and the debate over their

Greekness might not have been revived and the development of modern Greek popular music might have been quite different. That event was the Greco-Turkish war of 1919–1922.

So symbolic of tragedy is the defeat of the Greek forces in Asia Minor and the fire that destroyed Christian Smyrna in 1922, that it is simply referred to as 'The Catastrophe.' The city, which had been ceded to the Greeks as a reward for support to the Allied cause during the First World War, was the center of a rich and multi-ethnic culture where Greeks formed a substantial part of the population. Despite the difficulties of enforcing the treaty of Sèvres which granted Greece the right to administer Smyrna and its hinterland, the Greek army, supported by Allied warships, landed in Smyrna in May, 1919. The landing was not only an attempt to gain a foothold in Asia Minor. It was a symbol, for most Greeks, of the cherished dream of recovering some part of their former Byzantine glory. Approximately a million and a half Greek Christians still inhabited Anatolia and the Aegean coast and they were faced with increasing persecution as the Ottoman Empire declined.

With the hope of realizing the 'Great Idea' of a restored Greek presence in Asia Minor, and with the more valid excuse of protecting the Christian population of Anatolia, the Greek government began a disastrous attempt to occupy western Asia Minor. The details of the Asia Minor campaign cannot be elaborated here, but it ended with the defeat of the Greek forces and their retreat to Smyrna. After the Greek troops had been evacuated, Turkish troops entered the city and a wholesale massacre of the Christian population of Smyrna ensued. Finally, the Greek and Armenian quarters of the city were burned to the ground. So ended the ambitions of creating a greater Greece that would include the eastern Aegean and its cultivated population of Christians who had lived in relative peace with their Muslim neighbors for centuries.

The effects of the Asia Minor war on the young Greek nation were both psychologically devastating and physically overwhelming. By the treaty that followed the end of hostilities, Greece agreed to give back almost all the territory it had gained at the end of the First World War. Greece and Turkey also began an exchange of Christian and Muslim populations. Many thousands of Greeks had already fled to mainland Greece before the signing of the treaty; now over a million were made refugees by the terms of the treaty. In a nation of approximately five million people, with limited resources of land and almost no industrial development, the effects of such an influx are almost impossible to imagine.

Most of the refugees coming from Asia Minor had left without their possessions and were economically destitute. The Greek government made some official attempts to resettle the refugees, but most were left to fend for themselves in an environment that was often hostile to them. Culturally they stood out as being markedly different from local Greeks. Coming from a more cosmopolitan society they were often better educated and more skilled than their new neighbors. Despite this, in the years following the exodus, they were forced to accept an inferior status and settle in the shanty towns that grew up on the edges of Piraeus and Athens. The sudden increase in the urban population created, for the first time, a sizable proletarian audience for songs that dealt with themes of poverty, nostalgia, hashish smoking and low life. The expulsion of Asia Minor Christians also became enshrined in Greek popular culture as a metaphor for loss and grief.

The musicians among the refugees did not move into a musical vacuum, but they brought with them a level of professional skill unusual on the mainland. Constantinople and Smyrna were musically sophisticated towns where Turkish, Greek, Jewish, Armenian and Gypsy musicians played together and exchanged repertoires. The refugees were accustomed to playing all kinds of music and adapted quickly to the tastes of the day, whether they were asked to play foxtrots, tangos or *amanethes*. However, given the large numbers of refugees now living in Greek cities, it is not surprising that there was a revival of oriental, or what would retro-spectively be designated, 'Smyrna-style' music. Recordings of the so-called 'Smyrna-style' music were made in Istanbul and Smyrna before the exchange of populations. Some of the earliest Greek recording stars of the late 1920s and 30s were already established performers in Turkey before they came to Greece. Others left to record and perform in the United States. By the late 1920s, recordings of *café-aman* songs were also being made in Athens. Accompanied by ensembles of male musicians playing violin, santouri, cello, cymbalum and 'ud, women singers seem to have been at least as popular as men, and performed a wide variety of songs. Among the popular repertoire of these singers were stylized laments, variously called *amanethes, manethes* and *minores*. The most popular of the *minore* were associated with a particular city or neigh-borhood where Greeks had lived in Asia Minor. It is hardly surprising that these forms, already popular in the Asia Minor Greek communities, should have acquired not only a larger audience but an additional poig-nancy after the exchange of populations.

The poetic format of the *amanes* was usually a single four-line stanza with interjections and repeats of the exclamation 'aman' (Woe is me!). Beginning with an instrumental introduction that established both mood and mode, the piece continued with the sung verse that was usually on the theme of unhappy love:

> Ach, when I remember
> when I remember my mate
> who lives far, far from, aman, aman
> my mate who lives far from me
> (interjection) Oh, I'm so poor

> Ah, black smoke
> black smoke like a cloud
> comes from my heart, aman, aman
> My treasure, from my heart.

Whether performed by women or men, the *amanes* was a formulaic cry of anguish. The vocal style was tight-throated, usually high-pitched and always elaborately melismatic. The form and performance style of *amanethes* have more in common with Turkish classical music than Greek folk music, although the highly melismatic vocal style was familiar to Greeks from the chant of the Orthodox Church. The verse form of the amanes is probably derived from the Ottoman lyric *gazel*, but the unrelenting misery of the lyrics combined with the emotionally charged vocal style provokes comparison with an older, more universal form of expression. In a culture where women traditionally lament the dead, songs that express separation, exile and longing are often grouped with laments for the dead under the general head of *miroloia*. The *amanes* is a stylized form of lament and, as such, linked in the Greek folk tradition to a traditionally female form of expression.

In the repertoire of the *café-aman* music, such passionate songs occupied an important position, but many of the other songs performed by the Asia Minor singers and ensembles were quite light-hearted. Even songs that are closer in subject matter to the later rebetika – songs about prison, drugs or the urban demi-monde – were generally performed with humor and apparent detachment. One type of song for which there appeared to be an already-developed taste, among the Greek-speaking communities of Istambul, Smyrna, Athens and Piraeus, was about women who moved in the disreputable back streets of the town and hung out with hashish smokers. In the anonymous song 'Elli,' recorded in Smyrna about 1915, a song that must have been popular because it was later recorded in the United States and Athens, the disreputable milieu in which the young woman mixes is pointedly contrasted to the world of the Christian Greeks:

On the very day of Christmas, the bells were ringing
the bells were ringing
And the Christians in Church and Elli with the
Turks . . .

In the earliest recorded version of the song, Elli, who has abandoned her husband and children, is outside the bounds of respectability, but the tone remains playful, and Elli is described as a black-haired beauty who can be forgiven her misdemeanors for a kiss. By the time the song is re-recorded in the United States and Athens, Elli's behavior becomes a more serious crime and she 'deserves to be killed with a knife.' What is interesting about such songs, in which women transgress the boundaries of acceptable behavior and frequent the haunts of the hashish smokers and other disreputable types, is that they are often recorded by respectable women singers. Singers who performed the Asia Minor style rebetika, like Marika Papagika, Rita Abadzi, or Rosa Eskenazi, apparently catered to popular demand by including songs about low life in their repertoire. The song 'Mangas Girl,' which may have been recorded first in Smyrna and must have enjoyed considerable popularity judging by the fact that it was re-recorded a number of times by Smyrna-style musicians in Greece, is typical of such songs. The girl of the title is described as having driven the male protagonist crazy with her flirtatious ways. In this song there is no mention of drugs but women who are portrayed as hanging out with the rebetes, are also known to share the pleasures of the hookah, as in the equally popular rebetika song, 'The Hanoumakia':

On the sandy beach you had your hashish den
and I'd come every morning to drive the blues away.
One morning I ran into two lovely young girls,
Stoned poor things, they were sitting on the beach.

Come sit with us, you dervish
and listen to sad songs of love wrung from our hearts
take your little baglama and entertain us a while
light up a joint and smoke a while with us.

Fill me a hookah to get high with
and later, little ladies, I'll take my baglama
We'll fix you a hookah with leaf tobacco
at Uncle Yiannis' hashish den in Pasalimani.

Despite the devil-may-care attitude expressed by the female persona in some of the early rebetika and her resistance to conventional male-female relationships, there is often, in a gesture of protest that sets the woman outside conventional boundaries, a hard-luck tale. In Rosa Eskenazi's performance of 'Just so you know what's going on, Bum,' she lets her man know she's up to here with him, and complains that he wasn't content with beating her but took her money as well. Now she has found another desirable man who not only treats her well but even takes her out on the town. In such songs, composed by men and performed by women, we have at least the fiction of an independent-spirited woman who talks tough like a man. The popularity of songs that depicted a disreputable social milieu in which women enjoyed an unusual freedom is not necessarily a reflection of a change in social reality. As Evlyn Gould's study of 'Carmen' reminds us (1996), the woman in popular fiction who defies bourgeois norms also defines them. In a culture where the conventions of social and family life are strict, songs of daring women meet a demand for escape from everyday constraints. The type of the free-spirited woman found in these early Asia Minor songs would be revived in the 1940s, where the counterpart to the mangas or rebetis – the *rebetissa*, or *mangissa* — features in a number of the songs of the period.

During the same period when the Smyrna and Piraeus songs of low life became popular, the musical theatre or cabaret began to flourish in Athens. The song-writers who composed for this more bourgeois audience looked to the west for their models, producing Greek versions of the dance crazes that were sweeping Europe – the fox trot, the waltz and the tango. In the lyrics of many of these songs, too, we find daring women with names like 'Sonia,' 'Carmela,' or 'Lolita.' Like their Asia Minor counterparts, the exotic, liberated women of the cabaret songs are representatives of a forbidden world, one that is the antithesis of Greek reality.

Piraeus Style Rebetika

It was in the 1930s that male singers accompanied by bouzoukis began recording in Greece and a different style of rebetika emerged. In this early stage, there seems to have been considerable overlap between Asia Minor style songs and what was to become an increasingly distinct Piraeus-based style. This Piraeus style was initially dominated by the quartet of Markos Vamvakaris, Anestis Delias, Yiorgos Batis and Stratos Payioumdzis, two of whom were refugees from Asia Minor. These men were amateur singers and musicians who met to play and smoke hashish. One of them, Delias, would die in the streets of an addiction to a more dangerous drug that had begun to circulate in the streets of Piraeus: heroin. In the voices, the instruments and the lyrics of the songs they recorded, a rougher, tougher quality emerges. These songs present the fiction, at least, of lived experience, of the amateur musician who lives the life he sings about. They also establish a new male ethos, not overtly political but proletarian and street-wise. If the drug addict, the jilted lover or jailbird is a victim in these songs, he counters adversity with a swagger, dressing like a dandy, wielding his knife, playing his music, poking fun at authority. Superficially, at least, he is the epitome of the 'angst-free' side of Kazant-zakis's characterization. The song 'Koutsavakis' gives a good picture of the Piraeus tough-guy:

Hey mangas, if you want to use that knife of yours
you'd better have the guts, dude, the nerve to take it out.

That stuff don't wash with me, so hide your blade
Because I'll get high, dude, and come to your pad.

Go somewhere else and strut your stuff
Because I've smoked too, dude, and I'm mighty high.

I told you to sit down nicely or I'll zap you
I'll come with my pistol, dude, and I'll straighten you out.

This is a long way from the Smyrna-style of lamenting one's pain or playfully describing the low life of the city. Here, instrumentation, vocal style, dance rhythms dominate the music while the lyrics continue to mix love songs with songs of low life, drugs, jail, poverty and the subculture of the rebetes or manghes. I have suggested elsewhere that from the earliest recordings of rebetika in Greece, the lifestyle presented in the songs, even though it may mirror the life of some performers, is con-sciously exaggerated and presented to a bourgeois public as a fiction (Holst-Warhaft 1990: 183–96). There was, we know, a constant demand for songs dealing with hashish, the underworld, knife fights, tough-guys, and uninhibited women. The fact that many of the musicians who played rebetika smoked hashish and some had served jail sentences does not diminish the self-conscious display of songs like 'The Voice of the Hookah,' where we are presented with a tableau of the manghes world. The song begins with a comic dialogue between the composer, Vangelis Papazoglou (a Smyrna refugee) and the guitarist and arranger Stellakis Perpiniades:

'Hi there. Stellakis, my friend!'
'Good to see you, Vangelis.'
'What's that you're holding?'
'A hookah.'
'A hookah?'
'Well, what did you expect me to be holding, an ocean
liner?'

In the song that follows, Stellakis tells Vangelis that he has just come from prison where his only comfort was the company of the manghes who passed their time smoking dope together. The chorus of the song ('Blow it, suck it, draw it back; turn on and light it up/ Keep an eye out for those dummies, the dreaded prison guards') seems to be a sort of sing-along for smokers. The lively Asia Minor rhythm of the *karsilamas* and the use of Turkish-derived slang both add to the light-hearted humor of this song which is clearly catering to a taste for sampling low life at a safe distance.

The voice of Markos Vamvakaris is the model for a new and gravelly vocal style, one that suits the image of the tough underworld figure well. Together with the new voice comes a toughening of the male singer's attitude towards women. It is unwise to generalize too much about the lyrics of the rebetika songs, but a series of songs from the 1930s to the 1960s takes as its theme women as betrayers, witches who have ensnared their men, cats with claws, heartless dolls and shameless flirts. The fact that the haunts of the early rebetika singers were usually all-male establishments may have contributed to the disparagement of women in many of these early songs; it also clearly appeals to a public taste for macho songs that is not peculiar to Greece, but reflects the similar appeal of flamenco, apache and tango. In any event, the combination of rough male voices, the smart-dressing tough-guy image adopted by many of the early performers, and the disparagement of women, turn the rebetika songs of the Piraeus style into a more macho genre than anything the refugees had brought with them.

In the new Piraeus-based music the instrumentation becomes centered on a single instrument, the bouzouki. Almost all the songs are written in one of three dance rhythms: *zeibekiko, hasapiko* and *tsifte-teli*. Within that narrow framework, one dance comes to represent the new male ethos: the *zeibekiko*. If the *amanes*, the feminine wail of Smyrna, is the vehicle for expressing pain in the *café-aman* repertoire, the bouzouki and the solo male dance come to symbolize the essentially male character of the rebetika. Like the male dancer of the flamenco tradition, the *zeibekiko-*

dancer often appears to be in a state of possession when he dances. His inspiration comes from the bouzouki and the singer. The improvised footwork requires no skill; the importance of the dance lies in a combination of intensity and posture. The dead-pan expression of the bouzouki-player, often holding a cigarette between two of his fingers as he plays, and the dancer's apparent disdain for the audience together enhance the masculine image of the *zeibekiko*.

In contrast to the introverted *zeibekiko*, a dance men were prepared to pay high prices to the musicians for the privilege of dancing alone, the *hasapiko* was a dance of male camaraderie. Usually two, sometimes three men danced it with their arms around one another's shoulders. The *hasapiko* required practice if it was to be danced well. It was popular among sailors, young men doing their military service, men who hung out together without women. Its homoerotic possibilities are exploited, as I have noted, in the sequence from Zorba. What is attractive about the scene is the sight of two men dancing unashamedly and exhuberantly together. The upper-class Greek hero (played by Alan Bates) is introduced to a side of his manliness that has never been revealed to him; it may include adventures with the opposite sex, but it is mainly about male friendship. This is a world that not only excludes women, but celebrates their absence. Interestingly, even the one dance of the rebetika repertoire that was essentially a woman's dance, the *tsifte-teli*, was not uncommonly performed by men holding their genitals as they gyrated in a lewd parody of female dancing.

If rebetika could be said to have crystallized as a pan-Hellenic form of popular music in the 1930s, it is only in the post-war period that it was discovered by intellectuals and began to slowly make its way into more ambitious forms of popular culture. After the Metaxas dictatorship, which had banned rebetika songs and exiled many of the bouzouki-players, and the German occupation of Greece, when recording studios had closed down, rebetika songs enjoyed a wide audience during the late 1940s. This seems to have been due in part to the support of the genre by the state-controlled broadcasting services. Intellectuals of the Greek left, many of whom had played a leading role in the resistance to the Germans, were divided in their attitude to the rebetika. Many leftist intellectuals and musicians regarded the rebetika songs as decadent, especially because of the connection between the music and the smoking of hashish. But while some argued the songs were an opiate of the people, others saw them as continuing the tradition of Greek folk song and Byzantine music. The post-war debate about the rebetika has many similarities to the debates that had occurred about cante jondo in the Spain of the 1920s. On the one side were intellectuals who saw the genre as morally decadent and related to the decline of Greek culture; on the other were those who considered the songs tainted but quintessentially Greek and thus salvageable.

In 1949, the composer Mikis Theodorakis came to the defence of the rebetika, notwithstanding the unsavory nature of the lyrics of certain songs, because musically they belonged to the same tradition as Orthodox Church music and old demotic songs. Unlike the tango and Italian-influenced *cantadhes*, the rebetika were created from the 'eastern melodies' Greek children had learned from their parents (1974: 165). In fact, a number of the songs Theodorakis singles out for attention ('When You Drink in the Taverna,' 'I Lived Alone Without Love,' 'Captain Andreas Zeppos') have nothing oriental about their melodies. Theodorakis goes on to praise the tenderness and chivalry of many rebetika songs, pointing to the lyric descriptions of love such as . . . 'the beautiful song of love, like a spring flower . . .' 'When I kiss your two sweet lips like April roses . . .' (Ibid.: 166–7). Again, it would be easy to counter with rebetika songs that are decidedly unchivalrous, but it is difficult to argue with his conclusion that the figure of the mother, in the rebetika songs, remains as sacrosanct as she does in the folk tradition. Theodorakis concludes that in order to create new and more elevated forms of popular music, the Greek composer must assimilate the rebetika, or, as he prefers to call it, the popular song (Ibid.: 168).

Despite the championing of rebetika by certain artists and intellectuals, there was heated controversy in the Greek press during the forties, fifties and sixties about the value of such music. The main focus of the debate was whether the rebetika really represented the Greek people, and whether or not the songs were ethical. Composer Manos Hadjidakis added his support to Theodorakis's in a lecture at the Art Theatre in Athens. Echoing Theodorakis, he noted the parallels with folk and ecclesiastical music and the instrinsic Greekness of the genre (Holst 1977: 151–5). His talk was accompanied by a performance where rebetika singers Sotiria Bellou and Markos Vamvakaris both sang. The singer Sotiria Bellou, one of the few successful female post-war singers to rival the men in popularity, had been discovered by another intellectual, the playwright Kimon Kapetanakis and introduced to the young rebetika composer Vassilis Tsitsanis, who began to write songs for her. Listening to her perform rebetika is to understand the transformation that had taken place in the female voice of rebetika. Her voice is deep in pitch and has none of the melismatic ornamentation of the Smyrna-style singers. If the Smyrna-style song of pain is an adaption of an older feminine genre, and generally performed in a high pitch, the Piraeus style as sung by Bellou is the voice of a woman singing like a man. It is a voice admired and composed for because of its capacity to express pain, but as Washabaugh notes for the cante jondo of flamenco, it is 'the voice of a woman imitating a man mediating woman.'

Hadjidakis ended his lecture-demonstration in 1949 with the words:

> Someday the fuss over (the rebetika) will die down and they'll continue unhampered on their way. Who knows what new life the indolent and pessimistic 9/8 (of the *zeibekiko*) holds in store for us for the future. But in the meantime we will have really understood their strength. And we'll see them quite naturally and correctly raise their voice in our immediate surroundings and live, sometimes to interpret for us and sometimes to make us conscious of our deepest selves (Holst 1977: 155).

The presentation of rebetika to a sophisticated Athenian audience by a man respected as a 'serious' composer marked the beginning of the cultivation of rebetika by a significant group of Greek artists and intellectuals, some of whom, like the painter Tsarouchis, undoubtedly shared Hadjidakis's attraction to the exclusively male environment of the songs. The idealistic champions of the rebetika saw them as expressions of the downtrodden; songs that dealt with drugs or the underworld became marks of misfortune. To a predominantly left-wing intelligentsia that was marked by years of persecution, embracing the overtly a-political, wryly humorous rebetika necessitated some recasting of the music in terms of working-class oppression and protest. Tsitsanis's song 'The Factories' is about the only song in the repertoire that could be described as a stereotypical response to Marxist rhetoric, but dozens of songs from the repertoire dealt with poverty and hardship, including a whole sub genre of songs about tuberculosis. Besides, there was no doubt that the songs had emerged from and were popular with the urban proletariat. Tsitsanis was regarded by many of the new enthusiasts as the man responsible for 'cleansing' the rebetika both of its underworld associations and its more oriental characteristics. As one critic put it:

> It was immigration . . . that established the rebetika. From then on all that was needed was an internal cleansing: the foreign elements had to go so that the content of the songs could conform to more broadly popular themes, for the disgusting tendencies to disappear and the disparate voices to be absorbed so the rebetika could expand more broadly (Christianopoulos in Holst 1977: 158–63).

The rapid upward mobility of rebetika-based music continued to be the subject of controversy. Theodorakis's decision to set 'Epitaphios', a cycle of poems by the left-wing but non-proletarian poet Yiannis Ritsos, to music and have it performed by rebetika musicians set off a new storm of protest in Greek intellectual circles. 'Epitaphios' was originally written in response to a photograph of a mother kneeling above the dead body of her son, killed in the tobacco workers' march in Salonika in 1936. The poem was published in the Communist newspaper *Rizospastis*, where the photograph had originally appeared, and titled 'Lament.' During the next two decades, Ritsos, reworked the poem, adding more revolutionary and positive stanzas to what had been a poem cast in the model of a traditional woman's song of mourning. The poem was renamed 'Epitaphios'. The title reminded the audience both of the Good Friday service for the dead Christ, a ceremony in which women play a prominent role, and the ancient *epitaphios logos* or *encomium* given by a political leader for those who have died heroically in battle. Ritsos sent the verses to his friend and fellow-Marxist Theodorakis, who was studying classical composition in Paris. Theodorakis immediately set sections of the poem to music using elements from folk, ecclesiastical and the rebetika music. He returned to Greece and decided to record the music using a well-known bouzouki-player and a male rebetiko singer, despite the fact that the poems were all written in the voice of the bereaved mother. Hadjidakis, thinking the settings would be unacceptable, made his own arrangements of the songs, recording them with Nana Mouskouri.

Theodorakis's choice was vindicated by the popularity of the recording. Like the rebetika themselves, this striking new popular music was an invention, a patchwork of familiar elements that was consciously composed and received as a music of the persecuted Left, a music of passionate protest. The weeping mother who may wail in tones that betray the oriental origins of the Smyrna-style, has become thoroughly grounded on Greek soil. Her iconography is Orthodox and Christian but she wails in a male voice that comes from the back streets of Piraeus. Co-opted to a male world she is 'read' as an archetype not of female pain but of working-class martyrdom and incitement to revolution.

'Epitaphios' had been publicly burned during the Metaxas dictatorship, and the songs were banned by the 1967–74 dictatorship. No other composition in the history of modern Greek music has aroused such controversy, but the main bone of contention was neither the content of the poems nor the political affiliations of the composer. What caused the furor over 'Epitaphios' was Theodorakis's decision to use a rebetika singer (Grigoris Bithikotsis) and a bouzouki to perform songs that were settings of a high-brow poet, in other words, to combine the low-brow and dis-reputable rebetika with an intellectual if Marxist poet. The question of why Theodorakis chose a male voice rather than a female one was not central to the discussion, nor did the issue of gender feature in any of the discussions of rebetika. As Theodorakis departed further from rebetika prototypes and used singers like Maria Farandouri to interpret his lyrical and passionate songs, he still continued to use the male voice for his most *laika* or neo-rebetic songs. In his ambitious setting of Elytis' 'Axion Esti' for example, he used Bithikotsis to perform the songs written in popular style. The male rebetika singer's voice had, by the early 1960s, become a symbol of a broad-based proletarian ethic. There were female singers of the period, singers like Mary Linda and Polly Panou, who performed in a similar style, but for the songs that expressed the pain of the downtrodden *kosmaki* (the little people of Greece), nothing could substitute for the male voice.

Some would maintain that its transformation into *laiko* (popular) song removed rebetika so far from its original context that the designation could no longer be applied, but the characteristic instrumentation, rhythms and vocal quality of the rebetika have remained intrinsic to Greek popular music for approximately seventy years, and the revival of older style rebetika that began in the 1970s is still going on. No one can pronounce with confidence on the reasons for the success of the rebetika in their heyday or their influence on subsequent Greek music. It seems to me that one reason for their persistence is that, like all forms of urban music that are particular to a culture, they are built from musical elements that are deeply embedded in that cultural tradition. The oriental, Smyrna-style elements may have faded from the music as it took root in Greece, but traces of the music of the Ottoman period left their mark on the rebetika as they did on the music of other Balkan cultures. Like some forgotten mother-tongue, the oriental pain of the *amanes* still lingers in the macho swagger and wry humor of the later rebetika. If the songs mirror Kazant-zakis's description of the modern Greek character, it is perhaps because they match the vision that many Greeks have of themselves, a vision that is both self-deprecatory and pleased with the hybrid singularity of a culture poised between east and west.

The Zorba factor cannot be underestimated. Greek musicians recreate the rebetika, others revive it. We foreign and Greek scholars interested in the genre codify and analyze it. We are all attracted to it, at some level, for reasons that extend beyond its music and dances. The more we write, the more we contribute to the myth of the world of the rebetes, with their hookahs, their sharp clothes, their passionate dancing, their tough slang.

The myths were already present in the songs. The rebetika never expressed a sober reality, but like most popular songs, offered an escape, an exaggeration, a satirical or romanticized portrait of life in the back streets of Smyrna or Piraeus, one that combined a grieving, oriental mother with a tough, street-wise father.

9

The Tsifte-teli Sermon: Identity, Theology, and Gender in Rebetika

Angela Shand

Tsifte-teli is a Turkish word which literally means 'two strings' or 'double strings,' and refers to a style of playing the bouzouki or 'ud. In Greece this word has also come to signify a particular rebetika dance rhythm, as well as the physical performance of the dance itself, characterized by a shaking or shimmying of the chest and shoulders, and gyrating movements of the waist and hips. Greek tsifte-teli derives from Turkish belly dance, and utilizes its rhythms. In the old *café-aman* of Asia Minor cities, a woman would often sing while another danced in Turkish gypsy style, accompanying herself with finger cymbals (Holst 1977). Today, tsifte-teli is still usually danced by a woman, sometimes with a male partner, but it is not uncommon for women or men to dance together in same-sex pairs. The dance may even be performed by a solo dancer, in this instance always a woman, on top of a table laden with plates and glasses from an evening's revelry, surrounded by a circle of clapping friends. The latter image has become rather a cliché, and often graces the covers of tsifte-teli albums.

Despite its overwhelming popularity, tsifte-teli is problematic for many Greeks, along lines of identity, gender and the body. An incident from my experience, which I call the 'Tsifte-teli Sermon,' reveals the central issues that mark tsifte-teli as a source of difficulty in Greek culture.

One Sunday a few years ago, I attended the liturgy at a Greek Orthodox church in the upper Midwest. After the service was over, the priest announced that a Greek band from Canada would be playing at a local restaurant. He encouraged people to buy tickets, as the event was sponsored by a church-affiliated organization. I attended the party, though I arrived late. The entertainment lasted well into the night, in typical Greek fashion, and included *laika* (popular) and rebetika music, as well as folk songs, all of which were danced to by an enthusiastic crowd.

The next Sunday, the priest delivered a sermon, not on the Gospel reading of the day as is customary, but instead on this party. Although he himself had not attended, a parishioner had informed him that a belly dancer opened the show, complete with scanty costume and cymbals (a portion of the program I had missed). He stated that he felt betrayed, as he had publicly supported this event without having been told about the belly dancing. He went on to say that this type of dancing led to sin: Salome herself had danced in this manner and enticed King Herod to behead John the Baptist. Furthermore, he added, tsifte-teli is not even a Greek folk dance, but of Turkish origin, and therefore should not be danced or enjoyed by Greeks.

Although I had never heard this priest express himself so strongly before, it was common knowledge that he did not approve of tsifte-teli, whether danced by fully clothed women at parties, or by professional belly dancers in costume. Consequently, at church dances, his parishioners danced *syrto* (a folk dance performed in a line) to tsifte-teli rhythms if the priest was in attendance. However, he generally went home early, and local musicians would often save the 'good' tsifte-telia[1] for later, when they would be danced either as a solo or in pairs, but always with the classic snakelike arms and gyrating hips.

As dance is a form of bodily display, a consideration of the Orthodox Christian theology of the body may be helpful for understanding this priest's objections to tsifte-teli. Logically, our consideration begins with the concept of kenoticism, a term which derives from the Greek word *kenosis*, meaning 'emptying.' It refers to the Incarnation of Christ, of His emptying Himself of divinity to take on a physical body and become man. The Church struggled through four Ecumenical Councils to nail down the language of its beliefs on the Incarnation, '. . . to save the body of man from the absurdity of death, and to declare that the humble stuff of the world, the flesh of the earth and of man, has the possibility of being united with the divine life and the corruptible to be clothed in incorruptibility' (Yannaras 1991: 91–2).

The Eastern Orthodox emphasis on the Incarnation of Christ leads to a characterization of the body quite different from that maintained in much of Western theology, namely, that the body is not inherently evil. More-over, none of its functions – eating, drinking, working, sleeping, singing, dancing, or even sexuality – are wrong or sinful in their proper place. Rather, the body is called to salvation and sanctification along with the soul. Furthermore, the bodily senses are seen as sites of holiness as well as temptation. All the senses are incorporated into worship: sight, through the use of icons; hearing, through the chanting of hymns; smell, through incense; taste, through the Eucharist; and touch, through the sign of the Cross. There is also a large role for bodily movement in worship, through various prostrations and processions. Even fasting is pursued not so much to beat a sinful body into submission as to allow the body to experience God more fully.

The Church therefore does not teach that a bodily act such as dancing is inherently sinful. However, there are religious proscriptions on dancing during Lent and periods of mourning, and some priests disapprove of holding dances on Saturday nights, because according to Church canons it is a time of preparation for Holy Communion at the Sunday liturgy. Beyond these guidelines, however, great variation exists among priests and their attitudes toward dancing in general, and toward the tsifte-teli in particular. A few priests, like the one who delivered the sermon, not only disapprove of certain problematic dances, but themselves generally refrain from dancing, even in appropriate contexts. Other priests dance and sing frequently, and must make an effort to restrain themselves during Lent. I have even witnessed two Greek-American priests dancing tsifte-teli together in their collars, gyrating hips and all. In spite of all this variation, a dance performed to entice someone to sin would certainly be frowned upon at any time. This is where the priest's sermon applies. However, since he did not attend the event to which he referred, he had no way of judging whether the dancer performed in a lascivious way, or in an upbeat, lighthearted manner – (there is, after all, more than one way to dance tsifte-teli).

The priest's objections deserve careful consideration as *Greek* objections, not just Orthodox ones. His statement that tsifte-teli is 'not even Greek' points out the struggle for cultural identity that has played such a major role in the development of modern Greece. Nikos Kazantzakis encapsulated the identity crisis of modern Greeks when he called them 'double-descended' (1965: 167–8). Some elements of this double Greek identity are depicted below:

East	West
Romeic	Hellenic
female	male
body	mind
frivolous	serious
sin	virtue
private	public

While no doubt overly simplistic, this schema points to the highly dualistic nature of Greek identity, and the search for 'authentic' Greek culture which marks Greece's modern history. With the beginning of the Greek War of Independence in 1821, and the subsequent formation of the modern Greek state after 1830, the forging of a solid Greek identity was crucial, as was its perception outside of Greece. With the rise of Hellenism in nineteenth-century Western Europe, modern Greeks were cast as 'ancestral Europeans.' By asserting claims to the ancient Hellenic past, Greeks were able to convince European intellectuals to support their struggle for independence from the Ottoman Empire (Herzfeld 1987; Morris 1994).

During this period, Western Europeans held the view that anything Eastern was corrupt, bearing the taint of Constantinople's fall to the forces of Oriental barbarism (Herzfeld 1987: 20). Consequently, nineteenth-century Greek folklorists and linguists worked to remove Eastern elements from folk songs, dances, and even daily language. Simultaneously – and creatively – they developed new interpretations for folk traditions that might have seemed Eastern, constructing accounts that generated these traditions from pure Hellenic stock. The upshot of these views and discourses is still evident. Eastern, Romeic[2] elements are regularly recast in Western, Hellenic terms. Thus, 'Turkish coffee' becomes 'Greek coffee,' and some scholars maintain that the tsifte-teli is in fact an ancient Greek fertility dance (Petrides 1976: 69).

However, the problematic nature of tsifte-teli springs from more than just its Eastern versus Western roots. As a dance, it is closely tied to the deep-seated mother lode of traditional practices on which Greek national identity was built in the nineteenth century. Many of these practices were subjected, during this formative period, to *disemia*, which, according to Herzfeld, pitted fixed official rules and regulations against the shifting ground of everyday practice (1987: 152). Ironically, this *disemia* systematically promoted masculine officialdom and overshadowed feminine practices without acknowledging the fact that the homespun – including dance – practices of women served as the dynamo that powered the national discourses of men. This *disemia* is still at work in Greece today. For example, the appearance of a rural Greek grandmother in the city embodies 'the exposure of the inside to the outside, the rural to the urban' (Serematakis 1994: 221), and the prevailing national discourse requires that she be 'fixed up' and made presentable through setting aside her village kerchief and adopting modern dress.

But the female presence implies greater dangers to Greek national discourse than the exposure of its rural underpinnings. Herzfeld states:

It was the fall of Adam and Eve that divided human society and gave free rein to the play of self-interest. At the most localized level of refraction, this history informs the tensions between the unity of brothers and the insidious corruption of that unity that their wives, the lineal and ethical descendants of Eve, introduce through their gossip and backbiting (Herzfeld 1987: 153).

Since Greece became a modern nation-state, the official, the well-disciplined, and inevitably therefore the Adam-like dimensions of national identity have been celebrated over Eve-like practices that were either nonverbal or gossipy – and incidentally also *Romeic* – including dances such as tsifte-teli.

Thus, the deepest resistance to the tsifte-teli is cultural and highly gendered rather than purely religious. It is no accident that 'East,' 'female,' and 'body' appear on the same side of my structuralist schema, in opposition to 'West,' 'male,' and 'mind.' Greece as a modern nation-state encouraged an identity with the West which depreciated, if not repressed, connections to all things non-Greek, especially Turkish, and female (Herzfeld 1986: 228). Here is the link to the most significant and least explicit 'problem' with tsifte-teli, that of gender.

Tsifte-teli is primarily a woman's dance, and as Petropoulos (1968) notes, the only rebetika dance in which a woman smiles – it is a 'frivolous' dance in contrast to the 'seriousness' of male dance. This dance is a site of female bodily display. In spite of the presence of Eve-like images in Greek culture, the Church recognizes the female body as the very site of the Incarnation, and the Virgin Mary is most commonly referred to as *Theotokos*, or God-Bearer, to emphasize the bodily role she played in the salvation of humanity. In Greek folk dance as well, a woman's body may be revered and even celebrated, especially in the context of a wedding, where the bride is literally 'danced' (Cowan 1990). These positive images notwithstanding, the female body is also viewed as vulnerable, even dangerous in its attraction, and the reactions to a woman's dance reveal the significance of these dangers. Consequently, in traditional folk settings, Greek women dance proudly, but with restraint. They tend to keep their eyes downcast, and a female dancer's skill is determined by her grace and propriety, as well as her ability to occupy a minimum of space. In contrast, men are encouraged to make large, bold movements, and to take up greater amounts of space when leading the circle.

At the heart of the 'tsifte-teli sermon' are the issues of gender and bodily display, even more significantly than the Turkish origins of rebetika dances. After all, the priest who gave the sermon never criticized the *zeibekiko*, another classic rebetika dance with its roots firmly planted in the Ottoman East. However, zeibekiko is traditionally a man's dance, and therein lies the difference: the displays of unrestrained physicality and sexuality, including gyrations of the pelvis, which play a role in both folk and rebetika dances (Cowan 1990), may be acceptable for Greek men, but not for women.

Let us return, then, to the image that began this paper, that of a woman dancing tsifte-teli on top of a table covered with glasses, plates and ouzo bottles, while below her admirers clap, shout encouragement, and throw flowers and paper money. This scene is sometimes thought to represent the apotheosis of the female body (Petropoulos 1968: 80–1). However, even as she has been lifted up above the heads of her companions, the dancer's freedom of movement is severely curtailed by the tabletop debris; she is essentially reduced to jiggling in place. For many Greeks, the tsifte-teli remains an Oriental dance of a woman without restraint: beautiful and sensual, but also dangerous and tempting. Placing the dancer on the pedestal of the taverna table may celebrate the sensual and exotic elements of her dance, but it also restricts her movements and allows others to keep an eye on her. Her potential danger is thus averted, and the tsifte-teli is made safe for Western civilization.

Notes

1. The plural for tsifte-teli.
2. The term *Romeic* is commonly used to express this sense of private Greek identity, being a native term for Greeks (derived from 'Romios' or Roman, referring to the Byzantine or East Roman Empire).

10

Passionless Dancing and Passionate Reform: Respectability, Modernism, and the Social Dancing of Irene and Vernon Castle

Susan C. Cook

Although not alone in their career as professional dancers, Irene and Vernon Castle were by far the most popular performers associated with the widespread embrace of ragtime social dance in the five years preceding the entry of the United States into the First World War. Their brief career – from their marriage in 1911 to Vernon's untimely death in 1918 – can be amply documented in newspaper and journal coverage, film footage and hundreds of publicity photos.[1] The sheer amount of this documentary material attests both to the highly visible nature of their career and to the importance of social dance to American culture at the time.

The media coverage attending the Castles demonstrates the highly-charged nature of their social dance practices. As ragtime dancing became increasingly popular, it literally came to embody, through its music and movement, the purported freedoms and vitality of the modern age. For many, however, the new music, movement and social informality represented not the enticement of freedom but a threat to social order. Thus the public discourse surrounding the Castles's career and the dances they promoted relied on a set of historically-specific dichotomies of primitivism and modernism, passion and control, that reflected contemporaneous concerns about racial appropriations, class and changing constructions of white masculinity and femininity.

Even before the advent of ragtime dance, social dance has largely been viewed with suspicion in the United States if not as a very site of danger and trouble. Primarily due to Protestant denominational injunctions that reflect a gendered and racialized mind/body dichotomy, social dancing, as an embodied activity, has been deemed – like woman herself – irrational and unstable, yet frequently irresistible. Even the waltz, which came to symbolize the very essence of nineteenth-century gentility, was denounced by many when it became popular in the first decades of the nineteenth century because of its closed partnering hold. Decades later, pamphlets such as *From the Ballroom to Hell* (1894), still recounted in detail how the waltz's spinning movement induced a state of uncontrolled euphoria that made women prey to male sexual demands.[2] Social dance's potential danger has itself carried gendered outcomes. For women, dance, with its connection to courtship and its physical intimacy, carried an implicit threat of unleashing female sexual desire at odds with standards of feminine modesty and passivity. For men, dancing, through its connections to the body and its history as a site of female social activity, brought with it fears of effeminacy and emasculation.

Scholars have identified in Irene Castle's public image a reconfiguration of white womanhood, as she modeled a kind of active femininity – 'The New Woman' – that would become increasingly apparent in the 1920s.[3] Vernon's masculine role, however, has not been examined as a similar cultural construction of the pre-war age. This lack of attention demonstrates the ways in which scholarship, even that purporting to be explicitly feminist, perpetuates notions that only women's roles change while men remain universal and ahistorical subjects.[4] Vernon Castle's male identity was hardly invisible; he too performed white manhood on the social dance floor in ways not lost on social critics and writers of the time. Thus in an examination of the discourse surrounding the Castles, I want to pay particular attention to Vernon Castle, how his male behavior was judged, and how those judgments resonate with the dichotomous views surrounding the social behaviors enacted through ragtime dance.

The construction of manhood in the United States, by which some men claim authority through their anatomy, has been intimately tied to a discourse of civilization that was simultaneously, if often contradictorily, driven by ideologies of difference – racial, ethnic, class and sexual (Bederman 1995).[5] Bederman unpacks the nineteenth-century concept of American 'manliness' which, to quote from a dictionary of the time, identified 'what is noble in man or worthy of his manhood' (Ibid.: 19). Its attributes were independence and strong moral character as enacted through a self-restraint that demonstrated a transcendence of the so-called 'lower' passions. This ideology of civilization marked middle- and upper-class white men as superior on racial and cultural grounds, and the exercise of their manly behavior further separated them from both white women and non-white and lower-class men. Non-white men, especially men of

African descent, occupied an inferior place on civilization's ladder. As cultural primitives, they could never achieve civilized manliness because their racial ancestors had never evolved that capacity (Ibid.: 29).

Central to Bederman's historical study is how, through a powerful set of economic, political and social circumstances, this notion of manliness began to lose its power in the 1890s and came to be combined with a new notion of 'masculinity,' a term borrowed from French and rarely, if ever, used in English before this time. Masculinity, unlike manliness, was a term 'devoid of moral or emotional meaning' as it subsumed attributes available to all men and indeed invoked images of the uncivilized primitive freed from civilizing restraint (Bederman 1995: 18). Bederman tracks how Victorian manliness came to be taken over in the first three decades of this century by a new cultural construction of virile masculinity, which, in contrast to the manly virtues of self-restraint and morality, offered instead newly essentialized attributes of aggression, physical force and unchecked sexuality, attributes previously understood as the biological givens of the non-white male (Bederman 1995: 18–19).

Bederman notes that by 1917, when her study ends and a year before Vernon Castle's own death, proper manliness and aggressive masculinity were equally at play in American culture. This uneasy confrontation of civilized manliness and primitive masculinity can be seen in the discourse surrounding what might be called the first 'modern' disease, neurasthenia. Described in detail as early as 1881 by George M. Beard, neurasthenia was widely diagnosed and discussed well into this century and popularized by John Harvey Kellogg in his book *Neurasthenia or Nervous Exhaustion* from 1914.[6] This disease typically plagued the 'refined' and cultivated 'brainworkers' of the white Protestant upper class, and its pathology and treatment were similarly classed and gendered.

Beard, Kellogg and others diagnosed neurasthenia in men as a result of a loss of nerve energy through years of manly over-restraint and too much civilization. Hunting expeditions and other self-conscious forays into violent, aggressive primitive masculinity, such as those undertaken by that robust male specimen, Teddy Roosevelt, were prescribed as a means to recharge the overused and over-civilized male battery. Similarly, the pedagogic theories of G. Stanley Hall, a personal friend of George Beard, written and published in the first decade of this century, likewise subsumed the contradictions of manliness and masculinity. Among other things, Hall called for allowing young boys to explore their 'savage' sides in a kind of evolutionary preparation for achieving healthy civilized manhood after adolescence.

Ragtime

In 1899, the Association of American Dancing Masters held their annual conference in Chicago. As part of their activities, they reviewed newly-created dances of the past year and passed judgment on a shared social dance curriculum. Newspaper coverage of their conference stressed one major change: the Association publicly and reluctantly announced the passing away of the waltz, which had held sway in U.S. ballrooms since the 1820s, in favor of the two-step.[7] The easily learned two-step had grown increasingly popular in the U.S. with the rise of marching band repertory to which it could be danced. Like the waltz, the two-step would itself be supplanted within the first decade of the twentieth century by even newer and simpler dances. These duple meter dances, generically called 'one-steps,' originated from African American social dance practices and like the popular cakewalk of the 1890s, may have developed as parodies of or elaborations on white social dances or as continuations of Africanist practices. In these new 'trotting' dances, often given animal names such as the turkey trot, bunny hug, grizzly bear and camel walk, couples moved closer together, faced and embraced each other, and moved without prescribed steps in response to syncopated ragtime. Particular to these dances was a bent-knee body position that allowed swaying hip and shoulder movements.

Ragtime, a music widely associated with the growth of African American urban life at the turn of the century, had become increasingly popular and known among white Americans through widespread performance and sheet music publication, such as Scott Joplin's famous 'Maple Leaf Rag' of 1899. Black musicians had routinely provided music for black and white social dancing, and marching bands like John Phillip Sousa's began varying their repertory of duple-time marches and lively quicksteps with band arrangements of popular ragtime dance numbers like Kerry Mills's 'At a Georgia Camp Meeting' (1891). Musicologist Samuel A. Floyd has drawn an intimate connection between the two genres noting that ragtime, in seemingly 'borrowing' the march's form and rigid bass-line, demonstrates the powerful syncretism and signifying practices at work in so much African American culture, musical and otherwise (Floyd 1991: 271; 1995) Ragtime's rhythmic syncopation, present in the upper melody that pulls or 'throbs' against the marching bassline, called the strict duple meter into question with its 'hot rhythm.' As Ronald Radano has noted, white America soon became fixated on a black music which was seen and heard as racially marked through the 'metric difference' of syncopation (Radano, forthcoming).

The Association of American Dancing Masters had a reason to bemoan the changes in social dance. Relying as these new dances did on the individual responses of dancers to a music marked by improvisatory spontaneity and social informality, they rendered obsolete the kind of dance training and codification promoted by most dancing masters and their instructional academies. In marked contrast to earlier social dance practices where dance manuals cautioned against dancing without proper knowledge or without proper introduction to partners, these new dances could be performed almost anywhere under increasingly familiar circumstances as public dance halls opened in virtually all urban centers.[8] By 1910, according to historian Kathy Peiss, over 500 dance halls regularly offered such entertainment in New York City alone (Peiss 1986: 88). In 1911, Louise de Koven Bowen, writing as head of the Juvenile Protective Association in Chicago, estimated that as many as 86,000 individuals regularly participated in close to 300 dance venues available in that city (Bowen 1911). The vast majority of the participants were teenaged working-class boys and girls for whom such public dancing was their chief source of amusement and pleasure in lives often marked by the tedium of factory work and widespread economic deprivation.

Social reformers and cultural critics attacked ragtime dancing on various grounds, but chiefly over issues of movement, music and venue. Dubbed by its critics as 'tough' or 'rough' dancing, it was judged 'indecent' and 'vulgar' for the kind of wiggling, shaking, swaying and pivoting motions it permitted and even legitimated as these movements were read as explicitly sexual if not imitative of intercourse. Reformers argued that such dancing, especially when presented in unchaperoned environments as was becoming increasingly common in urban areas, held the very real danger of compromising working-class women who already faced inequitable economic situations.

Reformers, such as Chicago's Louise Bowen, documented both dance's popularity with the working class and the dangers from the unregulated venues in which it took place. Bowen and her Juvenile Protective Association documented that dance halls and so-called dance academies were often operated by saloon keepers and others who had well-known connections to prostitution. While some critics, especially those associated with religious institutions, called for an actual ban on dancing, Bowen and her reformer counterparts like Belle Israels of New York City, were well aware of dance's popularity with the working-class population they served. They sought instead new licensing restrictions and the stringent enforcement of current alcohol statutes.[9]

While reformers and others often focused their attention on the perils present for working-class women, there emerged in critical discussions of dance a new image of the parasitic male social dancer, one that frequently embodied an inconsistent sexual dichotomy. In keeping with older views, male dancers, with their connections to women and their seeming disinterest in manly careers of business or manly recreational pursuits, inhabited an effeminate space. These dancers were 'lounge lizards,' 'under-sexed butterflies' and male dandies whose dancing skill and popularity with upper-class women who might financially support them rendered them unnatural and unmanly. On the other hand as reformers noted, male dancers were also the victimizers of the unknowing working-class girls, the men who plied such girls with alcohol and then exploited them sexually. These men, the 'tango pirates,' embodied the powerful masculine sexual aggression that was understood as part of lower-class and non-white male behavior. Rather than displaying a manly control, they unleashed, through ragtime dance's provocative movement and music, sexual depravity that threatened social order.

Throughout the years ragtime dance was in vogue, roughly 1911-1918, media coverage of the Castles and others reflects social dance's threatening nature by referring to ragtime dance's popularity in pathological terms.[10] The body politic had gone 'dance mad' or had succumbed to a 'dance craze,' terms still widely used today by dance historians with little regard for their disruptive social meaning. While craze can suggest the excitement and even the indescribable pleasure of the experience, other writers, in keeping with a pseudo-Freudian imagery of mental disease, spoke of lunacy, dementia and hysteria. Ragtime dance was also an epidemic, an infection or a fever, images that reflect contemporaneous health concerns about bodily diseases that spread quickly often through germs that infected individuals without their knowing it. As ragtime dance was initially seen as a product of urban and largely immigrant working-class population, this discourse of dance pathology perpetuated notions of the growing 'immigrant menace,' which, according to Alan Kraut, embodied its own images of a germ-carrying, disease-ridden population of outsiders (Kraut 1994).

Closer to home for white native-born Americans and thus even more threatening was the ragtime music associated with the turn-of-the-century growth of a migrant urban black American population and its accompanying dance. This music was understood as central to the dance experience; indeed ragtime and its racially marked syncopation was often viewed as the very catalyst of the motion. If one was in earshot of this music, one could not help but dance, its rhythms caused bodily response. And black

Americans were widely acknowledged to be calling the shots, their music, uncivilized and primitive by evolutionary definition, had the power to cause civilized society to move. The hot rhythms of ragtime music – the image of heat itself suggesting fever – thus embodied the dichotomy of desire and dread, promising either vitality and/or more disease.

These were potent images indeed as ragtime dancing in its hugging embrace involved direct bodily contact that increasingly allowed transgressions of previous social code. Ragtime dance – like TB – spread through touch. And its music held the potential to cause this very bodily response to take place. Thus at the heart of the matter was the ultimate fear of touch and contact – the mixing of blood, of miscegenation. Central then to ragtime dance's supposed social danger were very real fears about social contact and social control, especially racial appropriations and transgressions of the careful boundaries of class, race and gender. If we carry this discourse back to the mind/body duality of Darwinian social theory at work during the years of ragtime dance, ragtime social dance acted like a woman or a non-white lower-class man; both presented a real threat to the social power of the white manly practitioner.

The Castles

In many respects the Castles were unlikely candidates for the celebrity status they attained. Irene Foote (1893–1968?) was the second of two daughters born to Annie Elroy Thomas, a European-educated woman, and Hubert Foote, son of the noted homeopathic physician E. B. Foote and himself a medical doctor. The Footes lived a comfortable upper-middle-class existence in the New York City suburb of New Rochelle. Irene Foote's childhood was not particularly unusual although the family's homeopathic health concerns allowed for an active life of bicycling, swimming and riding horseback. Her formal education ended at sixteen, and by 1910 Irene Foote was working in New York City as a chorus girl, a not uncommon occupation for young women desiring money and fame, although not one normally chosen by a daughter of privilege.

Tall, blonde and thin, Vernon Castle, born Vernon Blythe in 1887 in Norwich, England, was the son of pub owners and graduated with a degree in engineering from Birmingham University. Immigrating to the United States in 1906, Vernon Blythe followed his sister Coralie Blythe and brother-in-law Lawrence Grossmith into a stage career and subsequently took the name Castle as befitting his British background. He had attained success in a number of Lew Fields's productions in which he used his height and thinness to comic ends.

In 1910 Irene Foote met Vernon Castle, six years her senior, and they were married in May of 1911 when Irene turned eighteen years old. A French agent signed Vernon to perform in a French revue, and the couple left for Paris that same year. Vernon's comedy routine was a failure, but the ragtime dance numbers the couple concocted based on those they knew from theatrical productions – notably the Texas Tommy performed by Blossom Seeley in Fields' The Hen-Pecks – were well received. When they returned to New York City in 1912, Parisian cachet in place, the syncopated dancing of the working class had become increasingly popular through musical theater productions and was being widely imitated off-stage. While the considerable appeal of the new one-step dances preceded the Castles's return from France, the Castles would ride the wave of dance popularity and their ability to garner media attention and approval provided a new impetus for the white middle and upper class to participate.

Upon returning to New York City, the Castles first appeared on stage in *The Sunshine Girl* which opened in February of 1913. Vernon Castle, in the secondary male role as Lord Bicester, danced a tango with the show's star Julia Sanderson to the song 'The Argentine,' thereby helping to popularize another new social dance associated with ragtime and syncopated music. Despite Vernon's caballero costume and the song's title, this kind of tango was not Argentine tango as we know it today but rather had its origin in Parisian social dance stylizations already several times removed from its original. Yet the dance's popularity and certainly its notoriety drew on an understanding of that dance's connection with an exotic underclass and further associations of racialized passion and non-white immigrant.

Together the Castles performed a second trotting dance number to the song 'Little Girl, Mind How You Go.' Vernon's physical antics in his comic role as well as his dancing received great critical acclaim. The reviewer in the *New York Journal* noted: 'Vernon Castle in his role is an animated hairpin sort of person, full of his usual staccato dances, his surprising convolutions and his eccentric humor which combine to make a really remarkable comedian.'[11] Charles Darnton writing in the *New York World* noted as well: 'To keep the dancing honors in the family his pretty and graceful young wife joined him in a trot suggesting both wings of the turkey that proved the one real novelty of the evening.'[12] Within weeks of the show's premiere, Vernon was featured in newspaper stories that recounted his talent as a dance instructor charging as much as $1 a minute and provided his free advice for dancing the tango and one-step. The Castles were well on their way to becoming the most popular exhibition dancers on the social dance circuit.

Throughout their careers, the Castles responded to the discourse of dance pathology with their own carefully crafted one of propriety in which their dancing, self-described as 'modern,' was so identified by its calculated 'refinement' in opposition to the 'roughness' associated with its working-class and ethnic predecessors. They came to mark out a kind of middleground between the informality of working-class dance halls and the constrained rigidity of the Dancing Masters, a middleground that deconstructed and reconstructed the notions about male and female dancers.

In an article entitled 'How to Dance the Tango,' that appeared soon after *The Sunshine Girl*, Vernon emphasized bodily discipline as a means of rendering the tango legitimate. The body must be held 'perfectly straight,' 'erect'; their version of the dance was 'a stiff and proper affair compared to the tango of yesteryear' with 'none of the swaying that made the tango Argentine so objectionable.'[13] As controversy continued over the tango – a word often used to refer to all questionable ragtime dances – the Castles and other dance apologists stressed that the problem resided not with the dance but with the dancers. 'Vulgar people,' replied Mr. Castle, 'will make any dance vulgar.'[14] It is not surprising then that critical response to the Castles noted their grace, cool composure, the passionless nature of their dancing, even their platonic performance of the tango. Vernon's thin body type was frequently commented upon and caricatured, as in Figure 10.1, as was Irene's child-like or 'boyish' figure, both of which served to disconnect and further deflect eroticism and passion.

The Castles benefited enormously from the marketing savvy and upper-class connections of their agent Elisabeth Marbury, a highly-respected playwright's agent who had seen the Castles perform in France.[15] By 1914 she arranged for them to have their own exhibition and teaching venues, the Castle Club, a rooftop cabaret, and the Castle House, a dance school located across from the Ritz-Carlton Hotel. While the Castle Club maintained an exclusive, upper-class membership, the Castle House was central to their work of disciplining dance. Under the watchful eyes of society chaperones, it provided dance instruction for children of the well-to-do during the afternoon thereby precluding attendance by working-class youth. 'As scarletine is to scarlet fever, as vaccination is to smallpox, so is Castle House to the ordinary restaurant cabaret,' announced a newspaper story after its opening.[16] These connections with 'elite society' marked the Castles as refined and further legitimated their work for a growing middle-class audience.

To capitalize on their popularity, Marbury organized a 30-city tour in April–May of 1914 and published *Modern Dancing*, a dance manual

"WATCH YOUR STEP."

Figure 10.1 A caricature of the Castles following their 1914 performance in Irving Berlin's *Watch Your Step*, from *Detroit News*, 2 December 1914.

supposedly authored by the Castles, which was heavily anthologized in newspapers in the months prior to the tour. Together the tour and their book show how the Castles continued to further their careers by demonstrating how to recontain the social threat of unchecked dance madness. Their list of 'Castle House Suggestions for Correct Dancing', provided in Figure 10.2 and published in *Modern Dancing*, presents a veritable description of how to dance 'white.' Their descriptions of how to dance the one-step, hesitation waltz, tango and maxixe, carry further injunctions against certain kinds of bodily movement, a call for standardized steps, and justifications based on references to older court or folk dances: '(Tango) bloomed forth a polished and extremely fascinating dance, which has not had its equal in rhythmical allurement since the days of the Minuet' (Castle and Castle 1914).

CASTLE HOUSE SUGGESTIONS
FOR CORRECT DANCING

Do not wriggle the shoulders.
Do not shake the hips.
Do not twist the body.
Do not flounce the elbows.
Do not pump the arms.
Do not hop – glide instead.
Avoid low, fantastic, and acrobatic dips.

Stand far enough away from each other to allow free movement of the body in order to dance gracefully and comfortably.

The gentleman should rest his hand lightly against the lady's back, touching her with the finger-tips and wrist only, or, if preferred, with the inside of the wrist and the back of the thumb.

The gentleman's left hand and forearm should be held up in the air parallel with his body, with the hand extended, holding the lady's hand lightly on his palm. The arm should never be straightened out.

Remember you are at a social gathering, and not at a gymnasium.

Drop the Turkey Trot, the Grizzly Bear, the Bunny Hug, etc. These dances are ugly, ungraceful, and out of fashion.

Figure 10.2 From *Modern Dancing*, 1914.

Central to the Castles's claims of modernity, and directly countering the discourse of pathology, was their definition of dance not as mere entertainment, but as healthy fun. In her introduction to the book, Elisabeth Marbury stated: 'Refinement is the keynote of their method; under their direction Castle House became the model school of modern dancing, and through its influence the spirit of beauty and of art is allied to the legitimate physical need of healthy exercise and of honest enjoyment' (Ibid.: 20). Continuing along these lines, the Castles stressed in the book's foreword that once dance was refined along their guidelines 'social reformers will join with the medical profession in the view that dancing is not only a rejuvenator of good health and spirits, but a means of preserving youth, prolonging life, and acquiring grace, elegance, and beauty' (Ibid.: n.p.)

With chapters like 'Dancing as a Beautifier,' and 'Dancing and Health,' the Castles – often in Irene's voice – countered arguments against dance as dangerous in particular to white women with statements about its beneficial effects. 'What is more, we are unconsciously, while we dance, warring not only with unnatural lines of figure and gowns, but we are warring against fat, against sickness, and against nervous troubles' (Ibid.: 146)

'Nervous troubles' bespeaks 'neurasthenia,' and dancing, they argue, provides a cure for overly-civilized upper-class lifestyles. Under proper conditions, a woman might leave her confining home and take pleasure in the physicality of dance without necessarily falling prey to the danger always assumed in her public activity; she might dance her troubles, nervous or otherwise, away. For men too, dance became a physical activity which could recharge the worn-out male battery.

On tour the Castles continued their performance of refined modernity. Touring alone, they did not appear in the guise of vaudeville or variety shows but in spaces – such as Boston's Opera House – that were sites of legitimate theater frequented by elite box owners. While the overall tone of their exhibition was informal, at the center was the depiction of the distinction between the vulgar and refined, the tough and the modern, the passionate and the platonic. After the Castles exhibited their own dance versions, such as the Innovation Tango danced without touching, students from Castle House demonstrated the right and wrong way to dance, to a running commentary by Vernon, acting the part of teacher and patriarchal authority.

African American band leader James Reese Europe, six years Vernon Castle's senior, was central to the Castles's popularity and the dance experience they promoted. Indeed, given that he was an established figure in the New York City entertainment world as a band leader and through his organization of the Clef Club in 1910, it was their connection with him that helped insure the success of their New York ventures (Badger 1995).

James Reese Europe acted as the musical director for both Castle House and the Castle Club and accompanied the Castles on their tour. His music was regularly commented upon in newspaper coverage as were the band's antics suggestive of minstrelsy and the 'coon' clowning of other black vaudevillians. Europe played a key role in providing the Castles with their most famous dance, the foxtrot, as it, like so many other popular dances of the time, was derived from African American sources (Badger 1995: 116; Handy 1941: 226; Malone 1996: 143). During his tenure with the Castles, Europe published eleven original dance tunes, such as 'Castle

House Rag' (1914), and he and his High Society Orchestra became the first black orchestra to record, cutting eight sides in 1913–14 for the Victor label.

James Reese Europe is better known today for his participation during the First World War as leader and founder of the all-black volunteer 369th Infantry 'Hell Fighters' Band. His band entertained troops and French natives alike, providing European audiences with their first exposure to the syncopated dance music and early jazz that would become especially influential on European culture in the years following the war. The band was extremely popular and later made recordings in New York City after the Armistice.

While a leading figure in African American popular music, Europe himself remained, at least in print, ambivalent about this music, its popularity and especially the label 'ragtime.' 'In my opinion there never was any such music as "ragtime". "Ragtime" is merely a nick-name, or rather a fun name given to Negro rhythm by our Caucasian brother musicians many years ago' (Berlin 1994: 195–7). Europe further de-emphasized this kind of syncopated popular music in the concerts he organized for the Clef Club, choosing instead to focus on music by African American composers that showed 'refinement.' [17]

His mixed feelings about a music that was growing in popularity with white audiences is echoed by later proponents of race pride, such as Alain Locke, who ignored ragtime and early jazz, choosing instead to celebrate the Spiritual. Similarly, ragtime social dancing presented problems in the black community too, with members of black churches and service organizations expressing fear and calling for social controls.[18] Given the contested position this music and its dance had in mainstream society, it is not surprising that many African Americans chose to deny it. For African American men, to embrace this eroticized music of the 'dance craze' meant re-embodying pernicious stereotypes that identified them as irrational, oversexed and in need of civilizing discipline at the hand of their white male betters. Speaking to refinement for black Americans was a political act.

The Castles appear to have had a good working relationship with Europe and the band musicians and appeared prominently in a benefit for Europe's Tempo Club. Irene Castle made special arrangements, widely noted in the press, to insure that black musicians, in particular drummer Buddy Gilmore and composer/conductor Ford Dabney, were able to attend Vernon's funeral.[19]

The Castles, however, spoke little of their musical collaborator. Whereas four chapters of *Modern Dancing* dealt with dress alone, music is treated in a single chapter of a mere three pages that provides no specifics with regard to who, how, or what, reflecting both the flexibility of the music and its subservient nature. Likewise in her later autobiography, Irene Castle mentioned Europe only in passing, acknowledging that he composed all the music for their new dances and had been 'one of the first to take jazz out of the saloon and make it respectable.'

The relationship between the Castles and Europe was a clearly complex one, playing out the racism of American society. The Castles's true indebtedness to Europe might have been more than they, as white Americans maintaining class and race respectability, could admit let alone write about. Thus their silence on the music also speaks to the central importance of this racialized dance music and how it was changing notions about popular music and culture, and with it modern social behavior and relationships. Through James Reese Europe the Castles had direct access to African American culture which they subsequently repackaged and reworked for their white middle- and upper-class clientele. The Castles, whether they acknowledged it or not, depended on James Reese Europe and his musicians to complete their dance, and thus black and white America came together in another kind of power relation.

Both James Reese Europe and Vernon Castle died untimely deaths. In 1919, Europe, while in New York City and touring with his popular band, was stabbed by one of his musicians and died later in the hospital. His death was felt strongly in the black community and widely discussed in black newspapers. He did not live to see the flowering of the post-war Harlem Renaissance, to which his First World War volunteer service was a catalyst and to which he would no doubt have contributed greatly. Nor was Europe the beneficiary of the documentary procedures that might have provided some sense of his view of his dance/musical partnership.[20] We don't know how he saw his work with the Castles, how he judged them either as individuals, dancers, employers or collaborators, nor how he and his musicians coped with Jim Crow culture on the dance floor and off, or responded to the discourse of dance/music pathology.

Vernon Castle predeceased his musical collaborator. As a British citizen, he had volunteered for wartime duty in the RAF in 1916, and after flying many missions and being seriously wounded, he returned to the United States as a flight instructor for Canadian pilots training in Texas. He was killed in 1918 when his plane crashed while dodging one flown by a young recruit. His death was front-page news across the U.S., and he was mourned as a fallen hero, although he had not died in action. And yet, as the following extended quotations from two obituaries betray, Vernon Castle's male dancer persona was a questionable one.

He had always been spoken of as a 'lounge lizard' as an under-sexed butterfly, as a frivolous, unimportant youth. Then suddenly, with little fanfare, he enlisted and sailed away. Broadway couldn't believe it . . .. He will be missed, not as a dancer, for the great fickle public had ceased to be interested in his steps; but as a thoroughly likable chap who showed the world that a man can ball the jack in nancy clothes and still be a regular male beneath his fluffy exterior.

[Vernon Castle] became identified with a strange abnormal kind of girlish man which later developed into the afternoon tea party horror, known as the 'tango lizard.' This type it has been difficult to force into the war, impossible to eradicate from society and altogether exactly the thing Mr. Castle certainly was not and could not countenance . . . The Vernon Castle who has gone was not the Castle of the ballroom and the hothouse at all. It was the masculine, sterling, fighting Castle who idly, quizzically, put the 'Castle walk' over on his social idolators in clean disguise of the real big fellow in the flowerlike hide of him.[21]

In his public performance as a male dancer Castle had tried to balance the competing claims of manliness and masculinity. His British background, although nominally Other was hardly exotic, his attenuated body type, lack of conventional good looks and conventional marital status helped him construct a safe white Anglo-masculinity that removed threats of racial or sexual deviance. His humor, frequently commented upon in the press, gave him an air of not taking his dancing work too seriously; it was not a real career. As his RAF experience later showed, he could walk away from dancing and become proficient at a manly activity, one that would carry enormous social and gendered cachet after the war – the courageous First World War flying ace. Following his enlistment, newspaper coverage noted that his dancing had rendered him particularly fit for the physical demands of soldiering. Social dancing had indeed replaced the big game hunt as a means to render white civilized men virile subjects for patriotic pursuits.

But he also traded on ragtime dancing's embodiment of non-white masculinity, its racial primitivism, vitality and passion through the very visible presence of James Reese Europe and his band. Thus the Castles entered into their careful discourse of refinement and self-control invoked not only in how they actually carried their bodies on stage but in their call for the standardization of dances to constrain improvisatory movement. Such standardized dances demonstrated a kind of manly restraint over the lower passions that also put music back into its subservient position, but I would argue, with limited success. While the Castles might have been able to discipline, refine and sanitize dance movement and attendant behavior, ultimately they could not discipline or erase the black male bodies that made their music. The immateriality of the music, with its aesthetic of rhythmic difference and improvisational aesthetic, ultimately resisted attempts to control it. It remained, giving a voice to the Other that would only grow in power and stature in the following decades.

As the quotations from his obituaries make all too clear, Vernon Castle's dancerly manhood was not entirely recuperated until his death. Only a hero's death allowed for rewriting his story in which he had given up a lucrative, although potentially suspect, career to serve his country and, thus, make the ultimate male sacrifice, a sacrifice black men would later try to claim as their own as well. For the actual fortunes of social dance in white America, Vernon Castle exerted considerable posthumous influence. Having gone where other white men feared to tread, he helped recast the practices of white masculinity and reconfigure societal views about the white male dancer thereby making dancing safer for the men – like Fred Astaire and Gene Kelly – who quite literally followed in his footsteps.

Notes

1. There are sixteen scrapbooks of newspaper clippings in The Billy Rose Theatre Collection, Lincoln Center, of New York Public Library alone, as well as significant holdings in the Museum of the City of New York. Unless otherwise noted, all newspaper articles cited here are from the two scrapbooks in the Robinson Locke Collection, volumes 495 and 496.
2. Faulkner (1894) claimed to be a former dancing instructor whose own experience with the degradation of the dance world – particularly the post-dance seduction of a woman, her pregnancy and subsequent death in childbirth – caused him to speak out. Reflecting the sexual double-standard of the day, his reforms call for keeping women from the pleasure of dancing rather than condemning male predatory sexual behavior.
3. See Kendall (1979), Erenberg (1981), and my essay (Cook 1998).
4. I thank Paul Smith, whose introduction to his edited collection (Smith 1996) helped me realize my own complicity.
5. While aspects of these constructions of American civilization and manhood have been dealt with elsewhere and indeed my own research

has dealt with them from the outset, Bederman's book presents the best single discussion I have found which persuasively argues the intimate connections between gender and race as well as the need to see masculinity as historically created.

6. For more information on neurasthenia and its cultural implications, see Lutz (1991).

7. 'The Waltz No Longer Popular? Dancing Masters Say That it Has Been Supplanted by the Two-step,' *New York Sun*, 9 September 1899, and 'Passing of the Waltz,' *New York Sun*, 10 September 1899. Clippings found in the collection of the Chicago Historical Society, Bournique's Scrapbook, qF388RT/B66s/v.3.

8. A typical example of a dance-etiquette manual is Dick's Quadrille Call-Book and Ball-Room prompter (New York: Dick and Fitzgerald, 1878).

9. For a good introduction to Belle Israels's work, see Perry (1985). Perry has also written a full-scale biography of Israels (1987).

10. I have based most of my work on scrapbooks and collections of clippings on the Castles contained in the Billy Rose Theatre Collection of the New York Public Library and the theatre collection of the Museum of the City of New York.

11. '"The Sunshine Girl" so Gay that She Deserves Her Name,' *New York Journal*, 4 February 1913, v. 495.

12. Charles Darnton, '"Sunshine Girl" Bright, Dainty and Tuneful,' *New York World*, 4 February 1913, v. 495.

13. 'How to Dance the Tango,' *Atlanta Georgian*, 27 March 1913, v. 495.

14. 'Tango According to Castle,' *Metropolitan*, June 1913, v. 495.

15. Marbury's family, unable to accept her lesbian lifestyle, destroyed many of her personal papers, and thus she remains a shadowy figure whose importance to entertainment history has been undervalued. She authored an autobiography (1923) and was one of the featured women profiled in a book for young girls (Ferris 1940). More recently, she has been the subject of a dissertation (Strum 1989).

16. 'Castle House is Exclusive: Vulgar Mob Not Welcome at New York's Newest Fad/Well backed by Society/Unique Entertainment Enterprise Serves No Intoxicants and Insists on Correct Dancing,' *Rochester Herald* (n.d.), v. 495.

17. It is significant that refinement was a central concern of Scott Joplin as well. His wife noted his particular desire to affect refined speech.

18. Berlin (1994: 221) describes Joplin's struggles with Sedlia clergy and suggests that he later got his revenge through the character Pastor Alltalk in his opera *Treemonisha*.

19. 'Last Honors for Lieut. Vernon Castle: Flying Men and Negro Musicians at Aviator's Bier,' *New York Post*, 19 February 1918, v. 496. The article notes that Ford Dabney, as well as Charles Wilson, Allie Ross and Buddy Gilmore, all former members of the Castle House Orchestra, attended.

20. Examples of such documentary enterprises are (Kimball and Bolcom 1973) and the Jazz Oral History Project housed at the Institute for Jazz Studies, Rutgers University-Newark. Noble Sissle and Eubie Blake worked with James Reese Europe in New York and Sissle was a prominent member of the Hell Fighters Band.

21. The two quotations are from the *Detroit News* (1918) and from 'The "Real" Vernon Castle' by Amy Leslie, *The Daily News*, 15 1918, v. 496.

–11–

Social Theory and the Comparative History of Flamenco, Tango, and Rebetika

Gerhard Steingress

Part I

Ethnocentric, nationalist or essentialist approaches to ethnic music-styles afford little insight into the social and cultural significance of postmodern popular art, as the case of Andalusian flamenco demonstrates (see Steingress 1993). Indeed, romantico-nationalist illusions about popular ethnic music-styles – including for example those that pertain to Andalusian flamenco, Portuguese fado, Greco-oriental rebetika, Argentinian tango, Brasilian samba, Hungarian csárdás or, recently, Algerian rai – along with every exhalation of that mysterious *Volksgeist* generated out of nineteenth-century *Völkerpsychologie* – need to be set aside. This will allow serious investigations to reconstruct the origins of these styles in a more disciplined way, that is, as peculiar artistic results of the cultural *hybridization* of distinct musical, poetic and choreographic elements of traditional and modern culture, a hybridization process that characterizes the formation of 'national cultures' and corresponding identity concepts in the past, predominantly romantic century.

There is no doubt that recent cultural anthropology and comparative cultural sociology have fixed new standards of investigation with regard to flamenco and similar cultural manifestations in accordance with the notion that cultural differences have to be considered less a consequence of *isolation* than of mutual *relations* of different social and ethnic groups, or cultures themselves (see Lévi Strauss 1973). In contrast to the distinguishing and demarcating function ascribed to ethnic and cultural differences in the nineteenth century, contemporary cultural dynamics in the West tend towards a postmodern model of global culture – including its relativisms and eclecticisms. Once set free from its local, regional or national significance, ethnic aesthetics becomes a floating element of transnational and transcultural musical creation.

For our study, this means that we must apply modern social theory and methods to phenomena of contemporary cultural and artistic dynamics, subjected to social and cultural change in postmodern society. Almost immediately, therefore, we turn our attention to the crisis of identity that lies at the heart of these social dynamics. Identity demands new explanatory concepts, not only in spite of a necessary redefinition of deconstructed, obsolete collective identities, but also in order to establish new strategies through which to reformulate the historical project of Modernity itself (see LeRider 1990: 54 f.; but also Habermas 1990; Baudrillard 1992). In accordance with the generally accepted view of identifying ethnocentrism, racism and nationalism as concepts closely bound up to modernization, we could interpret the reformulation of differentiating cultural identities as a result of a peculiar intercultural communication with 'the others.' It allows one to avoid or correct the usual stereotypical perception and social evaluation of other attitudes, values and cultural life-styles.

According to these considerations, the above-mentioned modern urban ethnic music-styles can be understood as manifestations of an intercultural and even transcultural communication (see Pelinski 1995). But as we will try to demonstrate, intercultural communication, defined as a corrective theoretical, rationalist and discursive concept, has to be differentiated from other similar concepts of intercultural identity-construction, based on stereotyping 'mentality'-factors. This kind of identity construction characterized particularly the creation of European 'national cultures' during the nineteenth century: In view of the transcultural expansion of Modernity, anxious patriots embraced national culture, especially national music-styles in order to block foreign influences, considered decadent. Romanticism served to legitimize cultural nationalisms insofar as they were considered to be natural emanations of the people's spirit. In order to strengthen social cohesiveness in terms of national culture, intercultural communication within the frontiers of the nation states intended to create an organic popular national culture. In light of the debacle of the *ancien régime* and its traditional culture, as well as the cultural demands of the developing bourgeois society, this communication led to the artificial construction of popular culture as a functional folkloristic *pot-pourri*. It eradicated residues of the past culture, and also the manifestations of new urban middle-class cultural necessities. As nation and culture were considered to be synonymous, national culture was based on intra-national communication between social classes and ethnic groups in regard to regional and local peculiarities, although always subjected to the hegemony of the ruling classes and elites. When national cultures became an element of international communication – induced by the extension of markets, the intensification of transportation and, especially, by the rise of mass-media – cultural and ethnic particularities became objects of the basic economic dynamics, i.e. of a 'free' and arbitrary handling as exchange values. Once converted into economic factors of international mass-media industries, cultural and ethnic peculiarities drastically lost their capacity as elements of identity construction. Especially in advanced western societies, national culture was no longer considered a necessary basis for collective or personal identity. Ethnic music or roots-music became a peculiar genre for a global audience. This change can be considered as the basis of transculturation. The former identity-creating musical styles were now considered to be peculiar elements of a supranational artistic creation process, and its consequence was the rejection of these manipulated styles by those who still considered them to be manifestations of peculiar regions or ethnicities. The claim for a back-to-the-roots purity revealed the need for cultural identity based on continuity and authenticity.

As Kellner points out, 'many of the postmodern theories privilege popular culture as the site of the implosion of identity and fragmentation of the subject' (Kellner 1992: 144). This means that popular culture and especially traditional popular music still have preserved much of the fascination and social function within postmodern society that they had once acquired as a romanticized result of the social and cultural transition towards modern society.

According to these considerations, flamenco is considered to be a highly emotional, passionate musical style, created as a modern urban, post-romantic expression by Andalusian bohemian artists around 1850 and influenced by the nationalist movement in music. As a peculiar Andalusian popular manifestation within European romanticism, its links with traditional agrarian images, an idealized Gypsy-life, and a demonstrative Andalusian essentialism, are obvious. Romantics converted flamenco lyrics, expressive music and voluptuous dance into a new genre associated with the emerging Andalusian national identity in the second half of the nineteenth century. Due to the romantic concept of culture, and apparently uninhibited by growing social and political conflicts related to the gradual consolidation of bourgeois society after the War of Independence (1808–1814), the construction and/or imagination of the historical and cultural substratum of nation in the modern urban Andalusian society was advanced as a process of arrangement and public communication with a specific orientation in the historical past and its traditions. Accordingly, the new concept of popular art was a reaction to the endeavour to cover up social antagonisms, political arbitrariness and cultural backwardness – but nevertheless it reflected ambiguity and fatalism as prior manifestations of opposition. The lack of a significant liberal bourgeoisie, the continuing existence of a traditional agrarian, semi-feudal society, the strong patriotic identification with the past and the inclination to populism converted popular Andalusian music and dances into objects of a nation-wide 'remodelation' and an expression especially of the existing ethnic groups, urban subcultures and growing social marginalization. Indeed, Andalusian as well as Spanish culture went through a process of diffuse identity construction with clear tendencies to folklorism and mass-media popular music.

Part II

The present collection of essays on flamenco, tango and rebetika is an exemplary series of intensive analyses. Informed by anthropological and sociological thought, they generate insights by drawing from field-studies or by developing theoretical argumentation. But there still remains a need for a comparative and/or cross-cultural study that might explain regional musical styles in a broader and more systematic way as different and peculiar results of social, cultural and ethnic transition in modern society and its consequences for the evolution of contemporary music.

In order to respond to this problem, I will try to systematize some aspects of these musical styles with regard to two aspects of contemporary collective identity: a) music as an example of intra- and intercultural communication between different social and ethnic groups and traditions; b) music as a growing factor in transcultural processes, i.e. within the formation of elements of a future global culture.

To analyze modern popular music in terms of modernization in con-temporary society, it is essential to surrender the numerous neo-Romantic, traditionalist, nationalist, ethnocentric or cultural misconceptions about the origins and peculiarity of flamenco. A new and revolutionary approach to it began timorously after the heavy ideological impact of semi-official works, published and re-published in the 1950s and later by some distinguished and highly reputed flamenco-experts (*flamencólogos*), including Anselmo González Climent (1964), Domingo Manfredi Cano (1955) and Ricardo Molina/Antonio Mairena (1963). Soon, in the late 1970s, skepticism about this baroque flamenco-legend began to grow gradually as a result of increasing interest in flamenco music not only among a new generation of artists, but also among young Spanish intellectuals and students, related in one way or another to the political opposition to the dying Franco regime.

Indeed, flamenco always had been a challenge for intellectuals since its first years as an artistic style within emerging modern, urban popular music. With its strange, exotic music and corporeal sensuality, it was embraced with hopes of seeing more in it than mere passionate artistic expression. Specifically, it was considered to be the musical site of collective identity, a sign of the distinctive and much heralded *Andalusian essence*. Antonio Machado and Alvarez (Demófilo) is considered to be the first intellectual to summarize and condense, between 1879 and 1881, the romantic concept of flamenco as an object of ethnology or folk-lore (see Machado y Alvarez 1996). With him, flamenco became a manifestation of a millenary culture, but especially of the ambiguous soul of the Andalusian and the Gypsy community, a synthesis of conflictive, but artistically harmonized social relations. No doubt, we could understand this concept as the first attempt to see flamenco through the lens of inter-ethnic cultural communication in Andalusia, as a synthesis of different concepts of ethnic life-styles.

Later, in 1922, in order to oppose the onslaught of artistic decadence, modernist intellectuals like Manuel de Falla and Federico García Lorca tried to purify and re-animate the so-called deep song (*cante jondo*) as an assumed former manifestation of Andalusian Gypsy mentality converted into a neo-Romantic concept of popular Andalusian essentialism (see García Lorca 1984; Falla 1988). With the festival of *Cante Jondo* (Granada 1922), both responded to the political idea of Spanish regenerationism (*regeneracionismo*), i.e. to renovate the damaged Spanish national identity after the disaster of 1898, when its last colonies were lost. Political skepticism and cultural criticism motivated progressive Spanish intellectuals, such as Unamuno, Pio Baroja, Eugenio Nöel and others, to repulse the superficial, folkloristic *flamenquismo* embraced by decadent aristocrats, nostalgic *señoritos*, bohemians and pleasure-seeking lower-class individuals. After the Civil War, the Franco regime soon learned how to exploit nostalgia in order to create a new image of Spain as a future tourist attraction. Paradoxically, the decadence of the flamenco-opera with its folkloristic kitsch and meretricious social harmony (*España de pandereta*) provoked strong artistic and cultural reactions starting in the 1950s, reactions that were reinforced by the increasing influence of modern mass-media technology, such as television (see Washabaugh 1996). Especially since 1970, subcultural flamenco art turned into the very model of a rebellious, oppositional life-style, a kind of existentialist philosophy, a generalized cultural pattern and, in consequence, into an artistically performed object of collective identification in view of the upcoming democratic reorganization of the Spanish society. Certainly, the revitalized popularity of flamenco intensified its folklorization; but with reference to Antonio Mairena's dramatic and mysterious concept of *cante gitano*, it also stimulated a new artistic evolution of the genre in the shadow of political repression and opposition.

With the political transition to democracy, modern, polychromatic flamenco became a highly sensible politico-ideological manifestation of Andalusian identity, sponsored especially by the social-democrats (PSOE) and the Andalusian nationalists (PA). Once it was declared a 'sign of identity' (*seña de identidad*), flamenco artists and *aficionados* (flamenco fans) took increasing delight in periodic public promotions of this emblematic Andalusian art. Nevertheless, flamenco is still not comprehended by either Spaniards or Andalusians, who generally misinterpret its deeper cultural and artistic quality, and who consequently discount it as little more than a primitive and lower-class music.

In spite of the modernization of the educational system, the opening of the academic institutions and the growing influence of social sciences in post-Franco Spain, flamenco is still often discussed as if it was an object for study by some obscure neo-Romantic folklorists and old-fashioned ethnologists or anthropologists. Yet in 1976, Luis Lavaur published the first openly critical reflections on flamenco, although still within the tradition of late-nineteenth-century anti-flamenquismo, that is, from the point of view of cultural and ideological criticism (Lavaur 1976). It is worth noting that his book has not been re-published since that time and has been ignored by most of the flamenco experts. In addition, flamenco investigation developed gradually and hesitantly in the 1980s, producing new, mainly philological and historical insights (Mercado 1982; Gelardo and Belade 1985; Carrillo Alonso 1988a,b; Carbajo Gutierrez 1991). In the wake of this work, other scholars have dedicated themselves to analyzing the linguistic modes of flamenco poetry and its relation to Andalusian manner of speaking, its borrowings from slang and from the Gypsy language, depicting the flamenco mode of speaking as a peculiar subcultural linguistic construction (Fernández and Pérez 1983; Ropero Nuñez 1984), similar to the Argentine *lunfardo* in the case of tango (see Reichardt 1984: 161f.) or the oriental-Greek *mangika* or mangas slang, the secret hashish language associated with rebetika (see Holst 1977: 29). And with reference to the unconscious and semiologic aspects of flamenco, as well as its function within the system of cultural identification, some additional enlightening observations were made by Tarby (1992). To sum up: these and other works helped to inaugurate a line of comprehensive sociological and sociocultural analysis that permitted a critical balance of traditional investigation of flamenco, summarizing and condensing its results and emphasizing the ideological distortion that was a function of its acceptance of national and/or regionalist flamenco legends. But above all, these efforts made possible a new, modern approach of scientific flamencology (see Steingress 1989, 1993, 1997a,b; García Gómez 1993; Mitchell 1994; Washabaugh 1996). A similar tendency can be observed, however, in the case of Greek-oriental rebetika (Holst 1977) and Argentinian tango (Reichardt 1984; Pelinski 1995).

Part III

As we can see, the *extra-artistic* aspects of flamenco have been present since 1881, when Machado y Alvarez published the first annotated collection of flamenco-songs (Machado y Alvarez 1881). Even more so today, flamenco is extensively maintained by the Andalusian administration and considered to be an emblematic manifestation of modern Andalusian popular culture of which it is regarded as an *essential* expression.

Basically the same can be said in the case of Argentine tango: here, artistically accentuated and redefined erotic relations – between man and woman within the social marginalized subcultural milieu of Buenos Aires dock-area – became considered by the new middle classes to be a fascinating, lascivious manifestation of the modern Argentine identity, whose supposedly imaginary roots are sought in the form of an original tango (see Reichardt 1984), sung by an old gaucho-hero in the late nineteenth century. No doubt, as in the case of Andalusian *cante gitano*, that which never existed could not be found. Nevertheless, tango turned out to be something very close to what flamenco was in Spain: a manifestation of pain and sorrow, sensual eager desire, vitality, lust and an object of symbolic identification on the one side, and of something else, that was *added* to it, on the other: the legend of the collective self, which turned modern, urban and subcultural popular art into a mechanism of collective identity and cultural assignation of some essentialistic qualities of the region.

Such collective identity concepts are usually based on what Luhmann described as inclusion and exclusion in societies with a functionally differentiated social system (see Luhmann 1994: 15–45). Eighteenth-century patriotism and the 'ideologically accentuated contrast-metaphoric' of social communities (*Gemeinschaften*) in the following century refer to a kind of 'positive fact' in the sense of inclusion (Ibid.: 17), but the social organization of life also includes opposite strategies of exclusion and its corresponding strategies of legitimation (Ibid.: 20). Following Luhmann's concept, exclusion is based on an interruption of reciprocity in social relations, at the same time that this interruption realizes its fictitious, **symbolic compensation**. In accordance with what Freud considered to be the function of religion, art and sciences as auxiliary means in human culture, we can define modern popular music as one of the possible symbolic manifestations of non-reciprocity, i.e. social repression and its consequences in human attitudes (see Freud 1982: 206 f.). Symbolic legitimization as a sociological and psychological concept of identity-construction allows us to analyze modern popular art as a contribution to the process of establishing distinctive qualities between social classes, ethnic groups and national cultures in modern society.

The appearance or creation of Hungarian *csárdás* (as probably the first example of an artistic national popular music around 1830) shows us how artistic performance – based on preformed mentality-concepts of significant parts of the national population and its specific cultural and ethnic peculiarities – could be converted into artistic, cultural and ideological tools on the occasion of the search for national or ethnic origins within the frame of definition and application of imagined or eclectically constructed, popular national cultural identity.

According to the necessities of the national states and politically defined nations of the nineteenth century, popular art grew and developed within the cultural struggles established in particular by the new middle classes and cultural elites in order to fix political limits and also to separate their people and territory from others. National culture became an element of social exclusion: only those who share it belong to the community – this sharing apparently consisted in the conformity that was prescribed and expressed by popular culture.

This was the historical and ideological background not only of the previously mentioned *Völkerpsychologie*, but also of the utilization of artistic expression in order to demarcate cultural frontiers and national music-styles. But, ideologists and purists of national cultural mentality did not consider the spontaneous and transgressive forces in artistic creation: nationalized music-styles not only became popular within their pre-established context, but also outside of it. As the history of flamenco, tango and rebetika shows, these genres soon began to differentiate themselves and establish a peculiar, transcultural and transnational inclusion-exclusion dynamic.

One 'conservative' tendency remains controlled by those who consider themselves to be 'experts' in 'purity,' trying to fix certain standards of interpretation and instrumentation with the aim and/or effect of conserving it. This attitude led to a kind of restricted and paradoxical *classicism* in flamenco, tango and rebetika. The other 'heterodox' tendency (e.g. in New Flamenco or *flamenco-fusión*) is a development akin to that which Ramón Pelinski recognized in the case of Argentinian *tango-nomade*, and specifically in the international kind of tango that differed from the original *tango porteño* (tango from Buenos Aires). Evolution is differentiation, and in line with Pelinski's writings on tango, we define this second tendency as an evolutionary transculturation – a concept originally introduced by Ortiz (1940) and developed by Kartomi (1981). As Pelinski writes:

> En termes généraux, la transculturation est la synthèse du processus de déracinement progressif d'une culture combiné à la création d'une culture nouvelle et à la renégociation de l'identité première à travers le dialogue (généralement conflictuel) avec les autres cultures. Cette transition d'une culture à un autre implique, au niveau des éléments culturels, un emprunt réciproque, constant et innovateur (Pelinski 1995: 35).

As we can see, modern popular art tends to develop within the parsonian frame of pattern variables, in this case between 'particularism' and 'universalism.' But transculturation undermines and calls into doubt the cultural inclusion/exclusion mechanisms, so that most of the mentioned, supposed authentic ethnic music styles today are submitted to an international interpretation in line with the trends of global music. It is modern technology and mass media influence, which exposes both artistic creativity and consumers' attitudes in music to new standards and enhanced dynamics of social and cultural change. Indeed, these musics continue to be what they originally were: artistic *constructions* and effects of *acculturation* in accordance with social conditions and cultural necessities in modern society. Today's industrialized high-tech communication induces not only new ways of intercultural communication; it also stimulates a new feeling for other musical styles, assimilated into the processes of one's own artistic creation. The technological, economic and communicative changes point to a new kind of musical sensibility, and also to challenges and possible conflicts, insofar as these musical styles are still considered by many as objects for national and/or ethnic identification.

Part IV

Ethnic musical styles play a romanticizing role in the process of establishing different kinds of collective identities and of becoming an artistically defined and manipulated object of intercultural communication. However, new and critical scientific investigation must consider and analyze above all the historical, social and cultural determinants and backgrounds of these ethnic musical styles in order to localize common structures and dynamics that figure into transcultural processes in contemporary societies, characterized by a growing worldwide entanglement and implication of cultural patterns by art performance. But this phenomenon could not really be explained without considering the crucial influence of changes in consumers' attitudes: anybody interested in music avoids reducing his musical taste to what his own, national culture offers him. Today's musical experience extends far beyond national limits – an extension facilitated by modern technology, a highly developed entertainment-industry and a global market, all of which enables one to 'receive' world-wide musical expression at any moment and in any place.

Relying here on studies of flamenco, tango and rebetika, we emphasize the important sociocultural determinants and phenomenological particularities of this newly emergent musical experience, namely nationally defined, ethnically loaded, highly sensual types of 'passionate musics' (see Washabaugh 1996). These three previously mentioned styles originally appeared within the period of 1850 (flamenco), 1895 (tango) and 1920 (rebetika) as synthesized models of artistic popular music, related to urban subculture and marginalized groups, alcohol and drug-consumption, prostitution and crime. This social background created new attitudes in music, a kind of expressivity narrowly merged with ethnic musical traditions but adapted to the new necessities of urban subcultures. It was probably this ambiguous affinity not only to modern urban culture but also to nostalgic traditionalism that turned these musics into vehicles of identity construction in a supposed chaotic social environment. Due to professional artistic efforts, tourism and modern mass media, they became part of modern popular ethnic music. They point to a series of similar structural conditions and socio-cultural determinants within societies caught up in processes of modernization, i.e. the transition from traditional, agrarian, pre-capitalist society into modern, urban, national capitalistic society. Their common peculiarities are summarized below, refering to some of the characteristic manifestations of each of the discussed styles:

- In its origins we find a clear reference to certain kinds of marginalized social groups, outcasts and outsiders, who oppose the newly established social and political order of bourgeois society. The fact that these marginalized groups did not – would not – conform to the conditions of modern life may explain not only the intensity of emotion in their musical expression, but also their frequent ardent nostalgic attitude towards the past, traditional life-style and its values. So we find ballads and heroic poems (*romances*) related to romanticized popular heros: the *gaucho* (Martín Fierro)/tango; the *gitano* (Gypsy) and the *bandolero* (Diego Corrientes, *El Tempranillo*)/flamenco; the *koutsavakithes*, *vlamithes*, *tsiftes* and *rebetes* (outsiders)/rebetika.

- According to their social status as outsiders and/or immigrants, these groups appeared in the suburban and subcultural environment of big cities and with their typical social and ethnic local color of the *arrabales* (suburbs) of Buenos Aires (tango) or the Andalusian *corrales* (corrals), the prisons, brothels, taverns, cafés and hashish-shops (*Café Amán*, *teké*/rebetika, *cafés cantantes*/flamenco, *lupanares* (brothels)/tango).

- The subcultural origin of these styles is reflected in a peculiar music, dance and manner of singing, marked by extremely passionate, expressive and highly sensitive attitudes related to love, sorrow, pain, loneliness, death or to overwhelming delight and sensual eagerness expressed by the voice and the body. Explicit erotic female attraction is present especially in the *tsifte-teli* (belly dance/rebetika, the *buleria*/flamenco and the tango in general). In the case of flamenco and rebetika, eroticism is related to the image of sinful female Gypsies. What in tango history refers to the milonga (or *sandunguera*) as a charming, but superficial woman, is the Andalusian *flamenca*, both types of women were related to prostitution in certain moments of the history of the respective music-styles.

- All three kinds of music-styles originated in eclectic compositions based on different local and ethnic traditions of dances and songs (such as the *milonga, habanera, tango andaluz*/tango); *canción andaluza, bolero, seguidillas, tonás*/flamenco; *casaka* (cossack dance), *allegro* (Slavic dance), *tsifte-teli, zeibekiko* (jail-songs/rebetika)) and converted in new types of song and dance within the cafés, brothels and neighborhoods. Besides traditional influences in these musics, other modern tendencies in music also played and still play a decisive role, including the operetta, the chanson, jazz, rock and so on.

- The representative types of these styles are characterized by a pronounced male chauvinism (machismo) as a reflex of the general cultural attitude of the social environment: the Argentinian *compadrito* (fellow), *reo* (tramp, *rea*: bitch) or *lunfa*; the Andalusian *flamenco* (as the former Gypsy-like *majo* or fellow), and the Greek *manga* or *rebetis*. Pronounced extravagance in dressing and appearance, the attitude of carrying knives or sticks and the relation to the world of the Gypsies is frequent, not only in the case of flamenco, but also in rebetika (consider the *tsifte-teli* and the fact that *giftos* means 'musician' as well as 'Gypsy.'), although less in the case of tango (*La Moreira*).

– Regarding their manner of speaking, every one of these three subcultural groups generated and used their proper slang in their songs (*lunfardo*/ tango; *flamenco* or *caló*/flamenco; *mangika*/rebetika).

– The subproletarian, subcultural and ethnically multicolored environment of these musical styles found its artistic representation in the *tanguero* or *tanguera*/tango; the *flamenco* or *flamenca*/flamenco and the *rebetis*/rebetika. As a result, the former 'outsiders' became professional artists and representatives of a peculiar artistic subculture, which (at least in the case of flamenco) are often considered as objects of (national) identity (see Salillas 1898) especially by the lower social classes and the bohemians.

– In general terms, these musical-styles represent a kind of subcultural music characterized especially by the dialectics of social and ethnic factors. What in flamenco relates to *payos* and *gitanos*, in rebetika also points to the conflictive relation of Asia Minor Greeks and continental Greeks, as well as of Turkish and Greek culture. And in the case of tango, the massive immigration of European lower-class people at the end of the nineteenth century also created conflictive social, cultural and ethnic situations.

In a second step we will try to systematize the social, cultural and ethnic factors in a kind of **explanatory model** that takes into consideration the origins, functions and consequences of subcultural popular music as an artistic manifestation within societies in the process of transition towards modernity. According to this end, we propose the following:

– The above-mentioned subcultural musical styles appeared in conjunction with the transition of agrarian societies and traditional rural culture into modern industrial societies with civic urban and bourgeois culture as a hegemonic system of habits and beliefs, submitted to the necessities of the modern state. According to social class differentiation in high and folk culture, the former traditional rural culture became an object of reinterpretation and adaptation to the needs of lower and middle urban popular classes by a new generation of artists. The effect of this new artistic orientation was the transformation of the traditional agrarian culture in nostalgic folklore and the modern mass-produced popular culture (see Abercrombie et al. 1992: 131f.).

– This transformation included a double tendency: on the one hand, it expressed the necessities of popular classes to redefine their cultural identity within the newly established bourgeois society in a predominantly non-industrialized, agrarian area. On the other hand, it was strongly influenced and even submitted to the romantic idea of seeking this new identity proceeding from the re-animation of the heroic historic past and certain idealized popular social and cultural patterns. The newly created urban popular music stimulated enthusiasm not only in the lower and the marginalized social classes, but also in those sectors of the pauperized aristocracy that were unable to adapt themselves to the new social order. Accordingly, the Andalusian society of the second part of the last century constructed a spontaneous cultural expression out of the polychromatic *pot-pourri* of old-fashioned folklore, nostalgic reminiscences, imitations of the so-called traditional dances and airs – but at the same time mixed up with modern popularized Spanish operetta-romances and Italian opera-arias. In this sense, flamenco can be seen as a sensual solution to the needs of lost traditionalists as they struggled to adapt to the cultural exigencies of modern society while simultaneously embracing a time-honored cultural identity in the changing world.

– True to the ideas of Romanticism and Neo-Romanticism, cultural identity had to be sought in the traditional popular manifestations of the historical past of the new-born nations. But in order to demarcate one's own identity from those of others, only the most singular, most exotic and most fascinating elements of these societies were accepted in order to imagine national culture. By roughly 1850, Romanticism had already cleared the way for a more realistic perception of culture; thus, stereotypic ascription of 'mentality' was being advanced as a kind of positivistic reification of social and cultural patterns, that is cultural essentialism.

– The decline of traditional (folk) culture emphasized the existence of modern culture as a highly differentiated compound of social subcultures. The dominant romantico-idealistic approach towards identity construction converted certain marginalized social groups into objects of long-sought national representation (see Salillas 1898). Accordingly, the creation of a national image was based on the existence of certain, predominantly marginalized social groups, whose cultural attitudes and aesthetic expression became an independent (alienated) ideological construct in order to create national culture as an eclectic compound of what was considered popular art.

- This new kind of popular art mined the quarry of traditional folk-culture in order not only to invent a second-hand folklore and folklorism as an ideological concept, but also to strengthen popular identification with the nation state as the political institution of the social class system.
- In their origins, flamenco, tango and rebetika must be considered artistic expressions of marginalized and ethnically multi-structural urban social groups, but with a strong nostalgic (romantic) hang-over from the past traditional culture. Due to this fact their music and philosophy, were considered as elements of typical national representation: their manner of speaking, dressing, moving, singing and dancing, indeed, their music and their very philosophy, were considered by popular classes to be elements of mentality, worthy to be identified with. The music stimulated folklorism and populism and functioned ideologically to cover and conceal social and cultural antagonisms.
- Today, as the consequence of artistic popularization and nationalization of former subcultural styles, tango, flamenco and rebetika have lost much of their original notoriety and have become either national representations of regional folklore, or elements of the creation of transcultural musical styles within the phenomenon of world music.

As we can see, the existence of those marginalized social and ethnic groups (Gypsies along with cheats, robbers, beggars, prostitutes and souteneurs, immigrants, and so on) only influenced the latter musical styles in their origins. The *flamencos*, *lunfas* and *rebetes* were soon converted into models of *extravagant* behavior, represented above all by bohemian artists and imitated by members of (urban) lower and middle classes. In the course of stratification of the bourgeois society, these excluded 'others' became 'objects of desire' (Featherstone 1992: 283) and the identification with their artistic expressivity was received as a symbolic compensation for their social discrimination. According to the demands of the growing artistic market, the original, spontaneous music-styles were rapidly developed, transformed and adapted by professional or semi-professional musicians and dancers: the former wild and primitive music and dances received special attention and accentuation by the bohemian artists as specialists for subcultural behavior and emphasized sensual amusement. Given the Romantic appreciation of primitive, crude and unorthodox expressivity (e.g. of 'deep song'), related to the 'celebration of the *grotesque body* – fattening food, intoxicating drink, sexual promiscuity' (Featherstone 1992: 283; see also Mitchell 1994: 43 f.), the new genres responded to the psychology of the working and the new middle classes and to their need for erotic pleasure in a highly repressive environment. Hence, the craze for amusement or even for the melancholic thoughtfulness of working-class people was frequently criticized by factory owners as unproductive attitudes and idleness, as bohemianism or even anarchism. Voluptuousness and capitalistic labor-discipline did not mesh well.

Unlike the generally collective character of folkloric dances, the sensual attraction of the male and female body was cultivated and particularly pronounced by the new subcultural and highly individualistic popular genres as a mostly unconscious expression of ambiguous gender relations. Notorious in flamenco is the psychological drama of the male, involved hopelessly in the wickerwork of emotional relations between his mother and his bride as the reason both for his fear of castration and for his male-chauvinist reaction, which relates the flamenco personality with the alcohol-dominated *juerga*, the tough-guy image and the environment of prostitution. In the case of tango, it is the same (see Reichardt 1981: 167 ff.). Rebetika also deals with carnal desires of hashish-smoking and sexual attraction. Finally, Algerian rai confronts the explicit prohibition of alcohol and liberal sexual love in Muslim cultures as one of its main themes – similar to rock-music in the sixties, with its combination of drugs, sex and hot music.

Besides harboring these elements of individualism and corporeality, tango and flamenco, as well as rebetika – and probably other similar bohemian ethnic musics – can also be analyzed as sites of intercultural communication and interpellation (see Middleton 1989; Vila 1995; Frith 1996). According to this concept, it is the audience itself which assigns signification to the music. Collective identities consequently are constructed in the course of a bargain: 'What is adopted as a mark of identity has first to be negotiated' (Vester 1996: 99). This concept – based on earlier works of Collier and Thomas (1988), DeVos and Ross (1982), and McCall (1976) – allows one to analyze popular music styles as mass media supported artistic events that transmit symbols and significance, values, habits and rules of behavior all of which figure into the production of social identities. This 'sharing' of identifying attributes as a prerequisite of identification of the 'self' with 'the others' appeals, for example, to gender relations or to relations between different social or ethnic groups, national minorities or generations. In any case, one must attend to the historical background and situation where this aesthetically and musically edged production takes place. It is also necessary to include the dominant role of the market, as well as the socializing function of a music whose peculiarities are preformed by economic and hegemonic interests (see Adorno 1980).

Today's flamenco, for example, has changed very much with respect to its value and function in modern Andalusian culture, but it still represents an important medium for Andalusian (and Spanish) Gitano self-identification and cultural self-esteem. The origin of this kind of acculturated bargain of collective identities and self-concepts via popular music dates to the nineteenth century, when the disappearance of the *ancien régime* and the implementation of bourgeois social structure required new concepts of handling anachronistically ascribed statuses within the nation of formal equally entitled citizens. Capitalistic society staked out a claim for a new collective identity as an ideological basis for strengthening social cohesion in the face of increasing social and nationalistic conflicts. In general terms we can distinguish two fundamental concepts: a) positive or negative projection of certain attributes of personality to other social or ethnic groups or collectivities (self-assignment, assignment of 'the others'); b) interpretation of the existing culture system as a general frame of reference and point of departure for the conceptualization of a corresponding collective identity.

Both concepts result from the fixing of identities as a result of the definitions of social, ethnic or national groups as imaginary, fictitious collectivities in the sense of socialization patterns and models of identification, summarized in terms of cognitive psychology by Vester (Vester 1996: 85ff.). The relevant aspect here is the reference made in spite of the function of secondary socialization in this process. Popular music, seen as a cultural institution, belongs to this group of socializing agents. Nineteenth-century Romanticism turned it into a significant object of national cultural identification in society.

Part V

The individual, as well as the given stereotype of social perception and evaluation of everyday life, with its conscious and unconscious mechanisms and contents, is seen as the basis for the origin and the development of mentality as an empirical socio-psychological construct. Current sociological thought favors a conception of identity in terms of non-cognitive, slightly reflected, informally developed and applied opinions, orientations and habits. At this new horizon of thought, Bourdieu's concept of *habitus* is close to ours, especially with respect to the process of artistic creation which he describes as a singular way of merging an artist's individuality with a collective consciousness (see Bourdieu 1974: 132; also 1994: 277 ff.). But at the same time Bourdieu's concept allows for the communication of identity through corporeal expression as the basic condition of sensual perception of 'the other.' Therefore, according to these views, passionate musical styles are especially well disposed to serve as media for a sensual kind of inter-cultural communication, at the same time that they are used as empirical elements in ideology construction (see König 1967: 190 ff.). Due to their concreteness, such individual experiences of collective life are not only 'structuring structure' but also 'structured structure,' *opus operatum* and *modus operandi* (see Bourdieu 1977). But mentality is more than just a less-developed ideological mode of reality-perception: its relation with ideology is quite notorious, but its basic function has to be explained within the system of individual beliefs, orientations and habits related to the experience of daily life, where it reflects certain elements of the reference-frame of the person or group, the self-concept and the collective identity. Thus mentality must be seen as a category of mediation, inter-vention and transmission between personal and collective identity. Meanwhile, ideology tends to use these ambiguous, often contradictory but finally realistic visions in order to develop essentialist concepts of perception and evaluation of reality (e.g., ethnic groups, the nation, class and so on), as well as to shape mentalized personal identity. Ideologies use existing mentalities to become popular. At the same time, these mentalities reflect popularized ideological influences (hegemony) in everyday life.

Part VI

Concrete daily life experiences, like popular music and dance, with their capacity to stimulate socio-psychological and unconscious social mech-anisms, are of great importance for collective identity construction seen as the result of interpellation. They may work or be made to work in a way that helps to get the person into the mood, with the (intended) effect of creating or facilitating personal disposition to perceive the musical message or the virtual situation in a stereotypical way, that is, as elements of confirmation and verification of mentalized concepts of personal experience and beliefs. In accordance with our basic concept of explan-ation of passionate ethnic music-styles, we can conclude that popular music-styles are aesthetic conceptualizations of what should be considered as *identity-generators*. They participate and intervene in the construction of prosaic, common-sense identity concepts. Mass-produced popular music expresses the apparent reality of common desire. In this sense, popular musical styles can be considered as conscious and/or unconscious proceedings (bargains), the effect of which is the conversion of sensual pleasure into a basis of collective identification with their constructed message. And this kind of event turns out to be one of the possible mechanisms needed to define self identity and collective identity. Vester offers numerous psychological explanations: the concept of 'possible selves,' in accordance with the writings of Markus & Nurius (1986; see Vester 1996: 87), of 'self-identifications' (Schlenker and Weigold 1989; see Vester 1996: 88), and of 'self-narratives' or 'self-guides.' Other concepts point to the representation of basic social conditions and habits as mechanisms related to personality that create, disseminate and propagate 'conditional patterns' (see Vester 1996: 90), which, with the help of 'nuclear scenes' (Carlson 1981; see Vester 1996), can induce virtual reactions. Hence, from the point of view of social constructivism, ideology and mentality turn out to be unique and complex mechanisms of imaginary reality-creation; and it is especially the ethnic music-style, which softens or wipes out the difference between imagination and reality.

Part VII

If we consider modern popular music as an element of intercultural communication, we have to recognize that this identity-bargain between the 'self' and 'the others' (one's own group and the strangers) not only characterizes personal development, but particularly collective (cultural) identity. For example, we can explain the appearance of flamenco as a pronounced Gypsy style of music by way of two independent historical facts: the social and cultural integration of the Spanish Gypsies after 1783 on the one side, and the romantic European nineteenth-century Gypsy-vogue on the other. From this moment on, popular music, poetry and the popular theatre became public spheres and proceedings of mutual des-cription and definition of *gitanos* and *payos*, as hundreds of vaudeville performances (*tonadillas escénicas* and *sainetes*) demonstrate (see Subirá 1929, Caro Baroja 1969, Salaün 1983). Henceforth, and in accordance with the cultural change, we notice the paradoxical effect not only of a widespread European Gypsy-vogue, but also of an increasing gypsyfi-cation of the Gypsies (see Steingress 1993: 179) during the century of Romanticism as an effect of appellation and narratives in Andalusian identity construction. The real Gypsies reacted on public (and hegemonic) ascription and adapted themselves once more to the image produced parti-cularly in the popular theatre as society's identity-generator. As we can see, the artistically constructed 'structuring structure' produced the two Andalusian 'races' and their cultural peculiarities that Antonio Machado wrote about (Machado y Alvarez). Although the image of the *flamenco-habitus* was based in some way on real experiences and observations of Gypsy-life, these were accentuated, transformed and accommodated at the same moment to common **stereotypes**. The case of flamenco shows us how intercultural communication, mediated by the theatre as an important institution of the public sphere in civic society, may be conceptualized as an instrument which reduces social complexity (Luhmann 1994), but at the same time provokes the fixation of racial, national and/or ethnic prejudices. Therefore, in the same way as we consider music as an important element within this process 'to get people closer to each other,' we should not forget that the ethnic musical styles are based on mentality- and identity-concepts as *differentiating factors*.

This identity-creating differentiation not only refers to national or ethnic peculiarities, but also to gender relations in society: the highly emphasized lascivious attitude and posture, as well as simulated eroticism, the complementary aggressive encounter and the symbolic power-fight of the male and female dancers in the case of flamenco and tango, as well as the mostly solitary role of the male dancer or female belly-dancer of rebetika refer to different models of gender relations within different socio-cultural contexts. But ethnic musical styles also symbolize the significance of relations between ethnic groups such as *gitanos* and *payos* (flamenco), continental-Greeks and oriental-Greeks (rebetika) or *criollos* and *inmigrantes* (tango). The same happens in the case of young and old generations, between mother and son, friends, families and clans, regions and so forth. Not to forget the representation of social class relations such as those between the bourgeois and proletarian and/or subproletarian environment, between the powerful (often represented by the police or the judge) and the powerless, legitimacy and illegitimacy, the desire and the normative.

The effects of passionate musical styles are due to crystallization of attitudes and beliefs that refer to stereotypical concepts as well as to the collective identity of the individual, and to the function of these concepts as general models of cultural orientation. They usually are rationalized, although their origins are to be found in the collective unconsciousness as the deposit of collective inhibition and repression of needs: people always act in accordance with conscious and unconscious concepts; and music can arouse pent up energies and provoke states of outside-oriented ecstasy (*delirio*/flamenco) or experiences of an inner-directed personal psychological drama (*duende*/flamenco). But these socially induced and the mentalized psychological phenomena have to be analyzed in dialectical relation to ideology as a rationalized conceptualization of identifiable mentality-factors according to hegemonic interests.

Part VIII

As the history of the three ethnic music-styles demonstrates, modern society always considered popular music as an important element of mass manipulation, and this might be the decisive reason for the tenacity of neo-Romanticism, not only in nationalist, fascist and other totalitarian movements, but also operating within post-modernism. The actual transcultural manipulation of originally regional, ethnic music-styles as merchandise on the global market of world music has reduced considerably their value as objects of national or ethnic identification. Nowadays, identification refers to categories of markets and fans all over the world, who share their dedication to the same musical style as a collective attitude. The logic of the market has transformed those music-styles in accordance with world-wide musical trends. Given such denationalization it is no wonder that irritated fans recently have begun to demand respect for purity in view of the growing anxiety of young, creative flamenco artists. We can understand this demand as a new manifestation of the well-known necessity of popular objects of identification – in the same way as football and other sports – especially in times when the established and already traditional national and ethnic differences disappear or are submitted to a general devaluation in view of cultural standardization and worldwide hegemonization of Western civilization. Economic dynamics have started to abolish the nineteenth-century nation states and bring about the current postmodern identity crisis also in popular music. As one of the results of the internationalization of the markets, relations and means of expression provoke new problems related to the increasing dysfunctionality of traditional national identity concepts. This might be the primary reason why flamenco has shown a dispersing tendency: while the flamenco avant-garde (Enrique Morente, Juan Peña *El Lebrijano*, José Monge *El Camarón*, Paco de Lucía, *Tomatito* and others) have favored a polychromatic, multiform and still undefined hybridization of the genre in order to save it from fossilization by flamenco classicists (reassumed by Antonio Mairena between 1950 and 1970), the classicists – referred to more polemically as 'purists' – consider this innovative attitude to be fraudulent and even require public guaranties in order to save (once again) the flamenco purity that has been regarded as the most authentic manifestation of Andalusian uniqueness, its sign of identity and even its virtual banner. The perishability of life as a loyal companion to sorrow and eternal object of contemplation of human existence finds its echo in flamenco, expressed in the *copla* sung by *Bernardo el de los Lobitos* in tango-mode:

'Yo me fié de la verdad
y la verdad a mí me engañó,
cuando la verdad me engaña:
¿de quién me voy a fiar?

I trusted in the truth,
And it fooled me;
If truth itself plays me for a fool,
Who can I trust?

References

Abbate, C. (1991), *Unsung Voices: Opera and Musical Narrative in the Nineteenth Century*, Princeton: Princeton University Press.

Abercrombie, N., Lash, S., and Longhurst, B. (1992), 'Popular Representation: Recasting Realism,' in S. Lash and J. Friedman (eds), *Modernity and Identity*, Cambridge: Blackwell, pp. 115–40.

Adorno, T.W. (1980), 'Zur Gesellschaftlichen Lage der Musik,' in M. Horkheimer (ed.), *Zeitschrift für Sozialforschung*, München: Deutscher Taschenbuch Verlag.

Archetti, E. (1994), 'Models of Masculinity in the Poetics of Argentinian Tango,' in E. P. Archetti (ed.), *Exploring the Written: Anthropology and the Multiplicity of Writing*, Oslo: Scandinavian University Press, pp. 97–122.

Armbrust, W. (1996), *Mass Culture and Modernism in Egypt*, New York: Cambridge University Press.

Astarita, *G.J. (1981), Pasual Contursi, Vida y Obra*, Buenos Aires: Ediciones La Campana.

Attali, J. (1985), *Noise: The Political Economy of Music*, Minneapolis: University of Minnesota Press.

Badger, R. (1995), *A Life in Ragtime: A Biography of James Reese Europe*, New York: Oxford University Press.

Balderston, D. (1995), 'The "Fecal Dialectic": Homosexual Panic and the Origins of Writing in Borges. In 'Entiendes?,' E. Bergmann and P. Smith (eds), *Queer Readings, Hispanic Writings*, Durham: Duke University Press, pp. 29–45.

Bates, H. and Bates, L. (1936), *La Historia del Tango*, Buenos Aires: Taller Gráfico de la Compania General Fabril Vinanciera.

Baudrillard, J. (1992), *L'Illusion de la fin ou la Grève des Événements*, Paris: Éditions Galilée.

Bederman, G. (1995), *Manliness and Civilization*, Chicago: The University of Chicago Press.

Berlin, E. (1994), *King of Ragtime: Scott Joplin and His Era*, New York: Oxford University Press.

Berlin, I. (1990), *The Crooked Timber of Humanity*, New York: Knopf.

—— (1996), *The Sense of Reality*, New York: Farrar, Straus and Giroux.

Blas Vega, J. (1987), *Los Cafés Cantantes de Sevilla*, Madrid: Editorial Cinterco.

—— and Ríos Ruiz (1991), *Diccionario Enciclopédico Ilustrado del Flamenco*, Madrid: Editorial Cinterco.

Bohlman, P. (1988), *The Study of Folk Music in the Modern World*, Bloomington: Indiana University Press.

Borges, J. (1970), *The Aleph and Other Stories, 1933–1969*, T. di Giovanni (ed.), New York: E. P. Dutton.

—— (1989), *Obras Completas*, Buenos Aires: Emece Editories.

Boscagli, M. (1996), *Eye on the Flesh: Fashions of Masculinity in the Early Twentieth Century*, Boulder: Westview Press.

Bourdieu, P. (1974), Zur Soziologie der symbolischen Formen, Frankfurt: Suhrkamp.

—— (1977), *Outline of a Theory of Practice*, New York: Cambridge University Press.

—— (1979), *La Distinction: Critique Social du Jugement*, Paris: Les Editions de Minuit.

—— (1994), La Distinction: Critique Social du Jugement, Paris: Les Editions de Minuit, Edition 5.

Bowen, L. (1911), *Our Most Popular Recreation Controlled by Liquor Interests. A Study of Public Dance Halls*, Chicago: Juvenile Protective Association of Chicago.

Brandes, S. (1980), *Metaphors of Masculinity: Sex and Status in Andalusian Folklore*, Philadelphia: University of Pennsylvania Press.

Burt, R. (1995), *The Male Dancer: Bodies, Spectacle, Sexualities*, New York: Routledge.

Butler, J. (1990), *Gender Trouble: Feminism and the Subversion of Identity*, New York: Routledge.

—— (1993), *Bodies That Matter: On the Discursive Limits of 'Sex'*, New York: Routledge.

—— (1995), 'Melancholy Gender/Refused Identification,' in M. Berger, B. Wallis, and S. Watson (eds), *Constructing Masculinity*, New York: Routledge, pp. 21–3.

Caballero, A. (1995), 'Historia del Flamenco,' *El País*, 7 July 1995, pp. 27–31.

Canaro, F. (1957), *Mis Bodas de Oro con el Tango y mis Memorias, 1906–1956*, Buenos Aires: CESA Talleres Gráficos.

Canton, D. (1972), *Gardel ¿A quien le canta?*, Buenos Aires: Ediciones de la Flor.

Carbajo Gutierrez, F. (1990), *La Copla Flamenca y la Lírica de Tipo Popular*, Madrid: Cinterco.

Carloni, F. (1988), 'Mujer, Fiesta y Espaco,' *II Congreso de Folklore Andaluz*, Seville: N.P., pp. 127–32.

Caro Baroja, J. (1969), *Ensayo sobre la Literatura de Cordel*, Madrid: Revista de Occidente.

Carrillo Alonso, A. (1988a), *Las Huellas del Romancero y del Refranero en la Lírica del Flamenco*, Granada: Editorial Don Quijote.

—— (1988b), *La Poesía Tradicional en el Cante Andaluz. De las Jarchas al Cantar*, Sevilla: Editoriales Andaluzas Unidas.

Castle, I. (1919), *My Husband*, New York: Charles Scribner's Sons

Castle, V. and Castle, I. (1914), *Modern Dancing*, New York: Harper and Row.

Castro, D. (1982), 'The Quest for Immigrants: Argentina, Italy, and Immigration, 1860–1914,' *Paesi mediterranei e Paesi mediterranei e America Latina*, Rome: Centro di Studi Americanisti.

—— (1991), *The Argentine Tango as Social History: 1880–1955*, Lewiston: Edwin Mellen Press.

—— (1994), 'Women in the World of the Tango,' in G. Yeager (ed.), *Confronting Change, Challenging Tradition: Women in Latin American History*, Wilmington, Delaware: Scholarly Resources Books, pp. 66–76.

Cespi, B. (1995), 'Imagenes Fotograficas de Carlos Gardel,' in E. Moreno Cha (ed.), *Tango: Tuyo, Mio y Nuestro*, Buenos Aires: Instituto Nacional de Antropología y Pensamiento Latinoamericano, pp. 49–56.

Chab, N. (1995), 'Nacimiento y Muerte: las Dos Puntas de un Enigma,' in E. Moreno Cha (ed.), *Tango: Tuyo, Mio y Nuestro*, Buenos Aires: Instituto Nacional de Antropología y Pensamiento Latinoamericano, pp. 37–43.

Chinarro, A. (1965), *El Tango y su Rebeldía*, Buenos Aires: Continental-Service.

Cohen, A. (1985), *The Symbolic Construction of Community*, New York: Routledge.

Collier, M. and Thomas, M. (1988), 'Cultural Identity. An Interpretive Perspective,' in Y. Yun Kim and W. B. Gudykunst (eds), *Cross-Cultural Adaptation, International and Intercultural Communication Annual*, Vol. 11, Newbury Park: Sage Publications, pp. 99–120.

Collier, S. (1986), *Carlos Gardel*, Pittsburgh: University of Pittsburgh Press.

Connerton, P. (1989), *How Societies Remember*, New York: Cambridge University Press.

Cook, S. (forthcoming, 1998), 'Watching Our Step: Embodying Research, Telling Stories,' *Audible Traces*, Geneva.

Corbin, J.R. and Corbin, M.P. (1987), *Urbane Thought: Culture and Class in an Andalusian City*, Brookfield: Gower Publishing Company.

Corsini, I. (1959), *Ignacio Corsini, Mi padre*, Buenos Aires: Todo Es Historiam.

Couselo, J. and Chierico, O. (1964), *Gardel, Mito-realidad: Ubicación y Antología*, Buenos Aires: A. Peña-Lillo.

Cowan, J. (1990), *Dance and the Body Politic in Northern Greece*, Princeton: Princeton University Press.

Crapanzano, V. (1986), 'Hermes' Dilemma: The Masking of Subversion in Ethnographic Description,' in J. Clifford and G. Marcus (eds), *Writing Culture: The Poetics and Politics of Ethnography*, Berkeley: University of California Press, pp. 51–76.

Delias, A. (1988), *Anesthw Deliaw 1912–1944*, (Notes and Lyrics, LP Recording, Athens: Afoi Falhrea 98.

Desmond, J. (1991), 'Dancing Out the Difference: Cultural Imperialism and Ruth St. Denis's 'Radha' of 1906,' *Signs* 17 (Autumn).

—— (1997), 'Embodying Difference: Issues in Dance and Cultural Studies,' in J. Desmond (ed.), *Meaning in Motion: New Cultural Studies of Dance*, Durham: Duke University Press.

Deval, F. (1989), *Le Flamenco et Ses Valeurs*, Paris: Editions Aubier.

DeVos, G. and L. Ross (1975), 'Ethnic Identity: Vessel of Meaning and Emblem of Contrast,' in G. De Vos and L. Ross (eds), *Ethnic Identity*, Chicago: University of Chicago Press, pp. 363–90.

duBois, P. (1991), *Torture and Truth*, New York: Routledge.

Dunn, L. and Jones, N. (eds) (1994), *Embodied Voices: Representing Female Vocality in Western Culture*, New York: Cambridge University Press.

Eagleton, T. (1990), *The Ideology of the Aesthetic*, Cambridge: Blackwell.

Erenberg, L. (1981), *Steppin' Out: New York Nightlife and the Transformation of American Culture 1890–1930*, Chicago: The University of Chicago Press.

Escardó, F. (1966), *Geografía de Buenos Aires*, Buenos Aires: Editorial Universitaria de Buenos Aires.

Eugenides, J. (1998), 'The Burning of Smyrna,' *The New Yorker*, 73 (41): 62–7.

Falla, M. de (1988), El Cante Jondo, *Manuel de Falla: Escritos sobre Música y Músicos*, Madrid: Colección Austral.

Faulkner, T. (1894), *From the Ball-Room to Hell: Facts About Dancing*, Chicago: The Church Press.

Featherstone, M. (1991), *Consumer Culture and Postmodernism*, Newbury Park: Sage.

—— (1992), Postmodernism and the Aestheticization of Everyday Life, in S. Lash and J. Friedman (eds), *Modernity & Identity*, Cambridge: Blackwell, pp. 265–90.

Fernández Bañuls, J, María Pérez Orozco, J. (1983), *La Poesía Flamenca Lírica en Andaluz*, Sevilla: Consejería de Cultura.

Ferris, H. (1940), *Five Girls Who Dared*, New York: Macmillan.

Finnegan, R. (1989), *The Hidden Musicians: Music-Making in an English Town*, New York: Cambridge University Press.

Floyd, S. (1992), 'Ring Shout,' *Black Music Research Journal*, 11: 271.

—— (1995), *The Power of Black Music*, New York: Oxford University Press.

Folino, N. (1983), *Barceló, Ruggierito y el Populísmo Oligárquico*, Buenos Aires: Ediciones de la Flor.

Foster, S. (1995), 'An Introduction to Moving Bodies: Choreographing History,' in S.L. Foster (ed.), *Choreographing History*, Bloomington: Indiana University Press.

—— (1996), 'The Ballerina's Phallic Pointe,' in S. Foster (ed.), *Corporealities: Dancing Knowledge, Culture and Power*, London: Routledge, pp. 1–24.

Fox, I. (1997), *La Invención de Espana*, Madrid: Ediciones Cátedra.

Frank, W. (1969), 'America hispana,' in T. de Lara and I. L. Roncetti de Panti (eds), *El Tema del Tango en la Literatura Argentina*, Buenos Aires: Ediciones Culturales Argentinas, Ministerio de Educación y Justicia, Direccion General de Cultural, pp. 359–70.

Freud, S. (1982), 'Das Unbehagen in der Kultur' in *Studienausgabe. Band IX. Fragen der Gesellschaft. Ursprünge der Religion*, Frankfurt am Main: Fischer.

Frith, S. (1990), "What is good music?," in J. Shepherd (ed.), *Alternative Musicologies/Les Musicologies Alternatives*, *Canadian University Music Review*, (Special Number), pp. 92–102.

—— (1996), *Performing Rites: On the Value of Popular Music*, Cambridge: Harvard University Press.

Garcia Canclini, N. (1995), *Hybrid Cultures: Strategies for Entering and Leaving Modernity*, Minneapolis: University of Minnesota Press.

García Gómez, G. (1993), *Cante Flamenco, Cante Minero, Una Interpretación Sociocultural*, Barcelona: Antropos.

García Jiménez, F. (1976), *Carlos Gardel y su Epoca*, Buenos Aires: Ediciones Corregidor.

García Lorca, F. (1984), Importancia Histórica y Artística del Primitivo Canto Andaluz Llamado Cante Jondo, *Federico García Lorca. Conferencias I*, Madrid: Alianza.

—— (1984), Juego y Teoría del Duende, *Federico García Lorca. Conferencias II*, Madrid: Alianza.

Gauntlett, S. (1989), 'Orpheus in the Criminal Underworld: Myth in and about Rebetika,' *Mantatoforos*, 34, pp. 7–49.

Gay, P. (1995), *The Naked Heart: The Bourgeois Experience, Victoria to Freud*, New York: W.W. Norton.

Geertz, C. (1986), 'Making Experiences, Authoring Selves,' in V. Turner and E. Bruner (eds), *The Anthropology of Experience*, Chicago: University of Chicago Press, pp. 373–80.

Gelardo, J. and Belade, F. (1985), *Sociedad y Cante Flamenco. El Cante de las Minas*, Murcia: Editorial Regional de Murcia.

Giannuli, D. (1995), 'Greeks or "Strangers at Home": The Experiences of Ottoman Greek Refugees During their Exodus to Greece, 1922–3,' *Journal of Modern Greek Studies*, 13 (2).

Gill, S. (1987), *Mother Earth: An American Story*, Chicago: University of Chicago Press.

Gilmore, D. (1980), *The People of the Plain: Class and Community in Lower Andalusia*, New York: Columbia University Press.

—— (1990a), *Manhood in the Making: Cultural Concepts of Masculinity*, New Haven: Yale University Press.

—— (1990b), 'Men and Women in Southern Spain: "Domestic Power" Revisited,' *American Anthropologist*, 92: 953–70.

—— (1995), 'The Scholar Minstrels of Andalusia: Deep Oratory, or the Carnivalesque Upside Down,' *Man*, 1: 561–80.

—— (1996), 'Above and Below: Toward a Social Geometry of Gender,' *American Anthropologist*, 98(1): 54–66.

Gilroy, P. (1993), *The Black Atlantic: Modernity and Double Consciousness*, New York: Verso.

Gobello, J. (1995), 'Crónica del Tango,' *Un Siglo de Tango!* CD-ROM, Buenos Aires: Sierra 3.

—— and Bossio, J. (eds) (1979), *Tangos, letras, y letristas*, Buenos Aires: Editorial Plus Ultra.

González Climent, A. (1964), *Flamencología: Toros, Cante y Baile*, Madrid: Escelicer.

Goodwin, S.W. (1994), 'Wordsworth and the Romantic Voice: The Poet's Song and the Prostitute's Cry,' in L. Dunn and N. Jones (eds), *Embodied Voices: Representing Female Vocality in Western Culture*, New York: Cambridge University Press, pp. 65–79.

Gould, E. (1996), *The Fate of Carmen*, Baltimore: Johns Hopkins University Press.

Graham, H. (1995), 'Women and Social Change,' in H. Graham and J.

Labanyi (eds), *Spanish Cultural Studies: An Introduction*, New York: Oxford University Press.

Grande, F. (1979), *Memoria Del Flamenco*, Madrid: Espasa-Calpe, S.A.

—— (1992), 'Teoría del Duende,' in F. Grande (ed.), *Los Intelectuales ante el Flamenco, Cuadernos Hispanoamericanos 9/10*, Madrid: Gráficas, pp. 81–109.

Habermas, J. (1990), *Die nachholende Revolution. Kleine politische Schriften VII*, Frankfurt am Main: Suhrkamp.

Hacking, I. (1995), *Rewriting the Soul: Multiple Personality and the Sciences of Memory*, Princeton: Princeton University Press.

Hamm, C. (1996), 'Alexander and His Band', *American Music*, 14 (Spring).

Handler, R. and Linnekin, J. (1984), 'Tradition, Genuine or Spurious,' *Journal of American Folklore*, 97: 273–290.

Handy. W.C. (1941), *Father of the Blues*, New York: Macmillan.

Hanna, J. (1988), *Dance, Sex and Gender: Sign of Identity, Dominance, Defiance, and Desire*, Chicago: University of Chicago Press.

Hebdige, D. (1979), *Subculture: The Meaning of Style*, London: Methuen.

Herzfeld, M. (1986), 'Within and Without: The Category of Female: The Ethnography of Modern Greece,' in J. Dubisch (ed.), *Gender and Power in Rural Greece*, Princeton: Princeton University Press, pp. 215–33.

—— (1987), *Anthropology Through the Looking Glass: Critical Ethnography in the Margins of Europe*, New York: Cambridge University Press.

Hirschon, R. (1989), *Heirs of the Greek Catastrophe*, Oxford: Clarendon Press.

Holst, G. (1977), *Road to Rembetika: Music of a Greek sub-culture. Songs of Love, Sorrow and Hashisch*, Athens: Anglo-Helenic Publishing.

—— (1979), *Theodorakis: Myth and Politics in Modern Greek Music*, Amsterdam: Adolph M. Hakkert.

—— (1990), 'Resisting Translation: Slang and Subversion in the Rebetika,' *Journal of Modern Greek Studies*, 6, pp. 183–96.

—— Warhaft (1992), *Women's Lament and Greek Literature*, New York: Routledge.

Hooper, J. (1987), *The Spaniards: A Portrait of the New Spain*, London: Penguin Books.

Hutcheon, L. (1994), *Irony's Edge: The Theory and Politics of Irony*, New York: Routledge.

—— (1996), *Opera: Desire, Disease, Death*, Lincoln: University of Nebraska Press.

Huyssen, A. (1986), *After the Great Divide: Modernism, Mass Culture and Postmodernism*, Bloomington: Indiana University Press.

Iser, W. (1974), *The Implied Reader: Patterns of Communication in Prose Fiction from Bunyan to Beckett*, Baltimore: Johns Hopkins University Press.

Johnson, J. (1995), *Listening in Paris: A Cultural History*, Berkeley: University of California Press.

Kartomi, M. (1981), 'The Process and Results of Musical Culture Contact: A Discussion of Terminology and Concepts,' *Ethnomusicology*, 25: 227–49.

Kazantzakis, N. (1965), *Journey to the Morea*, New York: Simon and Schuster.

Kellner, D. (1992), 'Popular Culture and the Construction of Postmodern Identities,' in S. Lash and J. Friedman (eds), *Modernity and Identity*, Cambridge: Blackwell, pp. 141–77.

Kellogg, J. (1915), *Neurasthenia or Nervous Exhaustion*, Battle Creek: Good Health Publishing Co.

Kendall, E. (1979), *Where She Danced: The Birth of American Art-Dance*, Berkeley: University of California Press.

Kierkegaard, S. (1968), *The Concept of Irony, with Constant Reference to Socrates*, Bloomington: Indiana University Press.

Kimball, R. and Bolcom, W. (1973), *Reminiscing with Sissle and Blake*, New York: Viking.

Kittler, W. (1991), *Discourse Networks, 1800/1900*, Stanford: Stanford University Press.

König, R. (1967), *Soziologie*, Frankfurt am Main: Fischer.

Kramer, L. (1990), *Music as Cultural Practice, 1800–1900*, Berkeley: University of California Press.

Kraut, A. (1994), *Silent Travelers: Germs, Genes, and the 'Immigrant Menace'*, Baltimore: Johns Hopkins University Press.

Kunadis, P. and Papaioannou, S. (1981), 'H Diskografia tou Rempetikou sth Smurna-Polh prin apo to 1922,' *Mousikh*, 38: 39–45; 39: 43–8.

—— (1981), 'Anyologia apo thn Diskogrpafia tou Rempetikou Sth Smurnh-Polh Prin apo to 1922,' *Mousikh*, 40: 40–5; 41: 28–34; 42: 24–7; 43: 20–2; 44: 20–5; 48: 33–9.

Lacan, J. (1985), 'La significacion del falo,' *Escritos II*, Buenos Aires: Siglo Veintiuno Editories, pp. 665–75.

Lara, T. and Inés L. Roncitti de Panti (1961), *El Tema del Tango en la Literatura Argentina*, Buenos Aires: Ediciones Culturales Argentina.

Larroca, J. (1981), *Entre Cortes y Apiladas: Los Tangos de Prosapia Burrera*, Buenos Aires: Ediciones Cruz del Sur.

Lauretis, T. de (1994), *The Practice of Love: Lesbian Sexuality and Perverse Desire*, Bloomington: Indiana University Press.

Lavaur, L. (1976), *Teoría Romántica del Cante Flamenco*, Madrid: Editorial Nacional.

Leppert, R. (1993), *The Sight of Sound: Music, Representation, and the History of the Body*, Berkeley: University of California Press.

LeRider, J. (1990), *Das Ende der Illusion. Zur Kritik der Moderne*, Wien: ÖBV.

Lévi-Strauss, C. (1973), *Anthropologie Structurale*, Paris: Librairie Plon.

Levine, L. (1988) *High Brow/Low Brow: The Emergence of Cultural Hierarchy in America*, Cambridge: Harvard University Press.

Lipsitz, G. (1994), *Dangerous Crossroads: Popular Music, Postmodernism and the Poetics of Place*, New York: Verso.

López-Peña, A. (1965), *Teoría del Argentino*, Buenos Aires: Editorial Huemul.

Lott, E (1993), *Love and Theft: Blackface Minstrelsy and the American Working Class*, New York: Oxford.

Luhmann, N. (1994), 'Inklusion und Exklusion,' in H. Berding (ed.), *Nationales Bewusstsein und kollektive Identität. Studien zur Entwicklung des kollektiven Bewusstseins in der Neuzeit 2*, Frankfurt am Main: Suhrkamp, pp. 15–45.

Lutz, T. (1991), *American Nervousness, 1903: An Anecdotal History*, Ithaca: Cornell University Press.

McCall, G. J. (1976), 'Communication and Negotiated Identity,' *Communication*, 2: 173–84.

McCarren, F. (1995), 'The Symptomatic Act Circa 1900: Hysteria, Hypnosis, Electricity, Dance,' *Critical Inquiry*, 21: 748–74.

McClary, S. (1991), *Feminine Endings: Music, Gender, and Sexuality*, Minneapolis: University of Minnesota Press.

McNeill, W. (1995), *Keeping Together in Time*, Cambridge: Harvard University Press.

Machado y Alvarez, A. (1996), *Colección de cantes flamencos. Recogidos y anotados por Antonio Machado y Alvarez 'Demófilo,'* E. Baltanás (ed), Sevilla: Portada Editorial.

—— (1982), *De Soledades. Escritos Flamencos, 1879*, in A. Raya and V. Márquez (eds), Córdoba: Ediciones Demófilo.

Malefyt, T. (1997), *Gendered Authenticity: The Invention of Flamenco Tradition in Seville, Spain*, Unpublished Ph.D.dissertation, Providence, RI.: Brown University.

Malone, J. (1996), *Steppin' on the Blues: The Visible Rhythms of African American Dance*, Urbana: University of Illinois Press.

Manfredi Cano, D. (1955), *Geografía del Cante Jondo*, Cádiz: Universidad de Cádiz.

Manuel, P. (1993), *Cassette Culture: Popular Music and Technology in Northern India*, Chicago: University of Chicago Press.

Manzi, H. (1947), 'Prologue,' Francisco García Jiméz, *Vida de Carlos Gardel*, Buenos Aires: Editorial Crismar.

Marbury, E. (1923), *My Crystal Ball*, New York: Boni and Liveright.

Markus, H. and Nurius, P (1986), 'Possible Selves,' *American Psychologist*, 41 (9): 954–69.

Martínez Estrada, E. (1957), *La Cabeza de Goliat: Microscopia de Buenos Aires*, Buenos Aires: Editorial Nova.

Mascia, A. (1970), *Política y Tango*, Buenos Aires: Editorial Paides.

Matamoro, B (1969), *La Ciudad del Tango: Tango Histórico y Sociedad*, Buenos Aires: Editorial Governa.

Melgar Reina, L. and Marín Rújula, A. (1988), *Arte, Genio y Duende: Notas Flamencas*, Cordoba: Cajasur.

Mercado, J. (1982), *La Seguidilla Gitana. Un Ensayo Sociológico y Literario*, Madrid: Taurus.

Meregazo, J. (1971), 'Defensa humana de Carlos Gardel,' *Estudios de Tango*, 5 (Oct–Nov 1971), p. 210.

Middleton, R. (1989), *The Study of Popular Music*, Philadelphia: Open University Press.

Miller Frank, F. (1995), *The Mechanical Song: Women, Voice and the Artificial in Nineteenth-Century French Narrative*, Stanford: Stanford University Press.

Mitchell, T. (1994), *Flamenco, Deep Song*, New Haven: Yale University Press.

Molina, R., Mairena, A. (1963), *Mundo y Formas del Cante Flamenco*, Granada-Sevilla: Librería Al-Andalus.

Morena, M. (1983), *Historia Artística de Carlos Gardel*, Buenos Aires: Ediciones Corregidor.

Moreno Cha, E. (ed.) (1995), *Tango Tuyo, Mio y Nuestro*, Buenos Aires: Instituto Nacional de Antropologia y Pensamiento Latinoamericano.

Moreno Navarro, I. (1982), 'Hacia la Generalización de la Conciencia de Identidad,' in A. Miguel Bernal (ed.), *Historia de Andalucía*, Madrid: Cupsa.

—— (1993), *Andalucía: Identidad y Cultura*, Málaga: Librería Agora.

—— (1996), 'El Flamenco en la Cultura Andaluza,' in C. Cruces Roldán (ed.), *El Flamenco: Identidades Sociales, Ritual y Patrimonio Cultural*, Sevilla: Centro Andaluz de Flamenco, pp. 15–33.

Morris, I. (ed.) (1994), *Classical Greece: Ancient Histories and Modern*

Archaeologies, Cambridge: Cambridge University Press.

Mylonas, K. (1984), *Istoria tou Ellhnikou Tragoudiou, vol 1 (1824–1960)*, Athens: Kedros.

Ortega y Gasset, J. (1964), *Obras completas*, Madrid: Editorial Revista de Occidente.

Ortiz, F. (1940), *Contrapunteo cubano del tabaco y azúcar*, La Habana: G. Montero.

Ortiz Nuevo, J. (1990), *Se Sabe Algo? Viaje al Conocimiento al Arte Flamenco en la Prensa Sevilliana del XIX*, Sevilla: Editorial El Carro del Nieve.

—— (1996), *Alegato contra la Pureza*, Barcelona: Libros PM.

Ortner, S. (1974), 'Is Female to Male as Nature Is to Culture?,' in M. Rosaldo and L. Lamphere (eds), *Woman, Culture and Society*, Cambridge: Cambridge University Press, pp. 67–88.

—— and Whitehead, H. (1981), 'Introduction: Accounting for Sexual Meanings,' in S. Ortner and H. Whitehead (eds), *Sexual Meanings: The Cultural Construction of Gender and Sexuality*, Cambridge: Cambridge University Press, pp. 4–5.

Parker, A., Russo, M., Sommer, D. Yaeger, P. (eds) (1992), *Nationalisms and Sexualities*, New York: Routledge.

Peiss, K. (1986), *Cheap Amusements*, Philadelphia: Temple University Press.

Pelinski, R. (1995), 'Le Tango Nomade,' in R. Pelinski (ed.), *Tango Nomade. Etudes sur le Tango Transculturel*, Montréal: Triptique, pp. 25–70.

—— (1997) 'Homología, Interpelación y Narratividad en los Procesos de Identificación por Medio de la Música,' (unpublished manuscript).

Perry, E. (1985), 'The General Motherhood of the Commonwealth: Dance Hall Reform in the Progressive Era,' *American Quarterly*, 37 (Winter).

—— (1987), *Belle Moskowitz: Feminine Politics and the Exercise of Power in the Age of Alfred E. Smith*, New York: Oxford University Press.

Pescatello, A. (1976), *Power and Pawn: The Female in Iberian Families, Societies, and Cultures*, London: Greenwood Press.

Petrides, T. (1976), Greek Dances and How to Do Them, Athens: Lycabettus Press.

Petropoulos, I. (1968), *Rembetika Tragoudia*: Athens.

Phelan, P. (1996), 'Dance and the History of Hysteria,' in S. L. Foster (ed.), *Corporealities: Dancing Knowledge, Culture and Power*, New York: Routledge.

Pohren, D. (1980), *A Way of Life*, Madrid: Spanish Studies Society.

References

Portogalo, P. (1957), *Letra para Juan Tango*, Buenos Aires: Talleres Gráficos.

Quintana B. and Floyd, L. (1972), *¡Que Gitano! Gypsies of Southern Spain*, Stanford: Holt, Rinehart and Winston.

Puertas Cruse, R. (1959), *Psicopátologia del tango*, Buenos Aires: Editorial Sophos.

Radano, R. (forthcoming), 'Hot Fantasies: American Modernism and the Idea of Black Rhythm,' *Music and the Racial Imagination*, Chicago, University of Chicago Press.

Real Academia Española (1992), *Diccionario de la Lengua Espanola*, Madrid: Real Academia Española.

Reichardt, D. (1984), *Tango. Verweigerung und Trauer. Kontexte und Texte*, Frankfurt am Main: Suhrkamp.

República Argentina, Senado de la Nación (1975), *El tango y Gardel*, Buenos Aires Publicacíon Official.

Ríos Ruiz, M. (1972), *Introducción al Cante Flamenco*, Madrid: Ediciones ISTMO.

Romano, E. (ed.) (1974), *Las Letras del Tango: Antología Cronológica*, Buenos Aires: Editorial Fundación Ross.

Root, D. (1996), *Cannibal Culture: Art, Appropriation and the Commodification of Difference*, Boulder: Westview Press.

Ropero Núñez, M. (1983), *El Léxico Andaluz de las Coplas Flamenca*, Sevilla: Alfar.

Rosaldo, M. (1974), 'Women, Culture, and Society: A Theoretical Overview,' in M. Rosaldo and L. Lamphere (eds), *Woman, Culture and Society*, Stanford: Stanford University Press, pp. 17–42.

Rosales, L. (1987), *La Angustia Llamada Andalucia*, Madrid: Cinterco.

Said, E. (1979), *Orientalism*, New York: Vintage Books.

Salas, H. (1986), *El Tango*, Buenos Aires: Planeta.

Salaün, S. (1983), 'El "Género Chico" o los Mecanismos de un Pacto Cultural,' *El teatro menor en España a Partir del Siglo XVI. Actas del Coloquio Celebrado en Madrid, 20–22 de Mayo de 1982*, Madrid: C.S.I.C., pp. 251–62.

—— (1990), *El Cuplé (1900–1936)*, Madrid: Espasa Calpe.

Salessi, J. (1991), 'Tango, Nacionalismo y Sexualidad: Buenos Aires, 1880–1914,' *Hispamérica*, 20 (60): 33–53.

—— (1997), 'Medics, Crooks, and Tango Queens: the National Appropriation of a Gay Tango,' in Celeste F. Delgado and J. Esteban MuBoz (eds), *Everynight Life: Culture and Dance in Latin/o America*, Durham: Duke University Press, pp. 141–74.

Salillas, R. (1898), *Hampa: Antropología Picaresca*, Madrid: Librería de Victoriano Suarez.

Savigliano, M. (1995), *Tango and the Political Economy of Passion: Tango, Exoticism and Decolonization*, Boulder: Westview Press.

—— (1996), 'Fragments for a Story of Tango Bodies: On Choreocritics and the Memory of Power,' in S. Foster (ed.), *Corporealities: Dancing Knowledge, Culture and Power*, New York: Routledge.

—— (1997), *Nocturnal Ethnographies: Following Cortázar in the Milongas of Buenos Aires, Buenos Aires:* Etnofoor (in press).

Schlenker, B.R. and Weigold, M.F. (1989), 'Goals and the Self-Identification Process: Constructing Desired Identities,' in L. Pervin (ed), *Goal Concepts in Personality and Social Psychology*, Hillsdale, NJ: Erlbaum, pp. 243–90.

Schulze, L., White, A., and Brown, J. (1993), 'A Sacred Monster in her Prime: Audience Construction of Madonna as low-Other,' in C. Schwichtenberg (ed.), *The Madonna Connection: Representational Politics, Subcultural Identities, and Cultural Theory*, Boulder: Westview Press, pp. 15–38.

Schwartz, M. (1991), *Greek-Oriental Rebetika: Songs and Dances in the Asia Minor Style. The Golden Years: 1911–1937*, El Cerrito: Arhoolie/Folklyric, CD-7005.

Sedgwick, E. (1985), *Between Men: English Literature and Male Homosocial Desire*, New York: Columbia University Press.

Seigel, J. (1986), *Bohemian Paris: Culture, Politics and the Boundaries of Bourgeois Life, 1820–1930*, New York: Viking Press.

Serematakis, N. (1994), 'The Memory of the Senses,' in L. Taylor (ed.), *Visualizing Theory*, New York: Routledge, pp. 214–29.

Seymour, B. (1995), *Lola Montez: A Life*, New Haven: Yale University Press.

Shepherd, J. (1987), 'Music and Male Hegemony,' in R. Leppert and S. McClary (eds), *Music and Society: The Politics of Composition, Performance and Reception*, New York: Cambridge University Press.

Silverman, K. (1988), *The Acoustic Mirror: The Female Voice in Psychoanalysis and Cinema*, Bloomington: Indiana University Press.

Smith, O. (1989), 'Research on Rebetika: Some Methodological Problems and Issues,' *Journal of Modern Hellenism*, 6: 177–90.

—— (1991), 'The Chronology of Rebetiko – A Reconsideration of the Evidence', *Byzantine and Modern Greek Studies*, 15: 318–24.

Smith, P. (ed.) (1996), *Boys: Masculinities in Contemorary Culture*, Boulder: Westview Press.

Soffa, D. (1994), *Marika Papagika: Greek Popular and Rebetic Music in New York: 1918–1929*, Berkeley: Alma Criola Records, ACCD 802.

Steingress, G. (1989), 'La Aparición del Cante Flamenco en el Teatro Jerezano del Siglo XIX,' *Dos Siglos de Flamenco. Actas de la Conferencia Internacional. Jerez 21–25 junio 88*, Jerez de la Frontera: Fundación Andaluza de Flamenco, pp. 343–80.

—— (1993), *Sociología del Cante Flamenco*, Jerez de la Frontera: Centro Andaluz de Flamenco.

—— (1997a), *Soziologie des Flamenco. Zur Kultursoziologie der andalusischen Moderne*, Frankfurt am Main: Peter Lang. Europäischer Verlag der Wissenschaften.

—— (1997b), 'El Cante ante la Melancolía y el Mito Nacional,' *Candil, Revista de Flamenco*, 108: 2575–90.

—— (1997c), 'Der Flamencogesang als künstlerischer Akt, ideologisches Instrument und Bestandteil der kulturellen Identität Andalusiens,' *Österreichische Zeitschrift für Soziologie*, 3: 30–53.

—— (1997d), 'De fusiones y Confusiones (en pro de la Institucionalización del Cante Flamenco Clásico),' *Camarón. Cinco años después.* (*Revista Mensual de Flamenco*), Hefte 45/4, Villanueva de la Reina, pp. 75–88.

Steumpfle, S. (1995) *The Steelband Movement: The Forging of a National Art in Trinidad and Tobago*, Philadelphia: University of Pennsylvania Press.

Stoetzer, C. (1996), 'Krausean Philosophy as a Major Political and Social Force in Modern Argentina and Guatemala,' in M. Pérez de Mendiola (ed.) *Bridging the Atlantic*, Buffalo: State of New York University Press, pp. 83–105.

Strum, R. (1989), 'Elisabeth Marbury 1856–1933: Her Life and Work,' Ph.D. Dissertation, New York: New York University Press.

Studlar, G. (1993), 'Valentino, 'Optic Intoxication,' and Dance Madnesss,' Cohan and Hark (eds), *Screening the Male*, New York: Routledge.

Suarez-Orozco, M. (1982), 'A Study of Argentine Soccer: The Dynamics of its Fans and their Folklore,' *Journal of Psychoanalytic Anthropology*, 5(1): 7–28.

Subirá, J. (1929), *La Tonadilla Escénica*, Madrid: Tipografía de Archivos.

Tarby, P. (1991), *Eros Flamenco: El Deseo y su Discurso en la Poesia Flamenca*, Cadiz: Universidad de Cadiz.

—— (1992), *Anthologie de la Poésie Gitano-Andalouse*, Revues Marges: Université de Perpignan.

Taylor, J. (1976), 'Tango: Theme of Class and Nation,' *Ethnomusicology*, 20(2): 273–91.

—— (1992), 'Tango,' in G. Marcus (ed.), *Rereading Cultural Anthropology*, Durham: Duke University Press, pp. 377–89.

Terdiman, R. (1985), *Discourse/Counter-Discourse: The Theory and Practice of Symbolic Resistance in Nineteenth-Century France*, Ithaca: Cornell University Press.

—— (1993), *Present Past: Modernity and the Memory Crisis*, Ithaca: Cornell University Press.

Theodorakis, M. (1974), *Gia Thn Ellhnikh Mousikh*, Ayhna: Pleiaw.

Torgovnick, M. (1991), *Gone Primitive: Savage Intellects and Modern Lives*, Chicago: University of Chicago Press.

—— (1997), *Primitive Passions: Men, Women, and the Quest for Ecstasy*, New York: Knopf.

Uhl, S. (1991), 'Forbidden Friends: Cultural Veils of Female Friendship in Andalusia,' *American Ethnologist*, 18: 90–105.

Ulecia, A. (1976), *Las Confesiones de Antonio Mairena*, Sevilla: Publicaciones de la Universidad de Sevilla.

Vester, H. (1996), *Kollektive Identitäten und Mentalitäten. Von der Völkerpsychologie zur Kulturvergleichenden Soziologie und Interkulturellen Kommunikation*, Frankfurt am Main: IKO-Verl. für Interkulturelle Kommunikation.

Vila, P. (1995), 'Le Tango et la Formation des Identités Ethniques en Argentine,' in R. Pelinski (ed.), *Tango Nomade. Études sur le Tango Transculturel*, Montréal: Triptyque, pp. 77–107.

Vilariño, I. (1981), *Tangos, Antologa*, Buenos Aires: Centro Editor de la América Latina.

Washabaugh, W. (1996), *Flamenco. Passion, Politics and Popular Culture*, Oxford: Berg.

Wilshire, B. (1982), *Role Playing and Identity: The Limits of the Theatre as Metaphor*, Bloomington: Indiana University Press.

Wilson, J.Q. (1993), *Moral Sense*, New York: The Free Press.

Wilson, P. (1973), *Crab Antics: The Social Anthropology of English-Speaking Negro Societies of the Caribbean*, New Haven: Yale University Press.

Yannaras, C. (1991), *Elements of Faith: An Introduction to Orthodox Theology*, Edinburgh: T and T Clark.

Zubillaga, C. (1976), *Carlos Gardel*, Madrid: Editorial Júcar.

Index

Index

Index

Index